The EEC and Brazil

Euro-Latin American Relations—The Omágua Series

General Editor:

Peter Coffey, Europa Institute, University of Amsterdam

The Omágua were a civilised and peaceful Indian tribe living in the Amazon region between present-day Peru, Ecuador and Brazil in the fifteenth and sixteenth centuries.

THE EEC AND BRAZIL:
Trade, Capital Investment and the Debt Problem

edited by

PETER COFFEY
and
LUIZ ARANHA CORRÊA DO LAGO

Pinter Publishers London and New York

First published in Great Britain in 1988 by
Pinter Publishers Limited
25 Floral Street, London WC2E 9DS

British Library Cataloguing in Publication Data

A CIP catalogue record for this book is available from the
British Library

ISBN 0-86187-969-4

Library of Congress Cataloging-in-Publication Data

The EEC and Brazil : trade, capital investment, and the debt
  problem / edited by Peter Coffey and Luiz Aranha Corrêa do Lago.
  (Euro-Latin American relations—the Omágua series)
  Bibliography
  Includes index.
  ISBN 0-86187-969-4
  1. European Economic Community countries—Commerce—Brazil
2. Brazil—Commerce—European Economic Community countries.
3. Investments, European—Brazil.   4. Debts, External—Brazil.
I. Coffey, Peter.   II. Lago, Luiz A. Corrêa do (Luiz Aranha Corrêa)
III. Series.
HF3499.5.Z7B73   1988
337.4081—dc 19   88-2522

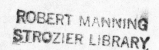
Typeset by Florencetype Ltd, Kewstoke, Avon
Printed by Biddles of Guildford

Contents

Notes About the
Contributors

Nelson Braga, a Brazilian national, was formerly a staff member of the Brazilian Foreign Trade Foundation (Funcex) and is now a staff member at the IPEM/INPES, the research institute of the Brazilian Ministry of Planning. He has also been a Professor at the Federal University of Rio de Janeiro.

Peter Coffey, a British national, is currently Head of the Economics Section of the Postgraduate Europa Instituut of the University of Amsterdam and General Editor of the Omágua series. He has lectured in most countries of the EEC and in many other parts of the world. He has published many books and articles on European and international economic and monetary issues.

Gustavo H.B. Franco, a Brazilian national, is currently engaged in a large research project on foreign investment (together with Professor Winston Frisch) and lectures on international economics and stabilisation policies.

Wolf Grabendorff, a German national, is currently Director of IRELA (the Institute for Relations between Europe and Latin America), in Madrid. He has, for many years, undertaken research on issues concerning Europe and Latin America and has published widely.

Luiz Aranha Corrêa do Lago, a Brazilian national, is currently a staff member of Brazil's Central Bank and is a Senior Research Economist at the Brazilian Institute of Economics of the Fundação Getulio Vargas. He was formerly Head of the Centre for Monetary Studies and International Economics at the same Foundation.

Marcelo de Paiva Abreu, a Brazilian national, is a specialist on Anglo-Brazilian relations since 1930. He is currently teaching and undertaking research at the Catholic University of Rio de Janeiro.

Philippe Pochet, a Belgian national, graduated in political sciences from the Université Libre de Bruxelles. He has worked at the Centre d'Etudes de l'Amérique Latine of the same university and is currently scientific collaborator with the Institute of European Studies.

Peter Praet, a Belgian national, is Professor of Economics at the Université Libre de Bruxelles and associate director of the Institute of European Studies of the same university. He is a former Staff member of the IMF and is currently chief economist in a private bank. He is editor of the *Cahiers Economiques de Bruxelles*.

Heinz G. Preusse, a German national, is head of the Foreign Trade and Development Division of Ibero-Amerika Institut für Wirtschaftsforschung, University of Göttingen, West Germany. He works on problems concerning the increasing interdependencies in the world economy and their repercussions on Latin American economic development. Recent publications are on the intra-industrial division of labour (1985).

Gilda M.C. Santiago, a Brazilian national, is an economist at the IBGE (Brazilian Institute of Geography and Statistics) and has been collaborating with Nelson Braga in his recent works.

Rolf Schinke, a German national, is head of the International Welfare Comparison Division of the Ibero-Amerika Institut für Wirtschaftsforschung, University of Göttingen, West Germany. His emphasis in current research is on indebtedness and welfare. He recently published articles and a book on debt equity swaps.

Acknowledgements

The authors are grateful to Mr Ben Kotmans, a secretary at the Europa Institut, University of Amsterdam, who has typed parts of this book. Likewise, thanks are due to Mr Geert van der Klis, a student assistant at the same Institute, who prepared the index.

Preface

This volume contains studies on all important economic aspects of relations between the EEC and Brazil, structured so as to present both Brazilian and Western European views on the same issues. Trade, investment and debt receive careful analysis, as do two special elements of the relationship: the effect of the third enlargement of the EEC and the Carajas Iron Ore project, which represents a unique feature in EEC relations with the developing countries.

The EEC dimension is, of course, only part of the overall relationship between Western Europe and Brazil, especially given the importance of bilateral policies of member states such as West Germany, France and Portugal, which have strong traditional relations with Brazil. Relations at the Community level, however, have a particular interest and importance. Moreover, there is a widespread assumption at present that relations between the EEC and Brazil are not good and are unlikely to become much better. This book shows that in fact these relations are by no means as bad as conventional wisdom seems to have it, and have considerable possibilities for improvement in the future.

Global economic conditions and their impact on Brazil and, to a lesser extent, the EEC, have certainly brought about a marked drop in trade between the largest Latin American countries and the EEC. Nevertheless, Brazil, with its promising industrial base, expanding internal market and successful export drive, remains the most attractive market for EEC exports in the region as well as a very interesting place for European investment. Brazil also has a special importance for the EEC related to its overall international position.

Brazil is, with India, one of the two Third-World spokesmen in international politics which have the weight of future great powers. Brazil's refusal to accept 'the freezing of the world power system' after the Second World War is shared by many states in the Third World and, since Brazil is not a country which manipulates these concepts for ideological reasons, has to be taken very seriously. Brazil's role in the United Nations, in international economical fora and the context of Latin American political cooperation, as well as its well-known diplomatic ability, makes the country a natural leader with respect to many issues which might not be shared but which have to be confronted by the EEC. As a result of its constant economic and various political conflicts with the United States, Brazil has always looked towards Western Europe as an area for diversification with regard to economic as well as political relations. In the fields of technology and armaments as well as with regard to private bank exposure the 'European Card' has proved to be a strong one. Frequent visits and countless exchanges on different levels have contributed to a mutual understanding of the importance of strong relations between Brazil and Western Europe.

Since the third enlargement of the EEC, political contacts with the two new member states have increased significantly. The visits of President Sarney to Portugal in 1986 and of Mario Soares and Felipe Gonzalez to Brazil in 1987 have proved to be important not only in the bilateral context. With the process of democratisation, transnational relations with Brazil are likely to increase and to strengthen economic relations at the same time as they will constitute a more pluralistic way of forging the profile of the relations in the years to come.

Looking at the trade figures, Luiz Avanha Corrêa do Lago shows that Brazilian exports to the EEC constituted as much as 41 per cent of total Brazilian exports in 1973 but averaged only 26.1 per cent between 1984 and 1986, and that since 1983 the US has taken over from the European Community as Brazil's principal market. The reasons for this are:

— the declining share of developing countries in international trade in general;
— the drop in prices for primary products;
— the difference in growth rates in those years in the United States and in the EEC; and
— the difference between Brazilian products entering the US market and those entering the EEC, since the latter are made up to a greater extent of primary products.

The shift in the relative importance of the EEC is even clearer if one looks at developments over a longer period. Between 1975 and 1985 Brazilian exports to the US increased by 438.5 per cent but exports to the EEC by only 158.3 per cent. In the same period, Brazilian imports from the US fell by 16.1 per cent, and those from the EEC by 38.7 per cent. EEC–Brazilian trade relations are also characterised by a great asymmetry: the EEC has in recent years taken about 25 per cent of Brazil's exports and supplied about 15 per cent of its imports, while Brazil accounts for no more than 0.3 per cent of the EEC's total exports and 1 per cent of its imports. The vulnerability of the trade structure is also manifested in the fact that over 60 per cent of Brazilian exports to the EEC are concentrated in three member states (the Netherlands, Italy and West Germany) while over 60 per cent of Brazil's imports from the EEC are purchased from France and West Germany.

In view of these sobering statistics and both sides' tradition of protectionism in sensitive areas, Marcela de Paira Abreu concludes that there are few possibilities for future EEC–Brazilian cooperation in the sphere of trade, pointing out that divergences are already becoming clear in the context of the Uruguay Round, especially with regard to the new issues such as services.

Nevertheless, the overall problem in the sphere of trade should not obscure the fact that the most successful of all bilateral agreements between the EEC and Latin America countries—which also include agreements with Mexico, Argentina and Uruguay—has been that with Brazil. Indeed, it has been so successful for Brazil that in the sectors of textiles and steel the Commission has even had to request some self-restraint on the part of Brazil with regard to its exports to the Community. Moreover, in the context of the new industrial cooperation which seems to be the foremost element of common interest between the EEC and Brazil, given the need to expand and modernise Brazil's industrial infrastructure, it is possible that there may be a wave of entirely new Brazilian exports to the Community in the 1990s.

European investments in Brazil, which have historically been very substantial, have fallen, because of both production cycles and the external economic problems which have affected Brazil since the oil crises of 1973, as Gustavo H.B. Franco points out in his chapter. However, European investment will certainly recover in the future, inasmuch as Brazil will very probably be one of the largest Third World markets for the EEC. At the same time, Brazil will use the possibility of debt–equity swaps, as a means to come to terms with the need for fresh capital inflows, in order to increase investment incentives. As Heinz Gert Preusse and Rolf Schinke argue, this may be one of the few possibilities for restoring economic growth in Brazil.

The other side of the investment picture is the increasing interest of Brazilian companies, both public and private, in improving access to the EEC market by direct investment in Portugal and Spain, basically through joint ventures. Although the enlargement in itself had little effect on Brazilian–EEC trade, as shown in the chapter by Helson Braga and Gilda M.C. Santiago, the Portuguese and Spanish connection might indeed allow the Brazilians to benefit from the increasing possibilities of the unified EEC market.

The new catchword fo EEC–Latin American relations seems to be 'industrial cooperation', an approach which goes beyond investment and technology transfer. There seems to be no country better equipped to take advantage of a cooperation programme of this nature than Brazil. If one looks at the historic document of the Community Council of 22 June 1987 entitled 'New EEC guidelines for relations with Latin America and for industrial cooperation with countries at an intermediate state of development', it is clear that most elements in the proposed programme, which centres upon the establishment of joint ventures between European and local enterprises, are designed for stronger cooperation with Brazil, which is obviously an ideal target country in all the areas mentioned, such as

— industrial standards,
— financial and technical cooperation,
— information on investment opportunities,
— scientific and technical cooperation, and
— training and economic information.

The second meeting of the mixed Commission between the EEC and Brazil in November 1987 showed that there is already a great interest on the part of Brazil in entering in that type of industrial cooperation with the European Community, especially in the field of small- and medium-sized industry. Brazil sees great advantages in cooperating with the EEC on an enterprise-to-enterprise level. The first step in that direction has already been taken with the creation of an EEC-Brazilian Business Council modelled after the successful body of this nature in the cooperation programme between the EEC and the ASEAN countries.

Practically all the chapters in this book make it abundantly clear that the debt issue, which threatens not only Brazil's prospects for economic recovery but also its political stability and governability, will loom over any further cooperation between the EEC and Brazil, and that some initiative will have to be taken by the EEC and member countries to share the costs of solving the debt problem. EEC banks are indeed Brazil's principal creditors, holding 27.7 per cent of the outstanding debt as compared to 24.7 per cent held by US banks. So far, however, the member states have avoided taking any clear stand on the issue of co-responsibility, and have given insufficient support to the very positive steps taken by Commissioner Claude Cheysson regarding an initiative on the part of the Commission.

One special field of EEC–Brazilian relations which deserves mention, although it is not the subject of a specific chapter in this book, is that of scientific and technological cooperation. Brazil has always found better access to modern technology in Europe than in the US, and the first formal relationship between the EC and Brazil was indeed a scientific and technological treaty between that country and Euratom signed in 1961 which came into effect in 1965. The treaty expired in 1985 without efforts to renew it, partly because the results were not as positive as hoped for by Brazil. Nevertheless, the 1975 nuclear cooperation treaty between West Germany and Brazil could have been seen as an extension of that Community-wide cooperation, since most technology transfer is done directly on a bilateral level, especially between Brazil and West Germany, France, Italy and the United Kingdom.

With regard to EEC scientific and technological cooperation with non-associated countries, Brazil has definitely benefited more than any other Latin American country and demontrated its interest in strengthening such cooperation by welcoming the creation of specific sub-commissions in this area, within the EEC–Brazilian Mixed Commission in November 1987. Given Brazil's advanced level of technical and scientific development, this form of cooperation is likely to be one of the most promising in the years to come.

As Peter Coffey argues in the first chapter, the prospects for increased cooperation between Brazil and the Community are by no means bad, especially if one takes into account that the ongoing integration process between Argentina and Brazil will likely create one of the most promising and advanced multinational development poles in the Third World in the 1990's. Nevertheless the relation will be characterized in the future by the vulnerability of the Brazilian economy and its relation with the EEC in two respects:

— the adjustments which will have to be made in response to changing international economic conditions, and
— the adjustments which will be required in order to create a different internal market, because of the social and political necessities of stabilising democratic development in Brazil.

In this respect the change from a coffee and soya bean exporter to a newly industrialised country which offers a wide range of industrial products means that Brazil's trading partners will have to accept, at least in part, a change from a complimentary to a competitive economic power.

Brazil's future role in the international economy will inevitably make it a more difficult partner for the EEC, even though both have an interest in trade liberalisation and both have protectionist tendencies in many sensitive sectors. Brazil's outspoken policy of no automatic alliances makes it sometimes a less predictable partner, even though its pragmatic attitude with regard to economic possibilities tends to reduce the risk of difficult economic conflicts.

The democratisation process in Brazil has been welcomed by the EEC but it has already become obvious that the decision-making process in foreign policy as well as in external economic policy has become much more complex and, as in all democracies, domestic political considerations have become an essential part of interest articulation in external economic relations.

The debt issue is the obvious case where the capacity of adaptation will be a test case for the EEC. The collected studies in this volume give both sides in this increasing complex relationship a unique possibility to understand better the interests and motives of both partners. The book is thus an important contribution to the strengthening of European–Brazilian relations.

Wolf Grabendorff

Introduction

The recent return of Brazil to democracy—together with the unrelated but important Brazilian foreign debt—have increased Western interest in that country's affairs. In particular, the European Economic Community, as Brazil's principal trading partner and main source of capital investment, is, inevitably, closely linked with Brazil's destiny.

At this moment in time, both Brazil and the Community stand at a crossroads. On the one hand, Brazil is in the process of strengthening its democratic process and introducing major economic reforms. On the other hand, the Community, in its decision to create a real common market by the year 1992, finds itself facing the choice of protectionism or 'openness'. Whichever choice is made by the EEC, it will affect Brazil and other Latin American countries.

Most recently, Argentina and Brazil have taken the historic decision—with all the attendant critical international implications—to work towards the creation of a common market between their two countries. In this connection, perhaps. the European Economic Community can serve as an example or model—especially if other Latin American countries join the two founder member states in their move towards economic integration.

These important historical changes, on both sides of the Atlantic, have prompted the two editors to bring together experts in Brazil and the European Economic Community to examine the most important current issues of mutual interest. The results of this examination are published in this book and the editors hope that they will increase understanding and deepen the links between the two partners.

Amsterdam and Rio de Janeiro,
October 1987.

PART 1: RELATIONS BETWEEN THE EUROPEAN ECONOMIC COMMUNITY AND BRAZIL: A HISTORICAL OVERVIEW

1

The European Economic Community and Brazil

Peter Coffey

Although the author has frequently complained that, until recently, the European Economic Community (EEC) has regarded Latin America as a kind of 'lost continent'[1] the EEC has, exceptionally, maintained formal links with Brazil over a number of years. Furthermore, among all Latin American countries, Brazil is the one that has most successfully used the concessions offered by the EEC. The aim of this chapter is to examine the main external economic policy options of the EEC and the types of concessions it offers to countries like Brazil. The specific trade and capital investment relations between the EEC and Brazil will be examined—with special attention being paid to the EEC's involvement in the Carajás Iron Ore Project. Proposals will be made for an improvement in relations between the two partners including the use of the ECU for EEC–Brazilian trade. Lastly, the author will assess the possibility of Brazil's success *vis-à-vis* the EEC being emulated by other Latin American countries.

THE EEC'S MAIN EXTERNAL ECONOMIC POLICY PRINCIPLES

The European Economic Community is the world's most important economic and trading bloc. Consisting of 12 Western European countries, it is a highly integrated customs and economic union and is also a *de facto* monetary union. In a recent work,[2] the author has discerned seven main principles upon which the Community's external economic relations are built. These are as follows:

1. The EEC (with the exception of the United Kingdom and its supplies of North Sea oil, and coal reserves in that and some other countries) is not self-sufficient in supplies of energy and raw materials. Therefore, these commodities have generally been allowed to enter the Community either free of duty or with very low tariffs.

2. At the end of the transitional period, the Common External Tariff (CET) would consist of the average of the existing (1957) tariffs of the member states. Subsequent participation by the EEC in a series of international trade negotiations has resulted in a rather low average CET. New member states are expected to introduce the CET after a transitional period.

3. It was agreed that special arrangements would be made for existing overseas territories, dependencies and the like for which member states exercised reponsibility. This policy has evolved over time from the special arrangements made for such countries to the two Yaoundé Agreements and further on to the present Third Lomé Agreement.

4. At the outset, the EEC decided to embark upon the construction of a Common Agricultural Policy (CAP), and until the Common Agricultural Market (CAM) actually came into being, the EEC was unwilling to discuss the question of agricultural matters in international trade negotiations. Since the full achievement of the CAM, its existence has tended to influence negatively the EEC's trade relations with most parts of the world—especially with Eastern Europe, Australasia and Latin America.

5. The Community expressed its willingness to enter into international trade negotiations with non-Community countries. Subsequently, the EEC has been (together with the United States and, more recently, Japan) the principal protagonist in (2), and following the Tokyo Round Negotiations, the average CET is now rather low.

6. Partly as a consequence of the low CET and partly due to the increased competitive ability of a growing number of Third World countries (particularly in the fields of clothing and textiles) the EEC has, since the 1970s, increasingly resorted to non-tariff barriers of a 'voluntarist' nature which are sometimes described as Orderly Marketing Arrangements (OMAs) or Voluntary Export Restrictions (VERs). Currently, efforts are being made to 'persuade' Japan to restrict exports of cars and electronic products to EEC member states.

7. Since the mid 1970s, the EEC has started to move in the direction of attempting to secure its supplies of energy and raw materials.[3] This more recent policy is an obvious reaction to the lack of self-sufficiency in these fields, which was mentioned in (1) and has been underlined by increases in oil prices made by OPEC countries.

Although these basic principles do clearly explain the Community's trading attitudes and policies towards imports and exports of agricultural products, raw materials, energy and some 'sensitive' products, they do not necessarily explain the choice or lack of choice of policies for specific geographical areas, about which so much has been written. Therefore, it is useful to examine such areas for which policies have or have not been made.

When examining these principles, it is important to bear in mind that the internal economic policies are at least as important as the official external economic policies of the EEC, if not more so, in influencing relations between the EEC and third parties. Thus, for example, the CAP has, according to Peter Praet, Philippe Pochet and Marcelo de Priva Abreu, had both positive and negative effects on Brazil. In the case of animal feedstuffs, Brazil has become a major exporter to the EEC. In contrast, the policies for beef and sugar have tended to have less positive effects for that country.

In comparison with the CAP, the EEC's industrial policies have tended to stop expansion of trade between the two parties. In the case of steel and in the framework of the Davignon Plan for restructuring the EEC's steel industry, have been imposed on Brazilian steel exports. Textiles have faced a similar fate in the framework of the Multi-Fibre Agreement (MFA).

Reference has already been made to the Lomé Agreements made between the EEC and the African, Caribbean and Pacific (ACP) states. These agreements give preferences to these states for exports of their traditional tropical products to the EEC. According to Marcelo de Priva Abreu, these policies place exports of similar Brazilian products at a disadvantage.

Although this chapter is devoted to EEC policies, it should be stressed that there are areas of cultural, economic and technological activity that are still very much more the responsibility of the individual member states than of the EEC itself. Indeed, in the specific fields of cultural affairs and capital investment, the EEC has laid down no policy for third parties.

ECONOMIC AND POLITICAL RELATIONS BETWEEN BRAZIL AND THE EEC

Economic and political relations between the two sides take place at two levels, at the EEC–Brazil and at a bilateral (Brazil–member state) level. The EEC, as represented by the Commission, is responsible for the trade relations of the individual member states *vis-à-vis* third parties. Here, one may say that each member state has transferred most of its sovereignty concerning trade policy to the EEC. This fact is underlined by the Commission's role as the negotiator for the entire Community in international trade negotiations and by the acceptance by member states of the inclusion of a 'Community Clause' in all trade agreements. Also, all the Community's trade policies are very much influenced by its internal economic policies.

In the case of a country like Brazil, economic relations with the Community are developed mainly in four ways:

1. Through multinational trade negotiations. As already mentioned,

since the implementation of the agreements reached in the Tokyo Round, the EEC's average CET has been rather low.

2. Through the generalised system of preferences (GSPs).
3. Through the MFA.
4. Through specific agreements with the country concerned. In the case of Brazil, the EEC's official relations have, since 1982, reached a particularly formal level.

According to the most recent report on EEC–Latin American trade,[4] trade between Brazil and the ten countries of the EEC[5] increased substantially between 1965 and 1982 and the EEC became Brazil's most important trading partner. Thus, in 1965, 17.51 per cent of the EEC's total imports from 20 Latin American countries[6] came from Brazil. In 1979, they had risen to 31.36 per cent, and in 1982 to 33.53 per cent. Similarly, in the same year, about 20 per cent of EEC exports to Latin America went to Brazil. Like a number of Latin American countries, Brazil has, except for

Table 1.1   Brazil's trade by area ($ million)

	1984			1985*		
	Exports	Imports	Balance	Exports	Imports	Balance
Total	27,005	13,916	13,089	15,992	8,141	7,851
Total excluding OPEP	24,530	8,348	16,182	14,338	5,158	9,180
EFTA	751	305	446	518	252	266
LAIA†	2,323	1,597	726	1,047	817	230
Argentina	853	511	342	320	298	22
Mexico	285	630	−345	124	208	−84
Chile	281	225	56	140	151	−11
Others	904	231	673	463	160	303
Canada	408	510	−102	249	215	34
EEC	6,157	1,726	4,431	3,943	1,095	2,848
West Germany	1,256	629	627	824	455	369
Netherlands	1,361	142	1,219	934	98	836
Italy	1,115	203	912	722	123	599
United Kingdom	708	278	430	417	157	260
France	836	371	465	508	200	308
Others	881	103	778	538	62	476
COMECON	1,359	420	939	648	185	463
USA	7,710	2,297	5,413	4,122	1,682	2,440
Japan	1,515	553	962	885	332	553
OPEC	2,475	5,568	−3,093	1,654	2,983	−1,319
Others	4,307	940	3,367	2,926	580	2,346

*   January–August.
†   Includes Puerto Rico.
Source: Central Bank of Brazil.

Table 1.2   The composition of Brazil's trade with the EEC

	As a percentage of total EEC exports to Brazil			As a percentage of total Brazilian exports to EEC		
	1970	1979	1982	1970	1979	1982
Food, drink, tobacco	2.88	3.03	2.82	54.22	50.82	51.28
Raw materials	3.81	2.83	2.73	37.18	26.09	20.91
Mineral fuels, etc.	1.08	1.20	0.90	0.36	0.05	1.71
Chemicals	21.41	22.25	20.62	0.97	1.51	2.09
Other industrial products	18.95	16.12	15.78	5.17	14.57	13.33
Transport equipment	50.99	52.10	55.53	1.89	6.74	10.47

Source: Eurostat.

the year 1975, tended to have substantial trade surpluses with the EEC. More recently, as the trade statistics in Table 1.1 indicate, the EEC has lost its position as Brazil's main trading partner to the United States.

The composition of the Community's exports to Brazil has shown very little change over the past decade, and recent trends observed by the Central Bank of Brazil tend to repeat the structure of the statistics for 1982 as shown in Table 1.2. However, in its exports to the EEC, whilst Brazil still continues to rely heavily on exports of food, drink and raw materials, it is substantially increasing its exports of industrial and manufactured goods. Brazil is thus competitive as well as complementary to the EEC on the international trade scene. Apart from exports of cars by European and American subsidiaries to Europe and the United States, it was symbolic that, in 1985, Brazil concluded an agreement with the United Kingdom to sell the Tucanor military training aircraft to the Royal Air Force.

In a paper given at the SLAS Annual Conference at the University of Cambridge in 1984,[7] the author suggested the following reasons for the great upsurge of trade between Brazil and the EEC in the late 1960s and in the 1970s.

1. Throughout the 1960s and into the early 1970s the EEC enjoyed a major economic boom which necessitated a great increase in imports of raw materials, notably from countries such as Brazil.
2. Likewise, during the same period, but lasting into the beginning of the 1980s, Brazil experienced a period of great economic expansion which encouraged imports of high-technology and transport equipment, which tended to favour the EEC.
3. Into the 1960s, Brazil had favoured the policy of a hard cruzeiro (which in fact taxed her exports) and the imposition of export controls. These policies were replaced by the institution of a 'crawling peg' for the cruzeiro[8] and the removal of export controls, thus encouraging

exports. Also, in the 1970s, Brazil subsidised the production of manufactured agricultural products—for export as well as for internal consumption.
4. The EEC has given concessions to a large number of Third World countries, which tend to have been fully used by Brazil.

In view of the important expansion of trade between the two sides so that, by the end of the 1970s, the EEC had become Brazil's most important trading partner, why, more recently, has the EEC been overtaken by the United States? It is difficult to give a clear answer to this question. However, the author would suggest the following basic (and by no means conclusive) reasons for this situation.

1. Both the EEC and Brazil have, in the early 1980s, experienced a recession, so that they tend to import less from each other.
2. As a result of this situation, Brazil has imposed very high tariffs (in some cases as high as 300 per cent) on imports—this has tended to penalise the EEC.
3. Despite the concessions given by the EEC, Brazil accuses the Community of trying to prevent her exports from entering the Common Market. Furthermore, some experts privately suggest that the United States is, in reality, less protectionist than the EEC. In any case, in recent years, the American economy has tended to boom—thus encouraging imports, notably from the economically more advanced Third World countries.

Apart these observations, Brazil has fully utilised the concessions given to her by the Community. Therefore, it is important to examine the Brazilian experience in this area since it could possibly provide an example for other Latin American countries.

The Generalised System of Preferences (GSP)

The GSP has, on the whole, been one of the more positive aspects of the external economic policies of the EEC. At the New Delhi meeting of UNCTAD, in 1968, a special group was created with the task of examining the structure and details of (and reaching agreement on) a 'generalised, non-reciprocal system of preferences'. The upshot was that the EEC agreed to put into operation such a system in 1971 (the EEC was the first group of countries to do so), renewable annually, for a period of ten years. As the agreement expired, the Community agreed to institute a new system on 1 January 1981, for a further period of ten years, the broad outlines of which (with annual revisions) were laid down for the first five. Apart from the basic principle of non-reciprocity, tariff-free quotas are granted for individual manufactures and semi-manufactures (though not for industrial raw materials) under headings 25–99 of the Brussels Tariff Nomenclature (BTN). Preferential treatment is also given for some processed and semi-processed goods under headings 1–24 of the BTN. A reduced tariff is offered for agricultural products.

On the restrictive side, no country may take up more than 50 per cent of the total quota for any one product (even where the other half is unused). Products have been classified into four categories: sensitive, semi-sensitive, non-sensitive, and hubrid. In the case of the first category (mainly textiles) the EEC imposes special restrictions.

The record of the first GSP was one of steady improvement. The global amount of quotas was increased and there was a relaxation in the case of processed and semi-processed agricultural products. Such an improvement was particularly useful for countries like Brazil.

Brazil was, in fact, one of the top five beneficiaries of the first GSP. Such was the success of that country that, in the second half of the decade, the EEC increased the number of 'sensitive' products (in the specific case of Brazil) which were subject to the reintroduction of customs duties, from four in 1974 to 15 in 1980. At the close of the first GSP (1980) the value of the quotas was approximately 10 billion ECU out of a total of approximately 130 billion ECU for EEC imports.

The new agreement, which came into force on 1 January 1981, shows some improvements and some negative features. In the case of agricultural products, there are improvements. Thus, in 1982, preferential margins were improved for 36 products, of which 14 were new ones. Industrial products have not fared so well. National quotas have been strictly 'individualised' for 'sensitive' products. Furthermore, quotas for textiles were frozen for the years 1980, 1981 and 1982.

Brazil clearly did rather well in the first decade of the GSP.[9] Alas, like similar countries, she has paid the price for success in that her opportunities in those areas of manufactures that really matter (the so-called 'sensitive' products) have been (at least temporarily) frozen. In contrast, in the field of partly or totally transformed agricultural products, possibilities exist for a continued improvement in the performance of Brazil's exports to the EEC.

According to Commission officials, the present Brazilian experience with the new GSP arrangement is quite fabulous. They are using up to and beyond 100 per cent of the concessions offered by the EEC. This contrasts markedly with a country like Mexico which normally does not manage to use more than 60 per cent of the concessions it could exploit.

Why should Brazil—of all Latin American countries—be able to rival and even to surpass some South-East Asian countries in its successful exploitation of these concessions? The author would suggest the following reasons for this success, which may well serve as a lesson for other Latin American countries.

1. The Brazilian economy has a much more varied structure than that of most Latin American countries. Thus when, as in the case with the GSP, concessions are offered both in the field of manufactures and in that of transformed agricultural products, Brazil is able to profit in both areas.
2. Brazil is currently pursuing an export-led boom and most of her commercial energies are devoted to the export market.
3. The country displays an unusual degree of flexibility in export markets. Thus, when the American state of Florida lost its share of the international orange juice market (through repeated frosts which destroyed the orange trees), Brazil moved in to replace Floridian sales in Europe and elsewhere. A similar experience was observed in the case of soya. Then, as has already been observed, when the EEC offered concessions for transformed agricultural products, once again the Brazilians swiftly moved in to corner a share of the market.

A further reason, which is as yet only hypothesis and which has still to be confirmed or rejected by research currently being undertaken by the author, is that the additional products included under the new GSP arrangement might have been particularly favourable to Brazil. The author is led to this hypothesis by the fact that, as has already been observed, under the first arrangement, the Brazilians became too competitive in a number of fields, and, by the end of that decade, the number of products for which export ceilings were imposed amounted to 15. Consequently, at that time, Brazil's effective use of GSP declined steeply to 44 per cent—as compared with 83 per cent for Venezuela, 59 per cent for Mexico, and 49 per cent for Argentina.

The Multi-Fibre Agreement (MFA): the special new arrangements for Brazil

According to the author, the MFA has been in recent times, one of the less glorious chapters in the history of the EEC. At the outset, during the course of the first agreement (1974–7), it had been agreed that textile imports (with some quite clearly defined exceptions) from developing countries should increase at a rate of at least 6 per cent annually. However, when the next series of five-year bilateral agreements came up for renegotiation, the EEC reduced quotas already achieved and curtailed other imports from Third World countries. Thus, what had been intended as a means of expanding trade was transformed into a means of protecting the textile industries of highly developed countries.

When the second agreement came up for renewal in 1981, there was great dissension among the EEC member states. The British and French wanted more protectionism whilst the Dutch, Danes, Irish and Italians called for a more open approach. Surprisingly, there were calls for more protectionism from West Germany. Such was the dissension within the EEC that, at the end of 1981, it did not possess a mandate to negotiate!

Finally, at the end of February 1982, the EEC ministers agreed to sign the third MFA (to run between 1983 and 1986). The particularly negative facets of this most recent renewal were:

1. The bilateral negotiations between the Community and 28 individual Third World countries were on a 'take-it-or-leave-it' basis.
2. The Community reserved the right to 'invalidate' its signing of the Third MFA if the bilateral negotiations did not prove satisfactory.
3. The 28 Third World countries were 'invited' to limit 'voluntarily' their textile exports to the EEC.
4. The quotas of the four major exporters—Hong Kong, South Korea, Taiwan and Macao—were reduced by 10 per cent on the 1981 quotas.

In the specific case of Brazil, the end result was a mixed one. Like the other countries, Brazil was forced 'voluntarily' to limit its exports of textiles to the EEC. Thus, in the case of cotton yarn and other woven fabrics (cotton), the levels for 1983 were frozen at those of the previous year (see Table 1.3). Thereafter slight increases were planned.

In contrast, a major increase was accepted in the case of woven fabrics (man-made fibres). This development was due to the fact that in 1982, the small quota was exported exclusively to the United Kingdom. Thereafter, the quota was enlarged to include the whole of the Community. On the other hand, a major cut was laid down in the quota for undergarments (shirts, T-shirts, etc.). The United Kingdom was one of the main instigators of this reduction. A controversial area is that of undergarments (pyjamas) where very strict quotas were instituted for France and West Germany. Even more worrying, the quotas for both outer garments and womens' and girls' undergarments (excluding pyjamas) were simply scrapped.

Understandably, the Brazilians were not happy with this new agreement. Like other similar highly developed Third World countries, they insisted that they were not being allowed to use their comparative advantage in the field of manufactures—more specifically, textiles. Consequently, the possibility of earning hard currency (needed so as to repay their debts) was reduced.

Although the feelings of the Brazilans are fully appreciated by the author, they may, in fact, have got rather a good deal from the Community when one examines other more developed Third World countries. In the case of Macao, Hong Kong, Singapore and South Korea, quotas were simply cut by 10 per cent! Brazil did not suffer such a fate. Instead, taking one product with another, she had 'asked' to freeze her quotas for 1982 and 1983, with slight increases to follow. Thus, in a time of crisis, whilst she did

Table 1.3 Brazilian textile export quotas to the EEC under the third MFA

Code no.	Description	Units used	1982	1983	1984	1985	1986
1	Cotton yarn (not for resale)	tonnes	27,644	27,644	27,671	27,699	27,727
2	Other woven fabrics (cotton)	tonnes	16,893	16,893	16,977	17,062	17,148
3	Woven fabrics (man-made fibres)	tonnes	409	1,350	1,377	1,405	1,433
4	Undergarments (shirts, T-shirts, etc.)	1,000 pieces	11,712	2,271	2,326	2,381	2,438
6	Men's and boys' outer garments	1,000 pieces	1,888	1,935	1,983	2,033	2,084
7	Other garments	1,000 pieces	118	150	152	154	156
				(United Kingdom only)			
8	Terry towelling, etc. etc.	tonnes	4,219	4,304	4,390	4,478	4,567
13	Undergarments (men's)	1,000	4,747	4,842	4,939	5,038	5,138
20	Bedlinen	tonnes	2,566	2,656	2,709	2,763	2,819
24/25	Undergarments pyjamas	1,000 pieces	1,511	1,571	1,634	1,699	1,767
	Quota limits:						
	France			25	26	26	28
	W. Germany			400	416	433	450
26	Outer garments	1,000 pieces	402	none	none	none	none
30B	Women's, infants' and girls' undergarments (excluding pyjamas)	tonnes	122	none	none	none	none
30D	Women's undergarments (others)	1,000 pieces	2,295	2,342	2,389	2,437	2,486
39	Bed/table/toilet kitchen linen	tonnes	1,655	2,738	1,825	1,916	2,012
46	Sheep's or lamb's wool	tonnes	9,233	9,787	20,374	10,997	11,656
80	women's, girls' and infants' outer garments	tonnes	90	96	102	108	114

Sources: EEC Regulations nos 661/82 and 3762/83.

Table 1.4 Foreign capital investment in Brazil (percentage of total)

Country of origin	1973	1979	1980	1981
EEC	32.51	33.1	33.1	30.5
(of which West Germany)	15.26	15.4	14.0	13.7
United States	27.82	27.4	28.6	30.0

Source: Central Bank of Brazil.

not receive the preferences she was seeking, basically, she did not lose her acquired benefits. All in all, it was not such a bad compromise.

Capital Investment and the Debt Question: the Community Attitude

According to the Central Bank of Brazil, the EEC is Brazil's most important source of capital investment (Table 1.4). This privileged position clearly encourages most Brazilian officials, bankers, businessmen and academics to call for a special EEC attitude towards the debt question.

The enormity of the debt question hit Brazilians in the winter of 1982–3 and again in 1983–4 with the drying-up of lines of credit, and has continued right up to the present time. The most eminent Brazilian economist, Celso Furtado, talks of the 'new dependence'.[10] Similarly, the wrath of a group of Brazilian economists has been heaped upon the International Monetary Fund,[11] which, perhaps understandably, demands that the Brazilian authorities reduce the public debt in exchange for the Fund's financial help. Unfortunately, all these problems tend to obscure the complexity of the debt question.

At the end of 1985, the Central Bank of Brazil calculated that the country's foreign debt amounted to about $100 billion. But they did not reveal the composition of this debt, and independent experts are attempting to disentangle its structure. It is almost certain that about 28 per cent of it is owed to the United States. Thus, contrary to received opinion, if one excludes some Arab and Japanese finance, a major share of the debt must be due to Western European states. Estimates suggest that the United Kingdom's share is about 8 per cent, while that of West Germany is, surprisingly, somewhat less than this. This leads to the conclusion that France, Switzerland and other Western European states have a very important stake in this problem. (See Chapter 2 for a more up-to-date analysis of the Brazilian debt problem which underlines the important role of the EEC.)

It is clear that a major part of the debt has been used to build up Brazil's manufacturing base. Despite the Brazilian moratorium on interest payments (February 1987), she continues to repay the principal. However, as inevitably happens under a military regime, a number of projects undertaken in Brazil in the 1970s, were superfluous loss-makers. According to Henri-Philippe Reichstul, head of the state companies division within the Planning Ministry, $60 billion of the $70 billion public foreign debt is owned by state companies. Of this, he said, 'as much as a quarter of $15 billion, has been irrevocably lost' through ill-conceived projects.[12]

Reference has already been made to repeated Brazilian calls, echoed by the EEC, for the adoption of a 'common Community attitude' to the Latin American debt problem. Rightly or wrongly, the Brazilians believe that the European attitude to this question is more understanding than that of the Americans. In this context, it had been hoped that such a common attitude would be adopted at the meeting of EEC Finance Ministers on 10 March 1986. Unfortunately, these hopes were not realised because the different countries of the EEC have different attitudes to this question. Thus, at one extreme, the Commission and France want to see the EEC adopt a common 'interventionist' policy which would view the question with understanding. At the other extreme, Britain and West Germany want the EEC to adopt a 'market approach' to the debt problem.

The author believes that everyone should adopt a more philosophical attitude to this question. He has frequently cited the case of the United States, whose balance of payments was persistently supported during the period 1850–1913 by massive capital inflows from European countries, notably France, Germany and the United Kingdom.[13] On some occasions, these countries exported as much as 10 per cent of their GNP in the form of capital investment.'

In the specific case of Brazil, there are some grounds for optimism. First, as has already been observed, the debt is being repayed. Second, rare among Third World countries, capital inflows have tended to outstrip capital outflows. Finally, there is an excellent example of a major Community initiative in the form of the EEC's participation in the Carajás Iron Ore Project. To the author, this seems to mark a real reawakening of EEC interest in Latin America and is an example of constructive co-operation which might be emulated in other parts of Latin America.

The ECU[14] versus the Dollar: the case for Brazil

In the context of the debt problem, the author has frequently suggested to colleagues in Brazil and other Latin American countries that they should quote the sales of their commodities in ECUs as well as in US dollars. Also, it would be more beneficial for them to take a greater amount of loans in ECUs. There are a number of sound reasons for making these proposals. Throughout history, it has been accepted international practice to quote the prices of commodities in the currencies of the principal trading partners. Thus, since the EEC is one of the most important trading partners of Brazil and is the world's greatest importer of commodities, it would be logical to quote a major part of sales of commodities in ECUs.

The use of the ECU for taking up loans as well as for selling commodities would have a number of advantages for Brazil and other Latin American countries. The main ones are as follows:

1. The ECU is the official unit of account of the EEC, which is the world's most important trading bloc. As such, it has the backing of the Community.
2. It is being increasingly used for private commercial purposes, as well as being the second international reserve asset.
3. Over the past eight years, its value has been stable. This contrasts strongly with such currencies as the US dollar, sterling, the yen and the Swiss franc.
4. ECU rates of interest have likewise tended to remain rather low. The composition of the ECU implies that it is a 'risk-spreader' for businessmen.
5. A greater use of the ECU by Brazilians and other Latin Americans would contribute to a strengthening of links between them and the EEC.

THE CARAJÁS IRON ORE PROJECT: A REALLY DIMENSION IN CO-OPERATION

A series of coincidences in the 1970s and the early 1980s paved the way for the EEC's involvement in the Carajás Iron Ore Project.[15] The initial development was the Commission's policy (to which reference has already been made) of seeking secure supplies of energy and raw materials. Then, a series of further developments, involving the EEC and Latin America—and, more specifically, Brazil—made EEC participation in the Carajás Project a strong possibility. These were:

1. A growing awareness within the Commission, especially under the leadership of Commissioner Haferkamp, that something should, at last, be done for Latin America. In the field of EEC external relations, Latin America had, until the late 1970s, constituted a kind of 'lost continent'.
2. A growing consciousness of the beginnings of a return to democracy in a number of Latin American countries. It was felt that the EEC should encourage this development.
3. A decision by the Brazilian government to develop the extensive mining deposits of the Serra de Carajás, in the Amazonian area. The Brazilians decided to embark upon this major enterprise in order to provide raw materials for their own growing industries, to earn foreign exchange from exports of metal ores and to begin a serious economic

Table 1.5 Carajás iron ore project: provisional financing plan, 1978–87

	$ million	(%)
A. *Equity*		
1. CVRD internal cash generation		
a. Expended to 12/81	565.0*	12.0
b. New from Southern operations	844.7	17.9
Subtotal	1,409.7	29.9
2. New capital subscription		
a. Reinvested government dividends	257.2	5.5
b. CVRD convertible debentures	125.0†	2.7
Subtotal	382.2	8.2
Total equity	1,791.9	38.1
B. *Debt*		
1. Local		
a. BNDE	700.0	14.9
b. FINAME	401.9	8.5
c. Banco da Amazonia	111.9	2.4
d. CVRD convertible debentures	125.0	2.6
Subtotal	1,338.8	28.4
2. Foreign		
a. IBRD	300.0	6.4
b. IFC	50.0	1.1
c. EEC	400.0	8.5
d. Japanese import loans	250.0‡	5.3
e. Japanese Exim direct loan	50.0	1.1
f. Japanese Commercial Bank syndication	150.0	3.2
g. Japanese bond issue	50.0	1.1
h. KFW	150.0	3.2
i. Morgan Guarantee	27.0	0.6
j. European export credits	47.5	1.0
k. Japanese export credits	33.3	0.7
l. US Exim Bank	67.8	1.4
Subtotal	1,575.6	33.5
Total debt	2,914.4	61.9
C. Total Financing	4,706.3	100.0

*   Total project expenditures as of 12/81 are estimated to be US$630.0 of which CVRD internal cash generation accounts for US$565.0, BNDE loan disbursements for US$38.0 million, and Morgan Guarantee loan for US$27.0.
†   Issue of CVRD convertible debentures totals US$250.0 million of which 50% is assumed to be converted into common and preferred shares.
‡   Of which US$175 million from Japanese Exim Bank and US$75 million from commercial banks.
Source: Lloyds Bank International.

development of the Amazonian region. The development of Serra would necessitate recourse to national and foreign sources of finance.

The Serra de Carajás, situated in the State of Pará (550km from Belém), contains high-quality deposits of iron ore, copper, manganese, tin, nickel, bauxite, gold and other metals. The area of mineral deposits extends over 100,000 sq km and contains an estimated 18 billion tonne of iron ore.

Estimates for the Carajás Iron Ore Project (the Small Carajás Project[16]) budgeted for an initial provisional financing plan for the period 1978–87 of $4,706.3 million, of which at least 33.5 per cent would come from foreign sources (see Table 1.5).

From the outset, Brazilian officials had made contacts with the World Bank, German, Japanese and American financial insitutions and the EEC. The World Bank expressed sympathetic interest in the project, largely because the Bank was already engaged in other projects in similar undeveloped parts of Brazil. The Germans, Japanese and Americans were very interested in being assured of regular, secure and almost limitless supplies of top-grade iron ore.

The EEC, while being interested in Carajá, experienced problems in associating itself with the project. First, there was a strong African lobby within the Commission which pointed out that African countries, with which the Community already had strong links, possessed important iron ore deposits. Logically, priority should be given to the further development of these sources rather than seeking new ones in Latin America. Second, even if the Community were to prove sympathetic to the Brazilian case, where and how were they to obtain the large amounts of finance involved? (Estimates of between $400 and $600 million were suggested as a possible EEC involvement). There was also a strong environmental and human rights lobby which would not make EEC involvement easy. Eventually, due mainly to the energetic lobbying by the Latin Affairs Division of the EEC, and notably the personal involvement of Commissioner Haferkamp, the Council of Ministers, acting within the framework of the European Coal and Steel Community (ECSC), agreed in July 1982 to make a loan of $600 million to the Companhia Vale do Rio Doce (CVRD), the Brazilian company responsible for the development of the Carajás Project, in which the Brazilian government has a 65 per cent stake.

The basic conditions attached to the Community loan are as follows:

1. The loan would be transferred to the CVRD in annual instalments.
2. These transfers would depend on:
   (a) the successful completion in the previous year of the planned technical parts of the project; and
   (b) the degree of satisfaction of the World Bank (which, like the Community, is also financially involved in the Project) expressed in its annual reports concerning respect by the CVRD for human

rights (e.g., adequate compensation for disabled persons and satisfactory housing and conditions for workers involved on the site) and the environment.

Although the EEC had, at the outset, been willing to organise a loan of $600 million to participate in the project, it was eventually not found necessary to go beyond $400 million. Community disbursements as at 11 July 1985 are given in Table 1.6. What is notable about this loan is that the Brazilian company has already started to repay its debt.

Table 1.6   EEC disbursements to the Carajás Iron Ore Project

Individual loan agreement	Date (day/month/year)	Value (million DM)	Rate of interest (% per year)
I	4 November 1982	165	8.05
II	5 June 1984	160	8.36
III	5 December 1984	150	7.58
IV	11 July 1985	250	7.75

Source: Agilberto Pires, Finance Director, CVRD.

On the technical level, the Carajás Project has been one of the few success stories in a tropical country. All the technical parts of the eneterprise have been completed ahead of schedule—these include the construction of the extraction and processing infrastructure at Carajás, a completely new railway, 887 km in length, across the jungle from Carajás to São Luís, port facilities in São Luís and townships in the Carajás area. In fact, the first consignments of iron ore started to be transported by rail in 1987.

There has, however, been some dissatisfaction with the record concerning compensation for disabled persons and working conditions for some of the workers. Earlier, in 1985, members of the European Parliament, together with their Brazilian counterparts, visited the Carajás area and voiced concern about these matters. The Brazilians promised to meet Community demands on these points.

FORMAL AGREEMENTS BETWEEN THE EEC AND BRAZIL

Reference has already been made to the fact that formal relations between the Community and Brazil have existed for 25 years. Thus, the first agreement between the two partners was signed between Brazil and the

European Atomic Energy Community (Euratom) in 1961 for the peaceful use of atomic energy. It came into force in 1965 for a period of 20 years.

A trade agreement between the two sides came into force in 1974. Its aim was the expansion of trade between the two parties, with the granting of the Most Favoured Nation (MFN) status by the EEC to Brazil. This agreement was replaced by the much broader co-operation agreement, signed on 18 September 1980, and which came into force on 1 October 1982. To the author, this agreement, which is examined in detail below, holds great promise for the future and could serve as a model for other Latin American countries. The other two agreements, the MFA and GSP agreement, have already been examined in this study.

Clearly, the co-operation agreement between Brazil and the EEC offers the most obvious field of co-operation between the two sides. This agreement consists of three basic parts, together with an annex giving Brazil preferences for her traditional products. The three main parts cover trade, commercial and economic co-operation.

At the trade level, the two parties granted each other MFN status. This is the very minimum that would be excepted from such an agreement. However, to give teeth to this status, article 2, concerning commercial co-operation, holds out the greatest hope for the future. Both sides agreed to promote to the maximum and to diversify trade between them. In order to facilitate this, they agreed to study means of removing obstacles—especially non-tariff barriers. In part 3 of this article, there is even the suggestion of organising favourable credit conditions on a national basis. Here, specific reference is also made to base products (obviously raw materials), but also to semi-manufactures and manufactures. Although, as the author understands it, a precautionary note was sounded in the call for account to be taken of the special needs of each partner, a major innovation was the clear call for a greater diversification of trade and the agreement to study and recommend promotional measures (marketing) for exports and imports.

Article 3 on economic co-operation is even more promising. Here, the aim is long-term and the special goals are:

1. The encouragement of the development and prosperity of their respective industries.
2. The opening-up of new sources of supplies and new markets.
3. Encouraging scientific and technological progress.
4. Contributing, in a general manner, to the development of their respective economies and standards of living.

In an apparent attempt to put teeth into these aims, seven precise areas are laid down for which the two parties should find the necessary (presumably economic) means so as to facilitate implementation of the above goals. These areas are:

1. An extensive and harmonious co-operation between their respective industries. Here, 'joint' enterprises are proposed.
2. Greater participation by both parties in industrial development, to their mutual advantage.
3. Scientific and technological co-operation.
4. Co-operation in the field of energy.
5. Co-operation in the area of agriculture.
6. Encouragement of an expansion of investment on mutually advantageous conditions.
7. Co-operation with third parties.

Both parties agreed to encourage the regular exchanges of information on commercial and economic co-operation.

A Mixed Commission, composed of representatives of both parties meets at least annually or by mutual request.

In the annex, the EEC accorded Brazil a preferential margin of 8 per cent for cocoa butter and of 9 per cent for soluble coffee.

The author considers that the aims laid down in this agreement are positive. Even more important are the seven areas of co-operation designed to facilitate the implementation of the goals. Among these, one of the most interesting is the proposal for setting up 'joint' enterprises. Perhaps in this way it might be possible to avoid investment in costly, prestige projects whose profit potential is questionable. Co-operation should also be easy to achieve in the fields of energy, agriculture and technology. Certainly, if Brazil wishes to increase her agricultural productivity in a substantial manner, the CAP could perhaps serve as a viable model.

The author is aware that the Commission is already (wisely) providing scholarships for young Brazilians to come to EEC countries for postgraduate training. This should, however, be greatly expanded.

OTHER CONSIDERATIONS

The enlargement

The entry of Portugal and Spain into the EEC will, in some areas, have important consequences for non-Community countries, notably Latin American. The author observed some years ago[17] that Portuguese and Spanish membership would increases EEC self-sufficiency in products such as steel, shipbuilding, textiles, wine, olive oil and Mediterranean food produce in general. In contrast, neither of these countries is self-sufficient in temperate food produce and formerly tended to make good its shortfall through imports from the cheapest third country sources—notably the Americas. Unfortunately for these countries, due to the acceptance of the conditions of the CAP by Spain and Portugal, they will henceforth tend to make good their shortfall through imports from internal EEC sources. Already, a violent trade war has broken out between the Community and the USA through Spain's substantial reduction in American grain imports. In contrast, as the Commission has pointed out, the former high Spanish tariffs will be reduced for imports of manufactures and industrial goods to the relatively low level of the CET.

In a more recent study, Alfred Tovias[18] points out that Portugal and Spain must henceforth give a certain degree of preference to the ACP countries in their imports of tropical produce. On balance, he believes, the second enlargement will be disadvantageous for Brazil.

Community policy changes

This is indeed a most opportune moment to examine the Community's trading policies because the EEC is on the verge of a most internal economic revolution. In the summer of 1987, the Single Eoen Act (SEA) became law. This means that by the end of 1992, we shall finally have a 'real' Common Market. In turn, this implies that there will no longer be any obstacles to the internal movement of goods, capital and services, and there will be no internal exchange controls. Also, only modest variations in the levels of value added tax (VAT) will be allowed.

All this should make the Community more efficient and more competitive internationally. Consequently, protectionism will be less of a temptation. This will have positive implications for Latin American countries.

At the same time, the EEC is finally adopting more drastic policies to control the argricultural surpluses associated with the CAP. Due to the shortage of financial resources, the CAP must be fundamentally transformed. These changes will also be positive for Latin American countries.

CONCLUSIONS

What conclusions may be drawn from this study of relations between the European Economic Community and Brazil? In order to answer this complex question, the author believes that it is necessary to place these relations in the context of the present international economic climate and against the background of the economic policies presently pursued by Brazil and the EEC. Despite current signs of an upsurge in economic activity in most EEC countries, both partners have been experiencing an economic recession which has had a negative influence on trade — and the EEC is now Brazil's second most important trading partner.

Both partners are protectionist in their economic policy and it is perhaps surprising that they still manage to conduct so much trade with each other. However, the Community does offer concessions to Third World countries and it is Brazil, more than any other Latin American country, which has used them to the maximum.

Probably of greatest importance are the most recent agreement between the two sides and EEC involvement in the Carajás Project. The agreement holds many possibilities for future co-operation and is certainly more comprehensive than the recently renewed accord between Mexico and the EEC.

Can the Brazilian experience serve as an example for other Latin American countries? To the author, Brazil's success is mainly due to a happy combination of a number of factors:

1. Its varied economic structure.
2. Its flexibility in quickly using new export possibilities whenever and wherever they arise.
3. Its own economic policies, particularly helped by the adoption of a 'crawling peg policy' for the cruzeiro.

To the author, the countries in Latin America which could most easily emulate the example of Brazil are those of the Andean Pact group of countries. One country which could be a most likely candidate for Community involvement in a Carajás-type project is Colombia. One has in mind that country's extensive deposits of coal which could be further developed.

In the case of smaller and/or economically weaker Latin American countries, it is unlikely that the trade concessions offered by the EEC would be of much help. The author considers that the Community might have to offer more generous concessions to these countries, almost certainly involving 'sensitive' products. Also, EEC involvement in Carajás-type projects could be mutually beneficial to both sides.

Finally, reference should be made to the somewhat disappointing Commission document on relations between the Community and Latin America which was published in 1984.[19] Although the Commission seemed to refute the accusations of protectionism levelled against the EEC—a refutation which would not be supported by many economists—and did not seem to hold out much hope for the granting of further concessions by the EEC to Latin American countries, a number of proposals were made for intensifying relations between the two sides. The European Investment Bank was invited to apply to Latin American countries its facilities for funding outside the Community. Likewise, calls were made for intensified industrial, scientific, energy, training, cultural and information co-operation and exchanges between the two sides. Trade promotion should also be facilitated.

Latin Americans tended to react rather negatively to this Commission document. Miguel Wionczek[20] has described it as negative and hopeless. Others consider that they should take up a common stand on trade and debt questions.

The author believes that countries should try to utilise the existing concessions more effectively, and, when agreements come up for renewal, they should try to widen their scope. Equally, where the Commission's proposals for co-operation (especially where they involve EEC financing) are accepted by the Council, Latin American countries should use them as fully as possible. The author is aware, for example, that the Commission is financing scholarships for a number of Brazilians studying in Europe. Lastly, it is possible that Latin American countries could obtain even more capital investment from the EEC, from the European Investment Bank, from Community backed loans, as well as from bilateral (country-to-country) public and private finance.

In these conclusions, the author has made a number of concrete proposals which might be accepted by both parties. There are no strong reasons why they should not be accepted.

To date, Brazil has used the trade concessions offered by the EEC with great flexibility and intelligence and it is assumed that this will continue.

Although Alfred Tovias considers that the second enlargement of the EEC will, on balance, be negative for Brazil, the author observes that Brazilian businessmen, using their traditional acumen, are already setting up businesses in Portgual. Furthermore, very few observers appear to be aware that Portuguese and Brazilians have the right to reciprocal citizenship. Does this imply that Brazil has a form of priviliged access, through Portgual, to the EEC?

However, the most important policy changes inside the EEC which appear to have positive potential for Brazil are current moves to restrict the agricultural surpluses of the CAP and the coming into force of the Single European Act which will create a 'real' Common Market by 1992. Both these moves mean that the EEC should be less protectionist in its external policies five years from now. In turn, relations between the EEC and Brazil should tend to improve.

NOTES

1. P. Coffey and M.S. Wionczek (eds), *The European Economic Community and Mexico*, Dordrecht, 1987.
2. P. Coffey (ed.), *Main Economic Policy Areas of the EEC*, Dordrecht, 1983.
3. The most important statement here was that made by the Commission in The Supply with Raw Materials of the EC, supplement to the *Bulletin of the European Communities*, no. 1/75. This statement called for the 'securing' of the Community's supplies of energy and raw materials. Since the publication of this statement the Commission has made a number of similar calls.

4. Eurostat, *Analysis of EC–Latin American Trade*, Commission of the European Communities, Luxembourg, 1985.
5. In December 1985, the ten countries of the EEC were Belgium, Denmark, France, West Germany, Greece, Ireland, Italy, Luxembourg, the Netherlands and the United Kingdom. In January 1986, Portugal and Spain became the eleventh and twelfth member states.
6. The group of 20 Latin American countries consists of Mexico, Guatemala, Honduras, El Salvador, Nicaragua, Costa Rica, Panama, Cuba, Haiti, Dominican Republic, Colombia, Venezuela, Ecuador, Peru, Brazil, Chile, Bolivia, Paraguay, Uruguay and Argentina.
7. P. Coffey, *Brazil and the European Economic Community*, Amsterdam and Cambridge, April 1984.
8. In its study, *Brazil: Economic Memorandum*, of 1984, the World Bank also underlines the role of these factors as contributing to the expansion of Brazil's exports.
9. OECD, *The Generalised System of Preferences*, Paris 1983.
10. C. Furtado, *A Nova Dependencia*, 5th edn, Paz Terra, Rio de Janeiro, 1983.
11. Notably: 'FMI x Brasil—A Armadila da Recessão', *Forum Gazeta Mercantil*, November 1983.
12. See *Financial Times*, 25 November 1985.
13. See P. Coffey, *Europe and Money*, Macmillan, London, 1977.
14. The ECU is a basket of the currencies of the ten (as at 31 December 1985) member states of the EEC. At the present time, its composition is as follows (the Portuguese and Spanish currencies will become part of the ECU at the end of the transitional period leading to their full integration within the Common Market).
15. Most of this part of the paper is taken from P. Coffey, *A Case Study—the Carajás Project*, Europa Instituut, Amsterdam, 1985.
16. The Large Carajás Project covers the whole area of thera de Carajás and includes the deposits of all the main metals. The Small Carajás Project covers only extraction and processing of iron ore. The Community is concerned exclusively with this latter project.
17. P. Coffey, *The Common Market and its International Economic Policies*, NUFFIC, The Hague, 1982.
18. A. Tovias, 'The Impact of the Second Enlargement of the European Community on Latin American Economies', in Coffey and Wionczek, *The EEC and Mexico*.
19. Commission of the European Communities, *Guidelines for the Strengthening of Relations between the Community and Latin America, Communication from the Commission to the Council, Brussels, 6 April 1984*.
20. *P. Coffey and M.S. Wionczek, The EEC and Mexico, Nijoft, Dordrecht, 1987.*

2

Economic Relations between Brazil and the European Economic Community: A Brazilian Overview

Luiz Aranha Corrêa do Lago

The recent enlargement of the European Economic Community (EEC) and the prospects of increased integration of the Brazilian and Argentinian economies seem to provide an adequate occasion for a revision of the economic relations between Brazil and the member countries of the EEC in recent decades. The main objective of this study is to examine trade and capital flows between Brazil and the EEC since the end of World War II, in order to appraise changes in the relative importance of Brazil's external economic transactions with member countries. This will be attempted from a Brazilian perspective so that those changes are studied in the context of Brazil's economic evolution in the last four decades and on the basis of Brazilian statistical data. However, domestic economic policies and more specific aspects of Brazilian development are treated rather briefly, only to serve as a frame of reference for the more detailed examination of trends in the external sector.

The first section of this study is an overview of Brazil's economic relations with EEC countries since the nineteenth century. It provides a historical background for the changes which occurred after World War II, which are then examined in greater detail.

The second section presents very briefly the general trends of the Brazilian economy in the post-war period, with an emphasis on the external sector. The evolution of Brazilian–EEC trade in four decades, in the context of a permanent rivalry with the United States, is the object of the third section.

In the fourth section, the question of foreign investment is treated, stressing the role of European countries in the process, in contrast to the United States and Japan. A short subsection is also devoted to immigration.

The fifth section deals with the debt problem, centering on recent developments and EEC participation in total Brazilian indebtedness. A brief conclusion restates the main trends in Brazilian–EEC relations. (A more detailed treatment of trade, capital investment and debt from a Brazilian perspective will be found in other parts of this book[1]).

HISTORICAL ANTECEDENTS

During the nineteenth century, Great Britain played a predominant role in the Brazilian economy. In fact, Britain was Brazil's most important commercial partner, and controlled most of its shipping. All Brazilian government foreign debt was placed through British banking houses. And Britain made significant direct investments in the country, notably in railway and other public utilities, but also in banking, insurance and manufacturing.

In the three decades which preceded World War I, Britain suffered from increasing competition from Germany and the United States, and, in certain areas, also from France and Belgium, so that its pre-eminent position in Brazil was gradually eroded. In 1911–13, it was still reponsible for slightly more than a quarter of Brazilian imports, but other countries had gained considerable ground, with Germany's share amounting to 17 per cent and that of the United States 15 per cent. The United States purchased more than a third of Brazilian exports, while Germany's share of one-seventh just exceeded Britain's. France, whose relative importance was declining, ranked fourth with a share of about one-tenth, both of the import and of the export trade, while Belgium was Brazil's sixth supplier, behind Argentina, and closely followed by Portugal. On the other hand, the Netherlands emerged as Brazil's fifth most important market (followed by Argentina) (see Table 2.1). The share of present-day EEC countries in Brazil's total exports reached 49.7 per cent and, in the case of total imports, 68.1 per cent. Thus, it is clear that the importance of present-day EEC member countries in Brazilian foreign trade was already clearly established on the eve of World War I, even if Great Britain were excluded.

With respect to foreign investment, Britain's early pre-eminence was maintained. It accounted for more than two-thirds of investments in government securities and possibly for more than half of direct investments and private portfolio investments. France ranked second in both cases, well behind Britain, while Germany, Canada, Portugal, the United States and Belgium played a minor role.

Europe's contribution to the formation of a free Brazilian labour force after the abolition of slavery in 1888 was also considerable. Gross entries

Table 2.1 Brazil's imports from and exports to selected countries, 1901–45

	Great Britain	United States	Germany	France	Belgium	Nether-lands	Italy	Denmark	Portugal	Spain	Japan	Argentina	EEC
Exports													
1901–10	17.0	39.7	15.2	9.4	2.4	4.0	0.9	0.2	0.7	0.3	–	3.1	50.1
1911–20	11.6	39.7	5.9	12.0	1.6	4.3	4.4	0.7	0.7	0.9	0.0	6.4	42.1
1911–13	13.4	35.7	14.3	9.9	2.5	7.3	1.2	0.2	0.4	0.5	0.0	4.2	49.7
1914–20	10.8	41.4	2.3	12.9	1.2	3.1	5.8	1.0	0.9	1.1	0.0	7.3	39.1
1921–30	5.7	42.7	8.2	9.6	2.7	6.0	5.7	1.0	1.0	0.4	0.0	6.1	40.3
1931–39	9.2	40.0	13.0	7.7	3.1	4.1	3.0	1.2	0.6	0.4	2.3	5.1	42.3
1940–45	14.2	49.6	0.6	0.8	0.5	0.3	0.4	0.2	0.6	2.0	1.6	10.7	19.6
Imports													
1901–10	28.4	11.9	13.6	9.0	3.6	0.6	3.4	0.2	6.4	0.8	–	10.2	66.0
1911–20	22.1	30.6	7.4	6.4	2.0	0.6	3.1	0.2	4.1	1.2	0.2	11.8	47.1
1911–13	26.2	14.9	17.2	9.2	4.9	0.8	3.8	0.2	4.8	1.0	0.0	7.5	68.1
1914–20	20.4	37.4	3.3	5.1	0.7	0.5	2.8	0.2	3.8	1.3	0.3	13.6	38.1
1921–30	21.9	26.4	11.3	6.1	3.9	1.5	3.6	0.4	1.9	1.0	0.2	11.9	51.6
1931–39	14.3	25.1	17.5	3.7	4.4	2.6	2.8	0.5	1.7	0.6	0.9	12.3	48.1
1940–45	5.8	55.9	0.7	0.3	0.2	0.1	0.2	0.0	2.0	0.2	0.7	16.7	9.5

Great Britain, Germany, France, Belgium, Netherlands, Italy, Denmark, Portugal, Spain. The share of other EEC countries was either totally negligible or non-existent.

Source: IBGE, *Anuário Estatístico do Brasil, 1939–40*, Rio de Janeiro, 1940, Appendix, pp. 1366–73; *Anuário Estatístico do Brasil*, 1946 and 1954.

Table 2.2 Immigration to Brazil from selected countries

Country of origin	1884–93	1894–1903	1904–13	1884–1913	1914–23	1924–33	1934–39	1914–39	1884–1939	1940–45
West Germany	22,778	6,698	33,859	63,355	29,339	61,728	16,243	107,310	170,645	1,641
Belgium	2,657	171	1,128	3,956	981	742	330	2,053	6,009	178
France	7,977	2,517	8,572	19,066	5,392	5,609	2,306	13,307	32,373	415
Netherlands	1,026	1,044	3,456	5,526	842	1,111	721	2,674	8,200	123
United Kingdom	2,870	825	6,710	10,405	3,964	5,829	3,547	13,340	23,745	475
Spain	103,116	102,142	224,672	429,930	94,779	52,405	4,604	151,788	581,718	684
Italy	510,533	537,784	196,521	1,244,838	86,320	70,177	10,928	167,425	1,412,263	687
Portugal	170,621	157,542	384,672	712,835	201,252	233,650	56,657	491,559	1,204,394	20,870
Subtotal	821,578	808,723	859,590	2,489,891	422,869	431,251	95,336	949,456	3,439,347	25,073
Poland, Lithuania, Russia	40,959	3,936	48,100	92,995	13,100	69,987	8,559	91,646	184,551	811
Austria and Hungary	13,684	32,456	24,660	70,800	7,506	13,768	2,271	23,545	94,345	
Turkey	3	6,522	42,177	48,702	19,255	10,227	271	29,753	78,455	
Syria	93	602	3,826	4,521	1,145	14,264	577	15,986	20,507	
Japan	—	—	11,868	11,868	20,398	110,191	43,342	173,931	185,799	2,816
United States	649	2,664	2,949	6,262	1,898	2,556	1,945	6,399	12,661	
Total	883,668	862,110	1,006,617	2,752,395	503,981	737,223	165,118	1,406,322	4,158,717	36,943

Source: 1884–1939: IBGE, *Anuário Estatístico do Brasil, 1939–40*, Appendix, p. 1307; 1940–45: *Anuário Estatístico*, various issues.

of immigrants to Brazil from 1884 to 1913 totalled 2.75 million, of whom 45.2 per cent were Italian, 25.9 per cent Portuguese and 15.6 per cent Spanish. Arrivals from the Russian Empire (including Poles and Lithuanians) accounted for 3.4 per cent of the same total while those from Austria-Hungary, Germany and France were respectively 2.6, 2.3 and 0.7 per cent.[2] British and Belgian immigration was much less significant in quantitative terms, but included many skilled labourers and technicians whose contribution was very important in qualitative terms (see Table 2.2).

During World War I, American influence increased considerably, as imports from the United States largely exceeded purchases from British suppliers. In spite of a brief British recovery in the mid-1920s, by the end of the decade the United States had definitely become Brazil's most important supplier and foreign market (see Table 2.1). On the other hand, in 1930 British direct investment still accounted for about half of the total, while the share of the United States had increased to slightly less than a fifth. As to Brazil's government debt, Britain still controlled about two-thirds of the total, while the proportion held by the United States was 30 per cent. France's share had considerably shrunk as a result of the devaluation of the franc. France and other European countries had direct investments totalling about the double of the American share and about two-thirds of Britain's share, but their holdings of foreign debt only reached 5 per cent of the total.[3]

European immigration recovered in the 1920s, but it now made a less important contribution to the overall demographic evolution of the country. On the other hand, Japanese immigration tended to accelerate.[4]

The Great Depression had very serious consequences for the Brazilian economy. Since the nineteenth century, Brazilian exports had depended heavily on coffee, which since mid-century had accounted for about 50 per cent or more of the total value of exports, and to a lesser extent on hides, cocoa, sugar, tobacco, cotton, matée-leaf and rubber, whose relative importance varied at different times (see Table 2.3). In the first decade of the twentieth century, rubber exports had reached 28 per cent of the total, still representing 12 per cent of the total exports from 1911 to 1920. In the 1920s, however, as the price of rubber fell steeply, coffee exports gained an unprecedented pre-eminence, averaging almost 70 per cent of the total between 1921 and 1930. The collapse of the international coffee market in the wake of the world crisis was thus bound to affect the country significantly.

A policy of coffee purchases coupled with significant destructions of coffee stocks by the Brazilian government during the 1930s helped to maintain a satisfactory level of activity in the coffee sector and to prevent further significant declines in the price of that product in international markets. Concomitantly, the significant decline in the value of total exports and imports created favourable conditions for the development of domestic industry and a diversification of agricultural activities.[5]

Table 2.3 Distribution of Brazilian exports by commodity, 1821–1845 (percentage of total)

	Coffee	Sugar	Cocoa	Maté-leaf	Tobacco	Cotton	Rubber	Hides	Total
1821–1880	18.4	30.1	0.5	0.0	2.5	20.6	0.1	13.6	85.8
1931–1840	43.8	24.0	0.6	0.5	1.9	10.8	0.3	7.9	89.8
1841–1850	41.4	26.7	1.0	0.9	1.8	7.5	0.4	8.5	88.2
1851–1860	48.8	21.2	1.0	1.6	2.6	6.2	2.3	7.2	90.9
1861–1870	45.5	12.3	0.9	1.2	3.0	18.3	3.1	6.0	90.3
1871–1880	56.6	11.8	1.2	1.5	3.4	9.5	5.55	5.6	95.1
1881–1890	61.5	9.9	1.6	1.2	2.7	4.2	8.0	3.2	92.3
1891–1900	64.5	6.0	1.5	1.3	2.2	2.7	15.0	2.4	95.6
1901–1910	51.3	1.2	2.8	2.9	2.4	2.1	28.2	4.3	95.2
1911–1920	53.0	3.0	3.6	3.0	2.6	2.0	12.1	6.2	85.5
1921–1930	69.6	1.4	3.2	2.7	2.1	2.4	2.6	4.6	88.6
1931–1940	50.0	0.5	4.2	1.6	1.5	14.2	1.1	4.4	77.5
1941–1945	32.0	0.5	3.3	0.9	1.1	8.6	2.4	3.7	52.5

Sources: IBGE, *Anuário Estatístico do Brasil, 1939–40*, p. 1380; *Boletim Estatístico*, vol. 3, no. 9, 1945. The data for 1939–45 are reproduced in H.W. Spiegel, *The Brazilian Economy: Chronic Inflation and Sporadic Industrialization*, Blackiston, Philadelphia, 1949, p. 123.

However, Brazil could not avoid a balance-of-payments crisis throughout the decade. After 1929, an interruption of the inflows of foreign capital occurred, reserves were rapidly exhausted (local currency had been made convertible into gold in 1926), and devaluation and exchange controls as well as restrictions on the service of the foreign debt had to be adopted.

In such a context, the United States was able to maintain its participation in Brazilian foreign trade, still absorbing 40 per cent of the country's exports and supplying one-fourth of its imports during most of the decade. Great Britain lost its second position to Germany as the share of the latter in total Brazilian exports and imports from 1931 to 1939 reached 13.0 and 17.5 respectively, while the corresponding figures for Britain were 9.2 and 14.3 per cent (see Table 2.1). German gains were to a great extent to the detriment of Britain, as Germany's share in Brazilian exports increased from 8–9 per cent in the early 1930s to a maximum of 19 per cent in 1939, a fact which resulted from the expansion of German compensation trade.[6] On the other hand, for the same reasons, from 1936 to 1938, the share of German products in Brazil's total imports averaged 24.1 per cent, exceeding the participation of the United States (23.1 per cent).

As far as Brazilian exports are concerned, France, with a share of 7.7 per cent, the Netherlands with 4.1 per cent, Belgium with 3.1 per cent, and Italy with 3 per cent, remained important European markets for Brazilian products (while Argentina also absorbed 5.1 per cent of the total). Present-day EEC countries as a group accounted for 42.3 per cent of total exports from 1931 to 1939, slightly more than the United States (see Table 2.1).

Included among other Brazilian main suppliers were Argentina, with 12.3 per cent of total imports from 1931 to 1939, Belgium with 4.4 per cent, France with 3.7 per cent, Italy with 2.8 per cent and the Netherlands with 2.6 per cent. The decreasing importance of Portugal and Spain in Brazil's foreign trade may be noted, while Japan emerged as an outlet for Brazilian products (absorbing 2.3 per cent of total exports, mainly cotton, whose importance in total exports increased in the 1930s, passing from 2.1 per cent of the total in the late 1920s to 18.6 per cent in 1935–9). But it remained a less important supplier, accounting for only 0.9 per cent imports.

Taken as a group, present-day EEC members supplied 48.1 per cent of Brazilian total imports from 1931 to 1939, almost twice the share of the United States.

From 1928 to 1938, the contraction of Brazilian trade accompanied that in world trade, as the share of Brazil in total world imports remained at 1.2 per cent, while its share of total exports fell from 1.5 to 1.3 per cent.[7]

There was a decrease in immigration to Brazil after the crisis, but from 1930 to 1939, 332,800 immigrants still entered the country, in spite of restrictions which were gradually introduced. Present-day EEC countries still accounted for the majority of the immigrants, but Japan's share was very significant. Between 1934 and 1939, as far as total immigration is concerned, only Portugal exceeded Japan and between 1930 and 1939 the Japanese were the main group of immigrants entering São Paulo, accounting for 51.3 per cent, while the Portuguese accounted for only 18.3 per cent of the total.[8]

Foreign investments, which had accelerated during the 1920s, fell sharply during the 1930s. According to the estimates available for 1938, Brazil's long-term obligations reached about $2,030 million. Britain still accounted for 39.4 per cent of the total, followed by the United States with 26.5 per cent and Portugal with 14.8 per cent. France held a share of 3 per cent plus a debt in gold francs which varied from 0.5 to 3.7 per cent of the total. The shares of Germany and the Netherlands were rather small (2 and 0.5 per cent respectively) while unidentified holders accounted for the remaining 10 per cent.[9]

According to official figures, Brazil's outstanding external public debt fell from £266.2 million in 1930 to £276.0 million in 1931 to £258.8 million in 1935 to £241.3 million in 1940.[10] Excluding small loans to two Brazilian states, Brazil's debt service had been 'substantially maintained until October 1931', through additional borrowing and refunding operations. After that date, 'debt payments declined sharply to about 20% and 30% of the amount due in most years until 1943, except for complete default in 1938 and 1939'.[11] This resulted initially from reductions in interest rates enforced by Brazil under the so-called Aranha plan, which also established priorities for the allocation of foreign exchange to payments of different types of debt.[12] Debt renegotiation would extend into the war period.

World War II interrupted Brazilian trade with many of its most important European partners. Brazilian–American economic relations were further strengthened as the United States purchased 49.5 per cent of Brazilian exports and supplied 55.9 per cent of Brazil's imports from 1940 to 1945. Brazil accumulated significant sterling balances against Britain, as that country supplied 5.8 per cent of the country's imports but absorbed 14.2 per cent of its total exports.[13] Trade with Argentina also became particularly important (see Table 2.1), as Brazil, in the absence of European competition, temporarily exported manfactured products to neighbouring countries and the share of coffee in total exports was reduced to only 32 per cent from 1941 to 1945 (see Table 2.3). The diversification of the economy, especially of the industrial sector, which was in progress during the 1930s, continued during the war though imports of machinery were again curtailed. Thus 'production of numerous types of machinery was initiated or expanded, including machine tools, time clocks, looms, silk-reeling equipment and looms, plastic molding equipment, distilling equipment, electric motors and scales'.[14]

British direct foreign investments declined by about 20 per cent in nominal terms during the 1930s to reach £100 million in 1940, but continued to fall during the war as some British firms were repurchased. By 1945 British direct investments amounted to only £85 million.[15] American direct investments, on the other hand, increased from $194 million in 1920 to $240 million in 1940, declining to £233 million in 1943.[16] British pre-eminence in direct investments persisted until the end of the war, but she lost ground to the United States soon afterwards.

As to the debt question, in 1943, after a decade of negotiations, 'a settlement was negotiated with representatives of the sterling and dollar bondholders, who held most of Brazil's public external debt.' By that adjustment, the nominal value of external bonds in those currencies was reduced by about 26%, and annual debt service, which had been $100 million in 1929, was reduced to $32 million in 1943. Before that settlement, in 1940, the American Export-Import Bank had granted a loan of $45 million to the Companhia Siderúrgica Nacional, a public company, for the construction of Brazil's first large-scale integrated steel mill. By 1945, Brazil's external public long term debt (which amounted to $1,059 million in 1929 and had reached $1,186.1 million in 1935) was reduced to $712.4 million.[17]

Finally, during World War II, immigration fell more significantly than in the 1930s, to reach only 37,000 from 1940 to 1945. Most of the immigrants were now European, arriving predominantly from Portugal (see Table 2.2).

In summary, by the end of World War II, American predominance in Brazilian external economic relations had been clearly established to the detriment of Britain and other European countries. In the post-war period several developments would lead to new changes in the relative position of the various countries *vis-à-vis* Brazil.

THE BRAZILIAN ECONOMY IN THE POST-WAR PERIOD

A detailed account of the evolution of the Brazilian economy in the post-war period would clearly exceed the scope of this study. However, a brief outline of some general developments is important for the understanding of Brazilian–EEC relations in the post-war period.

Any periodisation in this case is arbitrary, but it may be mentioned that from 1945 to 1961 Brazil went through an important phase of import-substitution during which the growth of the manufacturing sector was very rapid, so that by the mid-1950s the contribution of the secondary sector to Gross Domestic Product already exceeded the share of agriculture.[18] The growth of the real product was about 7.4 per cent from 1947 to 1961.

By 1961, the composition of Brazilian imports had been substantially altered in favour of intermediate goods and capital goods, as Brazil was producing most of the consumer durables consumed in the country.[19]

By this time the pace of inflation had quickened considerably. The average annual rise in consumer prices was 9.7 per cent in 1947–50, 17.9 per cent in 1951–5, and 24 per cent in 1956–60.[20] As a result of the evolution of domestic prices and of exchange policies, the cruzeiro remained overvalued during most of the so-called phase of import-substitution.

However, there was no significant diversification of Brazilian exports, which stagnated as the country continued to supply mainly primary products to its trade partners. This was true in spite of the fact that there was significant investment in manufacturing (including substantial foreign direct investment) during the 1950s and the creation of several new industrial branches, partially as a result of the introduction of government sectoral planning (Plano de Metas).

As regards exchange policy, Brazil had adopted a fixed exchange rate from 1947 to 1952 and multiple rates coupled with exchange auctions from 1953 to 1957, when the number of rates was reduced. Finally, in March 1961 a move towards greater 'exchange realism' was made, including a reduction of exchange subsidies to specific products.[21] But from then on, inflation rates increased rapidly so that the cruzeiro remained overvalued.

In the 1960s, Brazil entered a period of comparative stagnation, especially between 1963 and 1967. From 1964 to 1967 as inflation rates were gradually reduced, several important administrative changes occurred, including the creation of a Central Bank, a tariff reform, the 'unification' of exchange rates and a comprehensive fiscal reform. From August 1968, a new exchange policy of frequent 'mini-devaluations' was implemented, which would give significant stimulus to the export sector.

On the basis of the idle capacity which had developed in previous years, from 1968 to 1973 the Brazilian economy entered a period of unprecedented growth, with moderate inflation, led by the industrial sector, which was to be partially interrupted by the first oil shock.[22] By then, however, manufactured products were gaining an increasing weight in Brazilian total exports, while soybeans had emerged as another important primary export. After 1974, there was no immediate adaptation to the new 'energy environment', in spite of Brazil's heavy dependence on oil imports which resulted from a transportation system largely based on motor vehicles. In view of the low international interest rates and of political considerations, the country continued to grow until 1979 on the basis of an increasing external indebtedness towards commercial banks, while foreign direct investment, which had almost ceased during part of the 1960s, was again very significant during the whole decade. There was a new phase of import substitution, now involving capital goods and intermediate products and inflation rates reached a new higher plateau.

After the 'second oil shock' of 1979–80 and the 'interest rate shock' that followed, Brazil's external situation worsened, and the country entered a recession with high inflation rates. External problems would culminate with Mexico's suspension of payments in 1982, which soon led Brazil to a renegotiation of its external debt. The energy problem was partially faced through an increasing use of alcohol as fuel and by the increase in domestic oil production. The country continued in recession and conditions only began to improve after 1984 though inflation rates remained very high.[23] Since 1985 Brazil has resumed rapid growth but foreign direct investment has not recovered. It has been renegotiating its external debt, a process which has entered a new phase with the suspension of interest payments on the medium- and long-term debt held by commercial banks early in 1987.

BRAZILIAN FOREIGN TRADE AND THE EEC

In the four decades since World War II, the georgraphic and commodity distribution of Brazilian trade has shown considerable changes. The diversification of Brazilian exports after more than two decades of stagnation was accompanied by a significant increase in the total value of Brazilian exports, which, after oscillating between $1.2 and $1.7 billion from the 1950s till the mid-1960s, reached a maximum of $27 billion in 1984. Such a diversification and the increasing participation of manufactures has been associated with the opening of new markets, notably in developing countries, whose share in Brazilian trade has shown a long-term increase, unlike the share of more developed countries. The oil crisis has forced Brazil to expand its exports to its Middle-Eastern oil suppliers, so as to reduce the significant deficit in the trade with those countries. But Brazil was also successful in placing manufactured and other products in non-oil developing countries. It has also expanded its trade relations with centrally planned economies, with a net surplus. In 1985–6, Brazil showed favourable balances of trade with all groups of countries, except OPEC,[24] a fact which is at least partially attributable to a considerable import-substitution effort in the four decades since World War II.

In a longer-term perspective, it may be noted that the export coefficient (exports of goods and services divided by GDP) in the late 1940s reached 11.1 per cent, decreasing to a low of 6.4 per cent in the period 1965–60, and increasing again in recent years to reach 12 per cent in 1985. As for the import coefficient, this fell from 11.1 per cent in the late 1940s to 6.9 per cent in the late 1950s. It averaged about 7 per cent in the 1960s, increasing to little less than 10 per cent in the 1970s and 8.4 per cent in 1980–5.[25]

All these trends were bound to affect Brazilian trade relations with the EEC, which are analysed more specifically below.

Brazilian exports and the EEC

As was mentioned previously, by the end of World War II, Brazil presented an export structure typical of an agricultural country. From 1945 to 1949, coffee accounted for 41.8 per cent of total exports, while cotton, cocoa, hides and pinewood accounted for 13.3, 4.3, 3.5, and 3.5 per cent of

Table 2.4   Brazilian exports (fob), by category, 1984–86

	1984 US$ million	%	1985 US$ million	%	1986 US$ million	%
Primary products	12,077.5	44.7	11,054.1	43.1	9,273.7	41.4
Coffee (inc. instant coffee)	2,856.0	10.6	2,632.5	10.3	2,327.1	10.4
Soybeans (bean, bran, crude oil and refined oil)	2,565.6	9.5	2,540.1	9.9	1,640.0	7.3
Cocoa	656.0	2.4	775.7	3.0	625.6	2.8
Orange juice	1,415.0	5.2	748.9	2.9	682.6	3.1
Meat	867.3	3.2	844.4	3.3	678.6	3.0
Iron ore and other ores	1,784.8	6.6	1,795.7	7.0	1,728.9	7.7
Tobacco	449.5	1.7	437.4	1.7	394.6	1.8
Sugar (raw, crystal, refined)	586.3	2.2	368.7	1.4	381.4	1.7
Other	897.0	3.3	910.7	3.6	814.9	3.6
Industrialised products	14,927.8	55.3	14,584.9	56.9	13,119.8	58.6
Transport equipment and components	1,904.3	7.1	2,341.1	9.1	2,102.6	9.4
Machinery and mechanical instruments	844.8	3.1	939.6	3.7	941.1	4.2
Electric and electronic equipment	591.2	3.3	576.4	2.2	770.4	3.5
Metallurgical products	2,834.1	10.5	2,787.8	10.9	2,669.2	11.9
Chemical products	1,563.9	5.8	1,516.3	5.9	1,281.7	5.7
Wood and manufactured wood products	330.3	1.2	303.0	1.2	312.1	1.4
Footwear and leather products	1,358.4	5.0	1,231.1	4.8	1,276.2	5.7
Oil derivatives	1,792.5	6.7	1,605.8	6.3	674.0	3.0
Paper and pulp			544.9	2.1	677.5	3.0
Textile products	3,708.3	13.7	2,738.9	10.7	891.9	4.0
Other					1,523.1	6.8
Total	27,005.3	100.0	25,639.0	100.0	22,393.5	100.0

Source: Brazil—Economic Program, vol. 9, November 1985, p. 65; vol. 13, November 1986, p. 87; vol. 15, June 1987, p. 90.

the total, respectively. The shares of tobacco, sugar and rubber were 1.8, 1.2 and 1.2 per cent, respectively. These eight 'traditional' products accounted for 70.6 per cent of the country's exports.

In spite of fluctuations in the share of coffee, which occasionally reached more than 60 per cent of total exports during the 1950s, by 1967–8 the situation had not substantially changed. The share of coffee was still 41.9 per cent, while cotton, cocoa and sugar accounted for 6.2, 3.9, and 5.1 per cent of total exports, respectively. The same eight products accounted together for 62.5 per cent of the value of total exports, while iron-ore exports, which had been insignificant in the late 1940s (0.2 per cent of total

Table 2.5 Geographical distribution of Brazilian exports (fob) according to selected countries, 1945–86 (percentage of total)

	1945–49	1950–59	1960–69	1970–79	1980–86
Belgium and					
Luxembourg	3.90	1.74	2.47	1.80	2.09
France	2.13	4.41	3.62	3.61	3.64
West Germany	0.53	6.60	8.37	8.36	5.43
Italy	2.55	2.62	5.15	5.35	4.43
Netherlands	2.51	3.13	5.69	7.11	5.76
Original EEC members	11.62	18.50	25.30	26.23	21.35
Denmark	1.07	1.90	2.10	1.29	0.48
Ireland	0.47	0.04	0.06	0.12	0.12
United Kingdom	9.33	5.28	4.23	4.33	2.93
Greece	0.34	0.28	0.40	0.31	0.35
First-enlargement					
members	11.21	7.50	6.79	6.05	3.88
Subtotal	22.83	26.00	32.09	32.28	25.23
Spain	2.40	1.14	1.63	3.50	2.05
Portugal	0.60	0.34	0.35	0.77	0.49
Second-enlargement					
members	3.00	1.48	1.98	4.27	2.54
Total EEC	25.83	27.48	34.07	36.55	27.77
Memorandum items					
United States	44.76	46.90	35.29	20.74	23.22
Japan	0.05	2.36	2.74	5.95	6.03

Source: Annex 1, see Table 2.6.

exports) now reached 5.9 per cent of the total. However, the composition of Brazilian exports changed considerably from the late 1960s to the mid-1980s. By 1984–5, the share of iron ore remained at 6.2 per cent, but that of the other eight products added up to only 14.4 per cent as the share of coffee had fallen to 9.4 per cent.[26]

It is clear, then, that important structural changes affected Brazil's exports, reducing the share of its formerly traditional products. These changes are confirmed by the data in Table 2.4, which show that in 1986 'industrialised products' (under the Brazilian scheme of classification) accounted for 58.6 per cent of total exports. Primary products absent in the pre-war period (besides iron ore, whose share increased in the 1950s and 1960s) now include soybeans, meat and orange juice, which together accounted for 13.4 per cent of total exports in 1986, while coffee's share remained at 10.4 per cent.

Since the so-called 'traditional' export products of Brazil were mainly exported to Europe and the United States, the latter taking a substantial

Table 2.6 Brazilian exports (fob) to selected countries, 1945–86 (percentage of total)

	1945	1946	1947	1948	1949	1950	1951	1952	1953	1954	1955
1. Belgium and Luxembourg	1.38	4.30	4.70	4.75	2.54	2.36	2.06	1.50	1.41	1.27	
2. France	0.38	2.07	3.55	2.52	2.11	4.72	5.05	5.67	5.72	5.89	
3. West Germany	–	–	0.05	1.06	1.56	1.35	4.79	5.64	9.55	12.04	7.31
4. Italy	0.38	4.79	2.40	2.61	2.57	1.75	1.72	2.33	3.31	3.58	3.37
5. Netherlands	0.67	2.90	3.34	2.51	3.14	2.40	2.94	2.83	2.40	2.94	2.95
Original EEC members	2.81	14.06	14.04	13.73	13.45	12.76	16.86	18.53	22.48	25.86	18.48
6. Denmark	0.52	1.56	1.13	1.18	0.94	1.55	1.18	1.74	1.75	2.24	2.18
7. Greece	0.09	0.44	0.09	0.63	0.48	n.a.	0.38	0.25	0.26	0.32	0.35
8. Ireland	1.23	0.60	0.19	0.13	0.18	n.a.	0.05	0.01	0.07	–	0.14
9. United Kingdom	12.17	8.75	7.80	9.44	8.50	8.34	9.83	2.72	4.61	4.74	4.22
First-expansion members	14.01	11.35	9.21	11.38	10.10	9.89	11.44	4.72	6.69	7.30	6.89
Subtotal	16.82	25.41	23.25	24.83	23.83	22.65	28.30	23.25	29.17	33.16	25.37
10. Spain	1.65	2.80	3.54	2.36	1.63	1.11	0.34	0.38	0.71	1.54	1.97
11. Portugal	0.45	0.36	1.23	0.33	0.65	0.40	0.60	0.12	0.59	0.13	0.56
Second-enlargement members	2.10	3.16	4.77	2.69	2.28	1.51	0.94	0.50	1.30	1.67	2.53
Total EEC	18.92	28.57	28.02	27.52	26.11	24.16	29.24	23.75	30.47	34.83	27.90
Memorandum items											
United States	49.35	42.20	38.78	43.26	50.20	54.53	49.01	51.56	48.41	37.07	42.30
Japan	–	–	–	0.07	0.17	0.80	0.93	1.34	2.66	4.35	3.94
Total (in US$ million)	–	985	1157	1183	1100	1359	1771	1416	1539	1562	1423
Total exports (in million cruzeiros)	12198	18230	21179	21967	20153	24913	32514	26065	–	–	–

Table 2.6—cont.

	1956	1957	1958	1959	1960	1961	1962	1963	1964	1965	1966
1. Belgium and Luxembourg	1.75	1.08	1.45	2.03	1.97	2.14	2.47	2.56	2.94	3.01	2.24
2. France	3.71	3.16	3.30	3.27	3.39	3.64	3.38	3.84	3.56	3.51	3.45
3. West Germany	6.34	5.96	6.36	6.71	7.09	8.12	9.06	7.97	9.36	8.83	7.70
4. Italy	2.16	2.01	2.73	3.20	3.07	3.42	2.88	5.90	4.75	5.33	6.26
5. Netherlands	3.44	3.09	3.78	4.52	4.10	5.06	6.10	7.75	5.52	5.14	5.11
Original EEC members	17.40	15.30	17.62	19.73	19.62	22.38	23.89	28.02	26.13	25.82	24.76
6. Denmark	2.23	2.08	2.09	1.95	1.97	1.78	2.14	2.06	2.45	2.51	2.24
7. Greece	0.34	0.36	0.40	0.16	0.24	0.29	0.33	0.36	0.42	0.50	0.57
8. Ireland	–	–	0.08	0.08	–	–	–	0.07	0.07	0.06	0.06
9. United Kingdom	3.58	4.74	5.69	5.12	4.42	4.45	3.91	4.40	3.88	4.25	
First-expansion members	6.15	7.18	6.92	7.88	7.33	6.49	6.92	6.40	7.34	6.95	7.12
Subtotal	23.55	22.48	24.54	27.61	26.95	28.87	30.81	34.42	33.47	32.77	31.88
10. Spain	1.49	2.16	0.97	0.70	1.18	2.14	1.40	0.93	0.91	1.56	1.38
11. Portugal	0.20	0.29	0.32	0.16	0.24	0.21	0.33	0.21	0.35	0.38	0.34
Second-enlargement members	1.69	2.45	1.29	0.86	1.42	2.35	1.73	1.14	1.26	1.94	1.72
Total EEC	25.24	24.93	25.83	28.47	28.37	31.22	32.54	35.56	34.73	34.71	33.60
Memorandum items											
United States	49.60	47.41	42.96	46.18	44.44	40.13	39.95	17.77	33.12	31.26	33.37
Japan	2.50	2.66	2.01	2.42	2.44	3.06	2.39	2.28	1.96	1.88	2.35
Total (in US$ million)	1482	1392	1243	1282	1269	1403	1214	1406	1431	1596	1741
Total exports (in million cruzeiros)											

Table 2.6—*cont.*

	1967	1968	1969	1970	1971	1972	1973	1974	1975	1976	1977
1. Belgium and Luxembourg	2.24	2.39	2.77	2.66	2.17	1.95	1.82	1.34	1.23	1.28	
2. France	3.56	3.61	4.28	4.02	3.31	3.60	3.39	3.38	2.86	3.39	4.10
3. West Germany	8.16	7.87	9.52	8.62	8.81	8.42	8.95	7.17	8.08	8.86	8.94
4. Italy	6.58	6.22	7.10	7.23	6.99	6.62	5.68	4.49	4.15	4.12	5.57
5. Netherlands	6.77	5.47	5.84	5.62	6.06	7.69	10.02	7.61	6.46	7.34	7.64
Original EEC members	27.31	25.56	29.51	28.15	27.34	28.28	30.56	24.47	22.89	24.94	27.53
6. Denmark	2.30	1.75	1.78	1.97	1.31	1.35	1.39	1.28	0.89	1.52	1.18
7. Greece	0.42	0.43	0.43	0.40	0.21	0.17	0.22	0.23	0.20	0.32	0.28
8. Ireland	0.12	0.16	.09	0.11	0.17	0.12	0.10	0.14	0.07	0.12	0.11
9. United Kingdom	3.75	3.88	4.28	4.75	4.37	4.50	5.03	4.71	3.92	3.83	3.50
First-expansion members	6.59	6.22	6.58	7.23	6.06	6.14	6.74	6.36	5.08	5.79	5.07
Subtotal	33.90	31.78	36.09	35.38	33.40	34.42	37.30	30.83	27.97	30.73	32.60
10. Spain	1.45	2.39	2.90	3.91	3.24	3.59	3.40	3.80	4.20	4.36	4.01
11. Portugal	0.36	0.53	0.56	0.47	0.65	1.50	1.15	0.90	0.70	0.40	1.01
Second-enlargement members	1.81	2.92	3.46	4.38	3.89	5.09	4.55	4.70	4.90	4.76	5.02
Total EEC	35.71	34.70	39.55	39.76	37.29	39.51	41.85	35.53	32.87	35.49	37.62
Memorandum items											
United States	33.11	33.32	26.40	24.68	26.17	23.33	18.10	21.84	15.39	18.30	17.68
Japan	3.38	3.13	4.54	5.29	5.44	4.50	6.86	7.00	7.74	6.32	5.43
Total (in US$ million)	1655	1882	2311	2739	2904	4004	6199	7953	8668	10100	
Total exports (in million cruzeiros)											12152

Table 2.6—*cont.*

	1978	1979	1980	1981	1982	1983	1984	1985	1986
1. Belgium and Luxembourg	1.46	1.56	1.77	1.77	1.99	2.31	2.36	2.25	2.16
2. France	4.18	3.92	4.08	3.65	4.28	4.05	3.10	3.12	3.21
3. West Germany	8.39	7.31	6.64	5.64	5.86	5.17	4.65	5.11	4.92
4. Italy	4.02	4.59	4.87	4.12	4.88	4.47	4.13	4.48	4.07
5. Netherlands	6.19	6.51	5.71	6.30	5.61	5.76	5.04	6.08	5.82
Original EEC members	24.24	23.89	23.07	21.48	22.62	21.76	19.28	21.04	20.18
6. Denmark	1.12	0.85	0.65	0.40	0.45	0.47	0.46	0.47	0.49
7. Greece	0.50	0.59	0.60	0.27	0.30	0.36	0.31	0.24	0.34
8. Ireland	0.10	0.16	0.10	0.13	0.20	0.14	0.13	0.08	0.07
9. United Kingdom	4.05	4.64	2.73	3.15	3.33	3.30	2.62	2.46	2.89
First-expansion members	5.77	6.24	4.08	3.95	4.28	4.27	3.52	3.25	3.79
Subtotal	30.01	30.13	27.15	25.43	26.90	26.03	22.80	24.29	23.97
10. Spain	2.33	2.13	2.59	1.59	1.83	2.41	1.83	2.08	2.00
11. Portugal	0.51	0.47	0.76	0.45	0.34	0.48	0.60	0.53	0.29
Second-enlargement members	2.84	2.60	3.35	2.04	2.17	2.89	2.43	2.61	2.29
Total EEC	32.85	32.73	30.50	27.47	29.07	28.92	25.23	26.90	26.26
Memorandum items									
United States	22.66	19.29	17.43	17.62	20.48	23.16	28.55	27.13	28.20
Japan	5.13	5.82	6.12	5.23	6.51	6.53	5.61	5.45	6.77
Total (in US$ million)	12659	15248	20132	23329	20168	21853	27005	25639	22393
Total exports (in million cruzeiros)									

Sources: SEEF, *Comércio Exterior do Brasil por Países*, several issues; CACEX, *Intercâmbio Comercial*, 1953–1976; Banco do Brasil, *Relatório*, various years; International Monetary Fund, *Direction of Trade Statistics*, *Yearbook*, various years 1945–1952: shares calculated from figures in cruzeiros. Figures in US dollars, 1946–52 are from Gustavo H.B. Franco, *Estatísticas Históricas Relativas ao Setor Externo*, Pontifícia Universidade Católica, Rio de Janeiro, 1986.

fraction of coffee exports, changes in the destination of Brazilian exports in the last four decades should also be expected.

The distribution of Brazilian exports according to main markets is presented in Table 2.5. The share of several important countries has changed considerably since World War II. (Annual fluctuations, which are more pronounced, are reproduced in Table 2.6.)

A first very noticeable trend is the decline of the share of the United States, which fell from around 45 per cent from 1945 to 1959 to 23.2 per cent in 1980–6. In the last three years (1984–6) it increased to 28 per cent, but there was clearly a permanent reduction which is associated with the decrease of the participation of coffee in total exports. The share of the United Kingdom suffered a much more significant fall, from 9.3 per cent in 1945–9 to 2.9 per cent in 1980–6. Thus Britain's historical pre-eminence saw its definitive demise in the last forty years. The emergence of Japan as an important market for Brazil's products is a third aspect to be noted. From 1950 to 1959 the Country's pre-war share of 2.3 per cent was slightly exceeded, to reach 6 per cent in 1980–6. Finally, the share of West Germany, insignificant in the immediate post-war years, recovered to 6.6 per cent in the 1950s, to reach 8.4 per cent in the 1960s and 1970s, but it has since been reduced to around 5 per cent (5.4 per cent on average from 1980 to 1986).

Considering other important pre-war European partners, the decline of France, after a short recovery in the 1950s, must be mentioned, as its share has averaged only 3.6 per cent from 1960 to 1986. The share of Belgium and Luxembourg has also decline to around 2 per cent. On the other hand, Italy and the Netherlands have gained in importance as their respective participation in Brazilian exports has increased systematically from the late 1940s to the 1970s, to decline to 4.4 and 5.8 per cent respectively from 1980 to 1986 (see Table 2.5).

Taking groups of countries, it should be noticed that the original six members of the EEC increased their relative participation in the purchases from Brazil quite significantly from the late 1940s and 1950s to the 1970s, when on average they became Brazil's most important market. In fact, their share surpassed that of the United States in 1969, reaching a maximum of 30.6 per cent in 1973, to decline gradually to 21.8 per cent in 1983 when the United States recovered its former pre-eminence (see Table 2.6). From 1983 to 1986, the average share of the Six was 20.6 per cent, as opposed to 26.8 per cent in the case of the United States.

Considering the EEC before its last enlargement, the share of the Nine and of the Ten followed a path similar to that of the Six. It first exceeded the participation of the United States in 1964, but on a more permanent basis only after 1969, reaching a maximum of 37.3 per cent in 1973, only to be again surpassed by the United States in the last three years.

Finally, if the aggregate participation of the Twelve is considered, it exceeded the American share from 1964 to 1983, reaching a maximum of

41.9 per cent in 1973, but its average in 1984–6 was reduced to 26.1 per cent.

Such a comparative evolution of American, Japanese and EEC relative participations in the Brazilian export trade indicates at first an increase in the share of other countries. In fact, in the 1950s, when Europe and Japan had recovered from the war, the aggregate share of the 14 countries considered in Table 2.5 reached 76.6 per cent of Brazil's total exports, but in 1981–6 this share had declined to 57 per cent. Almost half of Brazilian export trade was now directed to other countries, a fact which is certainly linked to the present composition of Brazil's exports.

Though trade issues between Brazil and the EEC are treated in another study in this book,[27] some points may be raised to explain the fluctuations in the share of the EEC member countries in Brazilian exports, which once exceeded 40 per cent of the total but has since been reduced to 26 per cent (see Table 2.6).

The creation of the European Coal and Steel Community (ECSC) in April 1951 did not have any immediate impact on Brazilian trade with countries of the future EEC. Brazil had traditionally imported those two products mainly from Britain and the United States, and the ECSC countries were still recovering from the war.

When the treaties of the EEC and Euratom were signed in 1957, the recovery of the six initial members was well advanced and this new prospective large free-trade area appeared a promising market. The stagnation of Brazilian exports would, however, last until 1968, the year in which the elimination of tariffs between the member countries was achieved. The great vitality of the EEC in the following years may explain, from the demand side, part of the increase in Brazilian exports to the EEC, which clearly became Brazil's main market. It should be mentioned that the perspective of the enlargement of the community, and the consequent prospects of increased taxation of such products as soluble coffee and cocoa butter, for which the United Kingdom was one of Brazil's principal customers, and a potentially large market for Brazilian meat, prompted Brazil to negotiate and sign in December 1973 a trade agreement with the EEC, which in that same year had incorporated three new countries. Among the terms of the agreement was the creation of a Joint Commission to increase economic and commercial co-operation between Brazil and the EEC.[28]

In the following years and until the end of the decade the position of the Six and the Nine as Brazil's most important market would be consolidated. The entry of Greece in the Community in 1981 had no effect on Brazilian trade in view of the restricted economic relations with that country. As to the second enlargement in 1986, with the inclusion of Spain and Portugal, this is the object of another study in this book.[29]

While the general evolution of the EEC in recent decades and better diplomatic relations between Brazil and the Community are factors which have to be taken into account in explaining the changing geographic composition of Brazilian trade, a more specific economic aspect which should be mentioned are the fluctuations in exchange rates between the currencies of the developed countries. In fact, since the late 1960s, the Brazilian currency has been devalued in line with the dollar and not a basket of the currencies of its main trading partners. While Brazilian exports increased their competitiveness in European markets when the dollar was depreciating in the 1970s, during part of the 1980s the Brazilian currency appreciated against a basket of European currencies, damaging the penetration of Brazilian products in Europe and in third markets, where they competed with European products.[30]

A second factor explaining the decline of the share of the EEC is the considerable decline in the prices of primary products in international markets, as a significant part of the exports of Brazil to the EEC has traditionally consisted of primary products.[31] In 1975 and 1982, food products represented respectively 63.8 and 51.7 per cent of Brazilian exports to the EEC, and manufactures only 16.4 and 28 per cent, while iron ore accounted for 13.1 and 12.3 per cent. In those same years, while the share of the Ten in total exports was respectively 27.9 and 26.9 per cent, their share in the total Brazilian exports of food products was 32.8 and 35.1 per cent, while the corresponding share for manufactures was only 17.8 and 19.4 per cent. The share of concentrates and of iron ore was 34.4 and 37.6 per cent.

While fluctuations in Brazilian exchange policy are not under the control of European policy-makers, it would appear that the composition of Brazilian exports to the EEC can be easily affected by the overall economic policies of the Community, notably with respect to agricultural products. Thus, the decline of total sugar exports from Brazil has been frequently associated with protectionist measures in favour of EEC beet sugar, while in the 1960s and the 1970s former colonies of EEC member countries received preferential treatment. However, in spite of this, the Brazilian share of EEC imports from outside the EEC has systematically increased from 1980 to 1985, from 1.7 to 2.5 per cent, declining to 2.2 per cent in 1986. It should be noted that from 1980 to 1985 EEC imports from non-EEC countries declined in dollar terms, recovering somewhat in 1986.[32]

A third cause, therefore, for the decline in the share of the EEC in Brazilian exports, also pointed out in a recent study,[33] would be the differences in rates of growth between the United States and the EEC during part of the 1980s. But clearly the composition of Brazilian exports (showing a comparatively smaller penetration of Brazilian manufactured products in the EEC than in the United States and than in new markets in developing countries), and the evolution of the relative prices of primary and industrial products are more important explanatory factors.

The diversification of Brazilian exports in the post-war period may be seen, on the other hand, as a favourable factor, as Europe now absorbs a significant share of the Brazilian exports of soybeans (now under a more advanced phase of processing). In fact, the EEC accounted for around two-thirds of Brazil's exports of animal feed in the early 1980s. The share of the EEC in total coffee, meat, cocoa and iron-ore exports was around a third of the total and it exceeded 40 per cent in the case of other products such as tobacco and leather (now manufactured). Though the share of the EEC in exports of manufactured products in general is below average, it has become an important market for some specific products such as textiles and clothing (absorbing about a third of the total), but also for some types of machinery and transport equipment.[34] It would be most desirable if in the future equal success could be observed in the case of other branches of manufactures exported by Brazil.

The Brazilian import trade and the EEC

As in the case of exports, there were significant changes in the composition of Brazilian imports in the post-war period. From 1947–51 to 1967–71, the share of raw materials, including fuels, declined from 25.5 to 16.0 per cent and that of food and beverages (including mainly wheat) from 16.8 to 14.4 per cent, while the participation of chemical products and manufactures in general rose from 57.7 to 69.6 per cent.[35]

The spectacular increase in oil prices in 1973–4 and again in 1979–80 subverted the structure of Brazilian imports, as oil purchases were to account for as much as 52.2 per cent of total imports in 1982.[36] Import-substitution of intermediate products and machinery and equipment in the 1970s had contributed to reduce Brazil's dependence on foreign products.[37] In the 1980s, the intensification in the use of alcohol as fuel for motor vehicles and, more important, the significant expansion of Brazilian oil production, reduced Brazil's reliance on oil imports[38] and interrupted the increase in the share of oil in total imports, which more recently was also affected by the decline in the international price of oil.[39] Table 2.7 shows the distribution of Brazilian imports (FOB) by category. Oil and oil derivatives, which still accounted for 49.3 per cent of total imports in 1984, accounted for only 21.5 per cent of total imports in 1986 (though this share should increase to about 28 per cent in 1987), while the share of capital goods reached 24.7 per cent of the total. Among raw materials, chemical products were the most important group, accounting for 18.4 per cent of total imports, while the share of steel, non ferrous metals and other ores was 4.3 per cent.

Again, as in the case of exports, the changes in the composition of Brazilian imports are associated with fluctuations in the shares of specific countries. The absolute predominance of the United States, which in 1945–9 accounted for 54 per cent of total Brazilian imports, was gradually eroded after its share reached a maximum of 61.3 per cent in 1947. By

Table 2.7   Brazilian imports (fob), by category 1984–86

Discrimination	1984 US$ million	%	1985 US$ million	%	1986 US$ million	%
Oil and derivatives	6,866.6	49.3	5,693.6	43.3	3,020.1	21.5
Capital goods	2,151.6	15.5	2,479.9	18.8	3,463.9	24.7
Wheat	755.0	5.4	591.1	4.5	248.3	1.8
Raw materials	3,288.2	23.6	3,361.0	25.6	4,706.4	33.5
Steel, non-ferrous metals and other ores	390.6	2.8	393.6	3.0	598.2	4.2
Chemical products	1,766.5	12.7	1,837.3	14.0	2,583.8	18.3
Coal	453.7	3.2	460.3	3.5	477.9	3.4
Other raw materials	677.4	4.9	669.8	5.1	1,046.5	7.4
Other products	854.9	6.2	1,027.9	7.8	2,605.6	18.5
Total	13,915.8	100.0	13,153.5	100.0	14,044.3	100.0

Sources: Brazil Economic Program, vol. 5, November 1985, p. 66; vol. 13, November 1986m p. 88; vol. 15, June 1987, p. 91.

1980–6, it had fallen to 17.8 per cent, less than a third of the average observed in the immediate post-war period. Again, Britain's relative decline was even more dramatic. Its share of Brazilian imports fell from 8.3 per cent in 1945–9 to only 1.8 per cent in 1980–6. From the 1950s, West Germany rapidly became Brazil's second main supplier, as its share reached 7.8 per cent from 1950 to 1959, increasing to 10.8 per cent in 1970–9 (with a maximum of 12.8 per cent in 1971) and remaining at 5.8 per cent of total imports in the 1950s to 7.6 per cent in the 1970s, with a decrease in 1980–6 to 4.8 per cent. France never recovered its pre-war importance, but remains with Italy one of Brazil's principal suppliers of manufactures and especially of machinery.

In the post-war period, EEC countries never had the clear pre-dominance in Brazilian import trade which they showed in the 1970s with regard to exports. In fact, the share of the Six never exceeded that of the United States, regarding a maximum of 20.3 per cent in the 1970s. In view of Britain's decline, the share of the Ten was higher in the 1950s than in the 1970s. Finally, the Twelve did have a greater participation than the United States in the 1970s, when they accounted for slightly more than a quarter of Brazil's total imports (with a maximum of 32.8 per cent in 1972). From 1980 to 1986, however, their share fell to 15.1 per cent (see Table 2.8; annual figures are given in Table 2.9).

Several factors have contributed to that evolution. First, as was previously mentioned, the growing share of oil in total imports and balance-of-payments difficulties have forced Brazil to curtail other imports. On the other hand, imports from the EEC consist basically of manufactured

Table 2.8 Geographical distribution of Brazilian imports (cif), to selected countries, 1945–86 (percentage of total)

Countries	1945–49	1950–59	1960–69	1970–79	1980–86
Belgium and Luxembourg	2.16	1.96	1.34	1.43	0.63
France	1.47	4.31	3.61	3.16	2.88
West Germany	0.13	7.69	9.79	10.77	5.82
Italy	1.29	2.33	2.84	3.06	1.93
Netherlands	0.53	1.91	1.60	1.87	1.11
Original EEC members	5.58	18.20	19.18	20.29	12.37
Denmark	0.15	1.61	1.42	0.43	0.14
Ireland	0.04	–	0.00	0.06	0.10
United Kingdom	8.34	4.83	3.40	3.50	1.79
Greece	0.04	0.17	0.09	0.02	0.00
First-enlargement members	8.57	6.61	4.91	4.01	2.03
Subtotal	14.15	24.81	24.09	24.30	14.40
Spain	0.45	1.04	1.08	1.03	0.51
Portugal	1.86	0.36	0.28	0.28	0.21
Second enlargement members	2.32	1.40	1.36	1.31	0.72
Total EEC	16.47	26.21	25.45	25.61	15.12
Memorandum items					
United States	53.95	34.51	32.73	24.84	17.76
Japan	0.00	2.12	3.74	7.60	4.77

Surce: See Table 2.9.

products (94 per cent in 1980–2) and in particular of machinery (53 per cent in 1980–2). Increasing import-substitution of capital goods in the 1970s, as more sophisticated machinery began to be produced in Brazil (often by subsidiaries of European firms)[40] and a decrease in the rate of investment were bound to affect this category of imports. More recently, these were also affected by a reduction of suppliers credits, which resulted from the aggravation of the debt problem. Finally, direct restrictions on imports tended to increase as balance-of-payments difficulties developed.

It is therefore not surprising that from 1980 to 1985 the share of EEC exports to Brazil in total EEC exports showed a clearly declining trend with a recovery in 1986,[41] (which may be associated with a relaxation of controls on imports and with unusually high imports of food by Brazil in that year in view of a serious drought in the previous year).

In the near future, the prospects for Brazilian imports from the EEC will continue to depend on the country's reliance on imported oil and on the evolution of the international oil price, and also on the success of economic policy in the sense of guaranteeing a sustained growth rate and a recovery of domestic investment. The latter, on the other hand is linked to a

Table 2.9 Brazilian imports (cif) from selected countries, 1945–86 (percentage of total)

	1945	1946	1947	1948	1949	1950	1951	1952	1953	1954	1955
1. Belgium and Luxembourg	–	1.27	2.37	2.64	4.51	5.77	3.23	2.79	0.53	0.24	1.91
2. France	–	0.97	2.16	2.40	1.84	4.66	4.72	3.88	8.80	5.02	5.51
3. West Germany	–	–	–	0.10	0.54	1.74	5.57	9.41	8.19	9.61	6.73
4. Italy	–	1.01	1.94	1.92	1.30	2.21	1.96	1.97	2.88	3.75	3.75
5. Netherlands	–	0.51	0.50	0.86	0.80	2.29	2.20	2.34	1.21	2.08	2.60
Original EEC members	–	3.76	6.97	7.92	9.25	15.76	17.93	20.38	20.70	19.83	20.50
6. Denmark	–	0.11	0.12	0.18	0.32	0.75	0.91	1.18	2.20	2.14	2.07
7. Greece	–	0.04	0.04	0.08	0.03	n.a.	0.04	0.03	0.15	0.49	0.08
8. Ireland	–	0.11	0.07	0.05	–	n.a.	–	–	–	–	–
9. United Kingdom	3.96	6.79	10.08	12.91	12.34	8.49	8.55	3.71	1.04	1.38	–
First-expansion members	3.96	8.20	7.02	10.39	13.26	13.09	9.44	9.76	6.06	3.67	3.53
Subtotal	3.96	11.96	13.99	18.31	22.51	28.85	27.37	30.14	26.76	23.50	24.02
10. Spain	0.44	0.45	0.40	0.46	0.53	0.68	0.34	0.13	0.84	0.86	2.29
11. Portugal	2.98	2.99	1.38	0.63	0.64	0.70	0.63	0.15	0.18	0.31	0.31
Second-enlargement members	3.42	3.44	1.75	1.84	1.16	1.32	1.04	0.76	0.99	1.04	2.60
Total EEC	7.38	15.40	15.75	20.15	23.67	30.17	28.41	30.90	27.75	24.54	26.63
Memorandum items											
United States	55.11	58.20	61.32	52.67	42.47	34.48	41.84	49.66	27.75	32.86	23.64
Japan	–	–	–	0.01	0.01	0.12	1.06	0.95	0.83	4.83	3.44
Total imports (in US$ million)	–	–	–	–	–	1085	1987	1982	1319	1634	1307
Total imports (in million cruzeiros)	8617	13029	22789	20985	20648	20313	37198	–	–	–	–

Table 2.9—*cont.*

	1956	1957	1958	1959	1960	1961	1962	1963	1964	1965	1966
1. Belgium and Luxembourg	1.38	1.61	1.04	1.09	1.10	0.96	1.49	1.28	1.18	1.18	1.33
2. France	2.03	3.16	2.14	3.13	4.72	2.94	4.47	5.18	4.03	3.01	2.74
3. West Germany	6.48	8.53	10.42	10.27	9.30	9.66	10.31	9.01	8.14	8.74	9.02
4. Italy	2.35	2.55	2.14	2.18	2.60	3.01	2.91	3.03	2.13	2.37	2.47
5. Netherlands	1.13	1.41	1.63	2.18	2.39	1.44	1.29	1.48	1.19	1.73	1.67
Original EEC members	13.37	17.26	17.37	18.85	20.11	18.01	20.47	19.98	16.67	17.03	17.23
6. Denmark	2.35	1.61	1.18	1.68	1.98	2.67	1.15	1.28	1.26	1.28	0.80
7. Greece	0.41	0.07	0.15	0.29	0.14	0.21	0.07	0.07	0.16	0.09	0.07
8. Ireland	–	–	–	–	–	–	–	–	–	–	–
9. United Kingdom	3.48	3.42	3.25	2.69	3.49	3.22	3.12	3.56	2.92	2.82	2.94
First-expansion members	6.24	5.10	4.58	4.66	5.61	6.10	4.34	4.91	4.34	4.19	3.81
Subtotal	19.61	22.36	21.95	23.51	25.72	24.11	24.81	24.89	21.01	21.22	21.04
10. Spain	2.19	1.46	0.74	0.87	1.44	1.03	1.70	0.67	0.87	0.64	0.80
11. Portugal	0.32	0.27	0.22	0.22	0.20	0.14	0.20	0.20	0.16	0.27	0.27
Second-enlargement members	2.51	1.75	0.96	1.09	1.64	1.17	1.90	0.87	1.03	0.91	1.07
Total EEC	22.12	24.11	22.91	24.60	27.36	25.28	26.71	25.76	22.04	22.13	22.11
Memorandum items											
United States	28.77	36.80	35.70	33.55	30.30	35.27	30.98	30.73	34.44	29.69	39.41
Japan	4.05	1.54	2.44	1.97	2.60	5.41	5.07	4.17	2.69	3.37	2.94
Total imports (in US$ million)	1234	1409	1353	1374	1462	1460	1475	1487	1266	1098	1497
Total imports (in million cruzeiros)											

Table 2.9–*cont.*

	1967	1968	1969	1970	1971	1972	1973	1974	1975	1976	1977
1. Belgium and Luxembourg	1.74	1.50	1.59	1.54	1.59	1.48	1.59	2.44	1.88	1.08	0.94
2. France	2.63	3.38	2.96	3.12	3.85	3.44	2.39	2.76	2.72	2.99	2.99
3. West Germany	10.06	11.06	12.64	12.60	12.83	13.65	12.63	12.44	10.75	8.65	8.52
4. Italy	3.11	3.42	3.36	3.09	3.35	4.20	3.07	2.74	4.58	3.23	2.50
5. Netherlands	1.56	1.59	1.68	1.76	1.62	2.43	2.37	1.95	1.60	1.53	1.88
Original EEC members	19.10	20.95	2.223	22.11	23.34	25.61	23.10	21.96	21.57	17.21	16.83
6. Denmark	0.84	0.84	2.08	0.84	0.73	0.69	0.46	0.34	0.37	0.26	0.25
7. Greece	–	0.05	–	–	0.03	0.02	0.10	0.01	0.01	–	0.01
8. Ireland	–	–	0.04	–	0.03	0.04	0.14	0.04	0.04	0.04	0.17
9. United Kingdom	3.47	4.50	3.98	5.65	5.84	4.60	3.89	2.51	2.67	2.52	2.16
First-expansion members	4.31	5.39	6.10	6.49	6.63	5.35	4.59	2.90	3.09	2.82	2.59
Subtotal	23.41	26.34	28.33	28.61	29.97	30.96	27.69	24.86	24.66	20.03	19.42
10. Spain	1.26	1.40	1.02	1.13	1.32	1.53	1.23	0.97	0.85	0.84	0.94
11. Portugal	0.43	0.47	0.35	0.42	0.32	0.33	0.31	0.33	0.25	0.17	0.21
Second-enlargement members	1.74	1.87	1.37	1.54	1.64	1.86	1.54	1.30	1.10	1.01	1.15
Total EEC	25.15	28.21	29.70	30.15	31.61	32.82	29.23	26.16	25.76	21.04	20.57
Memorandum items											
United States	34.25	32.10	30.14	32.22	28.75	28.00	28.63	24.24	24.92	22.61	19.62
Japan	3.05	3.42	4.68	6.25	7.02	7.65	7.84	8.82	9.24	7.30	7.06
Total imports (in US$ million)	1670	2134	2263	2849	3701	4783	7000	14169	13592	13761	13254
Total imports (in million cruzeiros)											

Table 2.9—cont.

	1978	1979	1980	1981	1982	1983	1984	1985	1986
1. Belgium and Luxembourg	0.85	0.88	0.70	0.61	0.74	0.48	0.56	0.57	0.73
2. France	3.16	3.20	2.88	2.69	2.83	2.91	2.61	2.28	3.98
3. West Germany	8.12	7.50	6.98	4.90	4.43	4.51	4.48	6.51	8.93
4. Italy	2.22	1.67	1.66	2.75	2.46	1.36	1.42	1.40	2.44
5. Netherlands	1.45	2.10	1.05	0.95	0.71	1.02	1.03	1.24	1.77
Original EEC members	15.80	15.35	13.27	11.90	11.17	10.28	10.10	12.00	17.85
6. Denmark	0.21	0.17	0.13	0.11	0.10	0.12	0.11	0.13	0.29
7. Greece	–	0.01	0.01	0.00	–	–	–	–	–
8. Ireland	0.09	0.06	0.05	0.04	0.04	0.05	0.07	0.08	0.36
9. United Kingdom	2.60	2.54	1.94	1.52	1.28	1.51	2.00	1.90	2.41
First-expansion members	2.90	2.78	2.13	1.67	1.42	1.68	2.18	2.11	3.06
Subtotal	18.70	18.13	15.40	13.57	12.59	11.96	12.28	14.11	20.91
10. Spain	0.71	0.75	0.87	0.45	0.48	0.45	0.30	0.42	0.60
11. Portugal	0.21	0.23	0.19	0.20	0.12	0.10	0.08	0.12	0.66
Second-enlargement members	0.92	0.98	1.06	0.65	0.60	0.55	0.38	0.54	1.26
Total EEC	19.62	19.11	16.46	14.22	13.19	12.51	12.66	14.65	22.17
Memorandum items									
United States	21.14	18.32	18.56	16.34	15.02	15.63	16.61	19.71	22.42
Japan	8.87	5.96	4.78	5.73	4.62	3.68	4.00	4.28	6.29
Total imports (in US$ million)	15054	19804	24961	24075	21069	16803	15210	14332	15557
Total imports (in million cruzeiros)									

Sources: SEEF, *Comércio Exterior do Brasil por Países*, several issues; CACEX, *Intercâmbio Comercial*, 1953–1976; Banco do Brasil, *Relatório*, various years; International Monetary Fund, *Direction of Trade Statistics*, *Yearbook*, various years 1945–1952: shares calculated from figures in cruzeiros. Figures in US dollars, 1950–52 are from IBGE, *O Brasil em Números*, 1966, p. 83.

Table 2.10   Balance of Brazilian trade with the EEC, 1945–86 (1945–52: in million cruzeiros; 1953–86: in million dollars)

Years	The Six			The Ten			The Twelve		
	Exports	Imports	Balance	Exports	Imports	Balance	Exports	Imports	Balance
1945	343	–	343	2,052	341	1,711	2,308	636	1,672
1946	2,563	490	2,073	4,632	1,558	3,074	5,209	2,006	3,203
1947	2,974	1,588	1,386	4,925	3,189	1,736	5,936	3,590	2,346
1948	2,918	1,662	1,256	5,387	3,843	1,544	5,972	4,230	1,742
1949	2,767	1,911	856	4,803	4,648	155	5,263	4,888	375
1950	3,179	3,202	−23	5,642	5,860	−218	6,019	6,129	−110
1951	5,483	6,667	−1,184	9,203	10,181	−978	9,510	10,567	−1,057
1952	4,828	7,578	−2,750	6,059	11,205	−5,146	6,191	11,489	−5,298
1953	346	213	133	449	353	96	469	366	103
1954	404	324	80	518	384	134	544	401	143
1955	263	268	−5	361	314	47	397	348	49
1956	258	165	93	349	242	107	374	273	101
1957	213	257	−44	313	333	−20	347	359	−12
1958	219	235	−16	305	297	8	321	310	11
1959	253	259	−6	354	323	31	365	338	27
1960	249	294	45	342	376	−34	360	400	−40
1961	314	263	51	405	352	53	438	369	69
1962	290	302	−12	374	366	8	395	394	1
1963	394	297	97	484	370	114	500	383	117
1964	374	211	163	479	266	213	497	279	218
1965	412	187	225	523	233	290	554	243	311
1966	431	258	173	555	315	240	585	331	54
1967	452	319	133	561	391	170	591	420	171
1968	481	447	34	598	562	36	653	602	51
1969	682	503	179	834	641	193	914	672	242
1970	771	630	141	969	815	154	1,089	859	230
1971	794	864	−70	970	1,109	−139	1,083	1,170	−87
1972	1,132	1,225	−93	1,378	1,481	−103	1,582	1,570	12
1973	1,894	1,617	277	2,312	1,938	374	2,594	2,046	548
1974	1,946	3,111	−1,165	2,452	3,523	−1,071	2,826	3,707	−881
1975	1,984	2,932	−948	2,424	3,352	−928	2,849	3,502	−653
1976	2,519	2,368	151	3,104	2,757	347	3,584	2,895	689
1977	3,346	2,231	1,115	3,962	2,574	1,388	4,572	2,726	1,846
1978	3,068	2,378	690	3,799	2,815	984	4,158	2,953	1,205
1979	3,643	3,040	603	4,594	3,591	1,003	4,990	3,785	1,205
1980	4,644	3,313	1,331	5,466	3,843	1,623	6,141	4,109	2,032
1981	5,012	2,864	2,148	5,933	3,267	2,666	6,409	3,423	2,986
1982	4,562	2,353	2,209	5,426	2,652	2,774	5,862	2,779	3,083
1983	4,755	1,729	3,026	5,689	2,010	3,679	6,321	2,103	4,218
1984	5,206	1,536	3,670	6,157	1,867	4,290	6,814	1,925	4,889
1985	5,394	1,720	3,674	6,227	2,022	4,205	6,896	2,100	4,796
1986	4,519	2,777	1,742	5,368	3,253	2,115	5,881	3,449	2,432

Sources: Tables 2.6 and 2.9.

satisfactory solution of the debt question, permitting new inflows of foreign capital into the country.

The balance of trade

In recent years, the balance of trade between Brazil and the EEC has been very favourable to the former, as in certain years Brazilian exports to the EEC have been equivalent to three times Brazilian imports from the same countries. However, in a longer-term perspective, trade was more balanced and in several years the balance was in favour of the EEC. As regards the Six, this was true from 1950 to 1952, in 1955, from 1957 to 1960, in 1962, and again in 1971–2 and 1974–5. In the case of the Ten (or of the Nine, as the trade with Greece is not very significant), which are very much affected by the role of the United Kingdom, there were surpluses in favour of the EEC in 1950–2, 1957, 1960, 1971–2 and 1974–5. Finally, the inclusion of Portugal and Spain only changes the picture with respect to 1972, as for the Twelve, in that year, the surplus turned into a deficit[42] (see Table 2.10).

It may be noted that, in spite of commercial restrictions or advantages granted by the EEC to other countries, in the last 11 years trade balances in favour of Brazil have been systematically observed. However, those have been partially compensated by negative balances in the services account, notably with respect to profit remittances and interest payments, as will be shown in other parts of this study.

FOREIGN DIRECT INVESTMENT IN BRAZIL IN THE POST-WAR PERIOD:
THE COMPARATIVE ROLE OF THE EEC

The statistical evidence available on direct investment in Brazil in the post-war period permits us to draw a reasonably clear picture of the role of the principal investor countries. The distinction between private portfolio investments and direct investments becomes much clearer than in previous years[43] and though several caveats apply to the data, notably in view of exchange-rate fluctuations, the records of the Central Bank of Brazil for more recent years are quite reliable.[44]

The immediate post-war years

The available data on the immediate post-war years are incomplete. A British estimate puts British investments in 1945 (excluding government bonds) at around £85 million, 'on the basis of the par value of securities listed on the London Stock Exchange', a figure which possibly overestimated real values. On the other hand, 'the foreign Brazilian credits (arising out of Brazilian shipments during the war) amounted to £61.5 million in March 31, 1947 [but were] reduced to £50 million' at the time an Anglo-Brazilian trade and payments agreement was signed on 21 May 1948. 'This agreement made provision for the establishment of special accounts, bearing interest at 1% per annum, pending the liquidation of the credits through trade or otherwise'. Among the possible uses of funds were the purchase or repayment of Brazilian government sterling loans, or payments in respect to the taking over of British firms in Brazil. Thus the Brazilian government bought British railway companies for £15 million, contributing to a reduction of overall British direct investment in Brazil.[45]

American direct investment was still probably smaller than British investment in 1945, but soon exceeded it as a result of new capital inflows. The available data for 1943 on the 'value of Brazilian assets owned in the United States', compiled by the US Treasury Department show that 'interest in controlled enterprises reached $236.1 million, not including personal property and real property'.[46] By 1946, according to the United States Department of Commerce, American direct investment in Brazil totalled $323 million, 39 per cent of which was in manufacturing.

The interests of other countries in Brazil were smaller and may be surveyed according to sectors of economic activity. In fact, the only other country with a sizeable share of total direct investment was Canada, as Canadian nationals controlled the largest electric power company in the country (with a capital of about US$80 million), furnishing light, power, energy and gas to several cities through various subsidiaries, and which together with an American company generated and distributed about 75 per cent of the total power produced in Brazil in the late 1940s. There was also Canadian capital in banking and cement production and some in mining.

As for present-day EEC member countries, Belgium and Luxembourg had a substantial participation in a steel company founded in the 1920s, which produced pig iron and rolling mill products. The Portguese controlled a bank, and had an important participation in 'provisions trade, commerce and real estate'. The Dutch also controlled a bank, but little else.[47]

French investments had already considerably shrunk by 1938 when they totalled about £40 million, of which more than two-thirds was in the form of government loans. By 1945 there was no large company entirely controlled by the French, whose direct investments were not concentrated and went into such sectors as pharmaceuticals and cosmetics.[48]

German and Italian investments (not including the holdings of citizens who became naturalized in Brazil) which were not very significant by 1939,[49] were sequestered during the war and transferred to Brazilian ownership. This was the case with one of the airlines existing in 1940 'and of seven German and Italian insurance companies also liquidated during the war'.[50]

Table 2.11   Foreign capital registered in Brazil as at 31 December 1951, by country

	Million cruzeiros	%
West Germany	1.9	0.00
Belgium	213.8	0.74
Denmark	9.0	0.03
Spain	6.9	0.02
France	941.1	3.25
Netherlands	96.1	0.33
United Kingdom	3,495.6	12.08
Italy	90.6	0.31
Luxembourg	232.7	0.80
Portugal	193.4	0.67
Subtotal	5,281.1	18.23
United States	12,707.6	43.90
Panama	659.5	2.28
Canada	8,782.8	30.34
Japan	–	–
Sweden	106.1	0.37
Switzerland	284.1	0.98
Argentina	171.1	0.59
Uruguay	898.1	3.10
Other	56.4	0.21
Total		
Cruzeiros (million)	28,946.8*	100.00
US$ (million)[†]	1,546.3	

*   Of that total 14,819.0 million cruzeiros were registered in national currency, and the rest in 12 different currencies. There were US$677.3 million, £24.8 million and FS 13.9 million.
†   US$1 = Cr$18.72.
Source: Banco do Brasil, *Relatório 1951*, Rio de Janeiro, 1952, pp. 302–3.

The available information on the corporate capital of foreign businesses in 1945–6 shows a total of 3.44 billion cruzeiros, of which 63.9 per cent was invested in public utilities, 11.6 per cent in iron and steel, about the same in meat packing, 7.3 per cent in railways, 3.2 per cent in banks, 1.3 per cent in airlines and 1.2 per cent in insurance companies.[51]

The first official Brazilian estimates are apparently the figures on 'foreign capital invested in commercial firms and incorporated business enterprises' registered with the Banco do Brasil on 31 December 1950, which on the basis of the official exchange rate of 18.72 cruzeiros to the dollar, reached a total of $1,324.7 million.[52] More detailed data on foreign capital in cruzeiros are available for 1951 and presented in Table 2.11. It should be noted that 51 per cent of the stock of 28.5 billion cruzeiros had been registered originally in cruzeiros, and the remaining 49 per cent in 12 differenct currencies, so that the total of $1,546.3 million which results from conversion at the official rate of exchange may be an overestimate of actual past foreign investment and certainly includes reinvestments in local currency.

However, the distribution according to countries of origin confirms the United States as the most important investor country with 43.9 per cent of the total (to which should perhaps be added the 2.3 per cent attributed to Panama), while Britain, with only 12.1 per cent of the total, had slipped to third position, behind Canada, whose share reached 30.3 per cent. Present-day member countries of the EEC, including the United Kingdom, accounted for only 18.2 per cent of the total.

According to American estimates, American direct investment in Brazil reached $644 million in 1950,[53] a figure which is not inconsistent with Brazilian official data.

From the 1950s to the 1980s

During the 1950s, especially after the middle of the decade, foreign direct investment in Brazil increased considerably. Several factors seem to have contributed to larger capital inflows. Restrictions on capital transfers and remittances of profits were abolished in 1953. The system of multiple exchange rates introduced in that same year represented a '*de facto* devaluation . . . a market mechanism for equating exchange supply and demand' (World Bank), therefore stimulating local production and discouraging imports. Instruction no. 113 of SUMOC (a government agency which preceded the Central Bank) allowed imports of capital equipment without exchange cover. (The value of the machinery was registered as a direct investment in the firm and its equivalent value in foreign currency was accepted as the basis for future capital or profit remittances.) The tariff of 1957 was also designed to provide adequate protection to the industrial sector, further stimulating domestic production, while a set of rules known as 'the law of similars' (whose origins were in the early 1900s) restricted imports of goods 'similar' to local products. Finally, the new government elected for the period 1956–61 established various sectoral targets, granting incentives to new industrial sectors, and implemented investments in economic infrastructure notably in the production of energy, which were complementary to investments of the private sector. All those incentives and an 'anticipatory effect', out of fear of exclusion from the expanding Brazilian domestic market, led to particularly large investments in manufacturing.[54]

Though the United States had the largest share in new investments, among EEC countries the importance of West German investments was particularly remarkable. These were directed to new sectors such as the automotive and capital goods industries. According to official West German statistics, from 1951 to 30 June 1961, West German direct investment abroad totalled DM3.4 billion (about $850 million) and Brazil ranked first among receiving countries with DM598 million marks or 17.6 per cent of the total.[55] According to American data, on the other hand, the stock of American direct investment in Brazil reached $835 million in 1957 and $935 million in 1960, when the share of manufacturing in the total reached 54 per cent.[56]

Several EEC countries and Japan also made significant investments in various segments of manufacturing in the 1950s, which in several cases resulted in transfer of know-how. The data in Table 2.12 show mainly the values of operations authorised on the basis of Instruction 113 (which constituted a large fraction of total investments from 1955 to 1960), according to countries of origin and sectors of destination. The share of EEC countries in the total was 34 per cent (compared with an American participation of 44 per cent), and was largely explained by West German investments (19.4 per cent of the total) but also to a lesser extent by those of France, the United Kingdom and Italy. Canada did not increase its new investments in accordance with its share in the total shock, while Japanese and Swiss investments gained in importance.

As to the sectors of destination of these investments, the automotive industry, including trucks, buses and motor cars, received 48 per cent total capital inflows, while 2.6 per cent went into the production of tractors. West German (and to a much lesser extent French) capital was directed to the former sectors. Capital from West Germany and from other EEC countries was also invested in heavy and mechanical industries, which also absorbed a significant share of the total. Dutch capital (soon competing with a Japanese firm) was directed to shipbuilding and French and Belgian capital was also invested in chemicals. West German capital competed with Swiss capital in chemical and pharmaceutical products and Switzerland also invested in food industries.

According to balance-of-payments statistics, net annual foreign direct investment averaged only $17 million in 1947–50, and there was a negative investment of $4 million in 1951, followed by a positive average of $14 million in 1952–4. Net direct investment jumped to $43 million in 1955, and averaged $112 million from 1956 to 1961 (see Table 2.13).

A ranking of the 32 largest enterprises in Brazil in the early 1960s showed 14 firms with substantial foreign capital participation. These still included three large public utility companies (basically electric power) including two Canadian and one American; the already mentioned steel company under Belgo-Luxembourg control; another steel industry with government and Japanese participation; a large British tobacco firm; two West German and two American firms in the automotive industry; an American petroleum firm; a British company in gold mining; an American company in cotton and oils; and an Italian company in tyres and cables.[57] Capital from five EEC countries controlled six of the largest manufacturing firms in Brazil.

Table 2.12   Foreign direct investment in Brazil, by country of origin and sector of destination, 1955–60

	US$ million	%
Country of origin		
West Germany	93.9	19.4
Belgium	8.0	1.7
France	24.1	5.0
Italy	10.7	2.2
Netherlands	8.9	1.8
United Kingdom	19.0	3.9
	164.6	34.0
United States	213.4	44.0
Canada	20.3	4.2
Japan	18.4	3.8
Switzerland	34.9	7.2
Sweden	8.4	1.7
Other	24.7	5.1
Total	484.7	100.0
Sector of destination		
Shipbuilding	13.0	2.7
Mechanic and electric (heavy) industries	22.3	4.6
Mechanic and electric (light) industries	47.2	9.7
Non-ferrous metallurgy	10.9	2.2
Heavy chemical and petrochemical industries	42.6	8.8
Steel	9.6	2.0
Vehicles, motor cars, parts	233.0	48.1
Tractors and accessories	12.5	2.6
Chemical and pharmaceutical industries	19.3	4.0
Textiles	19.2	4.0
Food industries	12.6	2.6
Mining	6.3	1.3
Cement	4.7	1.0
Other	31.5	6.4
Total	484.7	100.0

Source: Annual data from Banco Central do Brasil, reproduced in IBGE, *O Brasil em Números*, 1966, p. 103.

Table 2.13 Net direct foreign investments and net remittances of profits and dividends, 1947–86 (US$ million)

Year	Net direct foreign investments	Net remittances of profits and dividends	Balance of investment flows
1947	36	23	13
1948	25	38	-13
1949	5	41	36
1950	3	47	-44
1951	-4	70	-74
1952	9	14	-5
1953	22	93	-71
1954	11	49	-38
1955	43	43	0
1956	89	24	65
1957	143	26	117
1958	110	31	79
1959	124	25	99
1960	99	40	59
1961	108	31	77
1962	69	18	51
1963	30	n.d.	—
1964	28	n.d.	—
1965	70	18	52
1966	74	42	32
1967	76	73	3
1968	61	84	-23
1969	177	81	90
1970	132	119	13
1971	168	118	50
1972	318	161	157
1973	940	198	742
1974	887	248	639
1975	892	235	657
1976	959	380	579
1977	810	455	355
1978	1,071	561	510
1979	1,491	636	855
1980	1,121	310	811
1981	1,584	370	1,214
1982	991	585	406
1983	664	758	-94
1984	1,077	796	280
1985	720	1,056	-336
1986*	-115	1,237	-1,352

* Provisional figures.

Source: Official data from various sources compiled in Luiz Aranha Corrêa do Lago, 'Investimentos Diretos no Brasil e a Conversão de Empréstimos em Capital de Risco', Discussion paper no. 161, Departamento de Economia, Pontifícia Universidade Católica, Rio de Janeiro, March 1987, p. 6.

After 1961, Brazil entered a period of political unrest. There were 'interventions' by the government in certain public utility companies and expropriations, which would only be the object of final settlement after 1964 (as a result, the total value of American investments in Brazil was reduced).[58] This was reflected in net direct investment, which fell to an average of $42 million in 1962–4. In the period 1965–8, the average increased to $70 million, but net annual inflows would really increase after 1969 when the levels of the late 1950s were again exceeded. (A new law on foreign capital had been passed in 1962, and complemented in 1964, establishing basic principles which have been maintained until 1987. It created a stable environment for new foreign investments.)

In fact, from 1970 to 1974, annual net inflows increased to $489 million, reaching $1,045 million from 1975 to 1979 and $1,232 million from 1980 to 1982. In the whole decade, direct investments from the EEC were particularly significant. After the debt crisis, net direct investments fell to $664 million in 1983, recovered to $1,077 million in 1984, declining again in 1985 to $720 million, to become negative and of the order of $115 million in 1986[59] (see Table 2.13).

The available data on the stock of foreign direct investments in the 1970s and in the 1980s are quite complete. Table 2.14 shows that from 1971 to 1986 the share of foreign capital registered as American fell from 37.3 per cent of the total to 29.7 per cent, while the share of the EEC became predominant in the 1980s, reaching 34 per cent of the total in 1986. As already mentioned, some variation in the shares of specific countries is due to exchange-rate fluctuations, but the predominance of the EEC seems at first sight clearly established and the amount of $9.4 billion is certainly very significant.

However, the presence of several 'fiscal paradises' in the statistics may mask the actual relative participation of European and American capital. In fact as Table 2.15 shows, Panama and Liberia, which traditionally harbour American investments, accounted for 6.3 per cent of total registered capital, while Liechtenstein and four Caribbean groups of islands accounted for another 2.5 per cent.

As for other countries, the Japanese share more than doubled from 4.3 per cent in 1971 to 9.3 per cent in 1986, while Switzerland, with 8.4 per cent, is the fourth most important investor in Brazil behind the United States, West Germany and Japan. With 5.3 per cent of the total, the United Kingdom definitively lost its historically pre-eminent role, and it closely followed by Canada which, in spite of the purchase by the Brazilian government of all Canadian-owned public utilities, still preserves a share of 5.2 per cent of the total.

With respect to reinvestments, it should be noted that their average share in the total investment of EEC countries (34.1 per cent) is not very different from their share in the total foreign capital in the country (31.5 per cent). While West Germany and the Netherlands are nearer the

Table 2.14 Registered foreign direct investments and reinvestments in Brazil, 1971–86 (in thousands of current US dollars)

	1971		1976		1981		1986*	
	US$ 1000	%	US$ 1000	%	US$ 1000	%	US$ 1000	%
Belgium	53,677	1.84	104,010	1.16	226,404	1.18	359,276	1.30
Luxembourg	36,309	1.25	253,037	2.81	396,063	2.06	447,813	1.62
France	129,941	4.46	326,261	3.62	682,484	3.55	1,055,651	3.81
West Germany	331,418	11.38	1,118,029	12.42	2,628,139	13.65	4,265,144	15.39
Italy	32,323	1.11	76,534	0.85	504,808	2.62	1,029,712	3.72
Netherlands	35,671	1.23	233,528	2.59	384,514	2.00	590,881	2.13
Denmark	4,629	0.16	22,016	0.24	31,082	0.16	47,052	0.17
Greece	—	—	—		—		10	0.00
Ireland	—	—	—		—		—	—
United Kingdom	273,089	9.38	420,674	4.67	1,017,887	5.29	1,461,278	5.27
The Ten	897,057	30.81	2,554,086	28.36	5,871,381	30.51	9,256,817	33.41
Spain	785	0.03	17,401	0.20	66,252	0.34	94,720	0.34
Portugal	4,933	0.17	36,221	0.40	46,666	0.24	58,866	0.22
The Twelve	902,775	31.01	2,607,708	28.96	5,984,299	31.09	9,410,403	33.97
United States	1,096,469	37.66	2,901,246	32.22	5,773,650	30.00	8,218,465	29.67
Japan	124,871	4.29	1,005,900	11.17	1,810,349	9.41	2,584,542	9.33
All countries	2,911,535	100.00	9,005,133	100.00	19,246,706	100.00	27,704,065	100.00
(at constant 1971 prices)	(2,911,535)		(5,607,181)		(7,480,259)		(10,610,519)	

* Position as at 30 September 1986.

Source: Banco Central do Brasil, *Boletim Mensal*, August 1984 and January–February 1987.

Table 2.15   Direct investments and reinvestments in Brazil, as at 30 September 1986 (US$ million)

	Investments	Reinvest-ments	Total	%	Reinvest-ments total (%)
Belgium	202.0	157.3	359.3	1.30	43.8
Luxembourg	370.8	77.0	447.8	1.62	17.2
France	522.4	533.3	1,055.7	3.81	50.5
West Germany	2,863.7	1,401.4	4,265.1	15.40	32.9
Italy	874.4	155.3	1,029.7	3.72	15.1
Netherlands	414.1	176.8	590.9	2.13	29.9
Original EEC members	5,247.4	2,501.1	(7,748.5)	(27.98)	(32.3)
Denmark	34.1	12.9	47.0	0.17	27.4
Ireland	—	—	—	—	—
United Kingdom	778.5	682.8	1,461.3	5.27	43.0
Greece	0.0	—	0.0	0.00	—
Original and first-expansion members	6,060.0	3,196.8	(9,256.8)	(33.42)	(34.5)
Portugal	53.3	5.5	58.8	0.21	9.4
Spain	88.9	5.8	94.7	0.34	6.1
Total EEC	6,202.2	3,208.1	(9,410.3)	(33.97)	(34.1)
United States	5,452.2	2,766.2	8,218.4	29.67	33.7
Canada	930.8	499.2	1,430.0	5.16	34.9
Japan	2,156.0	428.5	2,584.5	9.33	16.6
Switzerland	1,225.7	1,093.1	2,318.8	8.37	47.1
Sweden	306.9	128.8	435.7	1.57	29.6
Netherlands Antilles	216.8	17.5	234.3	0.85	7.5
Bahamas	78.3	27.5	105.8	0.38	26.0
Bermuda	195.4	39.4	234.8	0.85	16.8
Cayman	77.9	37.6	115.5	0.42	32.6
Liberia	467.7	17.1	484.8	1.75	3.5
Liechtenstein	147.4	29.8	177.2	0.64	16.8
Panama	889.1	381.5	1,270.5	4.59	30.0
Total	18,974.0	8,730.0	27,704.1	100.00	31.5

Source: Banco Central do Brasil, *Boletim Mensal*, January–February 1987, pp. 14–15.

average, France, the United Kingdom and Belgium show a higher re-investment participation and Italy, Portugal and Spain appear to have reinvested very little. Undisturbed earnings have been an important source of reinvestment in the immediate post-war period.[60] Reinvestments, however, are a function of the sectors of destination of the investments, of the length of the period of permanence of original investments in the country and of sectoral industrial policies of the government.[61]

Table 2.16 shows the distribution of direct investments and reinvestments by sector of economic activity as at 30 September 1986. Three-fourths of the total foreign capital of $27.7 billion in Brazil are in

Table 2.16 Distribution of direct investments by sector of economic activity and selected countries, ...

	Belgium	Luxem-bourg	France	West Ger-many	Italy	Nether-lands	Den-mark	Ireland	United King-dom	Greece	Portugal	Spain	United States	Canada	Japan	Switzer-land	Sweden	Panama	Total
Agriculture, cattle breeding, fishing	0.15	2.71	1.25	0.24	0.10	0.56	—	—	0.17	—	—	—	0.84	.02	1.77	0.85	0.14	3.12	0.90
Mining and extractive industries	—	0.02	0.43	1.99	0.13	1.68	—	—	5.98	—	—	3.99	3.80	2.94	1.72	0.14	—	5.83	2.60
Manufacturing	52.44	64.43	59.95	89.57	91.32	59.44	46.76	—	52.49	—	22.94	45.22	76.82	75.32	75.51	88.67	81.38	71.78	75.49
Steel	1.27	10.80	0.29	0.44	13.72	0.89	—	—	0.01	—	—	16.95	0.06	—	11.04	0.62	0.07	0.01	1.96
Metallurgy	0.88	2.50	2.17	10.03	8.32	2.52	3.14	—	1.53	—	—	0.78	5.51	10.74	8.54	1.13	15.63	1.15	5.78
Mechanical industries	0.23	13.31	3.93	14.30	9.44	4.11	16.51	—	1.57	—	—	1.64	11.20	11.76	7.70	4.76	12.31	5.12	8.50
Electrical and communica- tions equipment	—	5.13	3.26	6.72	0.99	9.78	—	—	1.22	—	—	0.54	8.95	13.34	12.07	9.52	25.13	0.80	7.57
Automotive vehicles	—	6.47	0.09	24.83	44.27	2.20	—	—	0.36	—	—	—	3.98	—	6.74	18.38	16.90	31.72	11.42
Autoparts	0.07	0.04	0.90	9.08	—	—	—	—	0.40	—	—	—	2.75	—	0.56	2.64	0.02	—	2.55
Basic chemical products	44.35	0.74	25.04	6.46	0.29	20.01	0.20	—	7.56	—	0.04	3.56	14.77	30.14	1.67	2.27	7.81	1.56	10.00
Oil & derivatives	—	0.02	0.01	0.02	0.18	—	—	—	30.27	—	—	3.87	3.86	—	1.07	0.10	—	0.01	2.91
Medical, pharmaceutical & veterinary	0.02	6.06	3.55	5.02	2.16	6.01	1.84	—	1.30	—	6.30	4.06	5.27	8.60	0.12	4.40	—	4.75	4.32
Textiles	0.02	0.92	1.87	0.19	0.01	0.11	—	—	3.67	—	—	0.46	0.70	—	7.28	1.78	—	0.67	1.70
Food	—	0.36	2.55	3.00	0.47	0.38	5.24	—	0.21	—	—	2.70	4.34	—	2.17	16.69	0.26	13.42	4.37
Tobacco	0.62	8.26	0.16	0.20	1.53	1.53	—	—	0.27	—	15.89	1.96	2.51	—	0.06	0.26	—	—	1.04
Other	4.96	9.84	16.12	8.48	11.47	11.52	19.84	—	4.33	—	0.71	8.72	12.91	0.74	16.48	26.13	3.24	12.57	12.99
Public services	—	3.37	0.28	0.18	0.01	0.29	2.06	—	0.11	—	—	—	0.08	0.42	0.01	0.21	0.60	0.02	0.21
Road transport	—	3.37	0.19	0.12	—	0.01	0.84	—	—	—	—	—	0.02	0.42	—	0.11	—	0.01	0.12
Other	—	—	0.09	0.06	0.01	0.28	1.22	—	0.11	—	—	—	0.06	—	0.01	0.10	0.60	0.01	0.09
Services	43.29	28.26	35.76	7.74	8.29	35.96	50.87	—	38.46	—	76.84	44.99	17.14	18.66	17.18	8.73	16.09	15.38	18.92
Banking	5.74	0.11	11.85	1.38	1.91	3.33	—	—	6.25	—	73.18	35.03	3.60	2.98	6.87	0.35	0.36	—	3.65
Consulting and property administration	20.87	18.33	18.48	2.65	5.18	6.89	0.03	—	27.08	—	0.28	4.91	8.38	15.49	2.98	4.96	8.41	10.27	9.44
Other	16.68	9.82	5.44	3.71	1.20	25.75	50.84	—	5.13	—	3.38	5.05	5.16	0.18	7.34	3.43	7.32	5.11	5.83
Other	4.13	1.22	2.33	0.39	0.15	2.07	0.31	—	2.78	100.00	0.22	1.39	1.56	2.63	3.81	1.40	1.94	3.88	1.88
Total	100.00	100.00	100.00	100.00	100.00	100.00	100.00	—	100.00	100.00	100.00	100.00	100.00	100.00	100.00	100.00	100.00	100.00	100.00

Source: Banco Central do Brasil, *Boletin Mensal*, January–February 1987, pp. 24–37.

manufacturing and only 0.9 per cent in agriculture. Mining absorbs 2.6 per cent and public services only 0.21 per cent. The share of banking is only 3.65 per cent, while that of consulting and administration of property reaches 9.4 per cent, and 'other services' 5.8 per cent.

However, these are overall averages. In the case of EEC countries, the share of manufacturing is also predominant. It is particularly high in the case of Germany (89.6 per cent) and Italy (91.3 per cent), but less so in the case of France (60 per cent), the Netherlands (52.4 per cent) and the United Kingdom (52.5 per cent). Agriculture and cattle breeding are irrelevant in all cases but that of Spain, but the latter's investments are small in absolute terms. Banking is the most important sector in the case of Portugal (73.2 per cent) and has some importance in the case of Spain (35 per cent), France (11.9 per cent), the United Kingdom (6.2 per cent) and Belgium (5.7 per cent). In all other cases its share is below 5 per cent. Consulting and property administration are relevant particularly in the cases of the United Kingdom (27.1 per cent), Belgium (20.9 per cent), France (18.50 per cent) and Luxembourg (18.3 per cent). Public services have become irrelevant with the nationalisation, in recent decades, of communications and electric energy services.

As regards the manufacturing sector, the relative importance of the various branches also varies considerably from country to country. Taking the four largest countries of the EEC, in the case of West Germany the shares of motor cars (24.8 per cent) and parts (9.1 per cent), mechanical industries (14.3 per cent) and metallurgy (10 per cent) appear as particularly relevant. The case of Italy is similar, with a great predominance of the automotive industry (44.3 per cent), followed by steel (13.7 per cent), mechanical industries (9.4 per cent) and metallurgy (8.3 per cent). The investments of France are more evenly spread among the various sectors, but the share of basic chemicals (25 per cent) is particularly high, as it is also the case of the Netherlands (20 per cent) and especially of Belgium (44.4 per cent). Finally, in the case of the United Kingdom, basic chemical products (7.6 per cent) and oil and derivatives (30.3 per cent) are the two most important manufacturing segments, and the country still preserves non-negligible investments in mining (accounting for 6 per cent of the total).

An examination of the 50 largest firms in Brazil in 1986 according to gross sales, including public companies, shows that the largest private firm and third largest of all the firms in the country is Anglo-Dutch and is engaged in oil distribution. A German motor-car manufacturer and a British tobacco firm are also among the ten largest, ranking fourth and fifth respectively. Five American firms rank from seventh to 14th. A second German bus and truck manufacturer and an Italian cable and tyre producer are also among the largest 25. From the 28th position to the 45th, there are an Italian automobile manufacturer, a French chemical firm, a Dutch cosmetics firm and a Dutch manufacturer of electronic products.[62]

Table 2.17 Remittances of profits and dividends, selected countries (thousands of US dollars)

Countries	Total direct investments and reinvestments, 31 December 1985	Remittances of profits and dividends in 1986*	(%)
Belgium	306,331	29,174	9.5
Luxembourg	432,492	12,590	2.9
France	925,828	62,529	6.8
West Germany	3,546,638	113,378	3.2
Italy	956,316	8,786	0.9
Netherlands	518,142	26,933	5.2
United Kingdom	1,429,796	38,169	2.7
EEC (7 countries)	(8,115,543)	(291,559)	(3.6)
United States	8,055,010	507,827	6.3
Canada	1,252,002	75,411	6.0
Japan	2,385,176	52,049	2.2
Switzerland	2,072,831	82,684	4.0
Sweden	407,580	35.984	8.8
Netherlands Antilles	229,899	12,623	5.5
Bahamas	153,480	15,397	10.0
Liberia	480,784	4,290	0.9
Panama	1,171,450	41,035	3.5
Total	25,664,484	1,237,000	4.8

* Preliminary.
Source: Banco Central do Brasil.

The distribution of the investments of specific countries by sector of economic activity is related to remittances of profits and dividends in view of the different rates of return in the various sectors. Though a more thorough examination of this question goes beyond the objectives of this study, those remittances in 1986 and their relation to the stock of capital as at 31 December 1985 are presented, for the most important countries, in Table 2.17.

While the ratio of total remittances of profits and dividends to the total capital stock was 4.8 per cent (historically it never exceeded the average of 6 per cent), there were significant variations from country to country and the remittances of the EEC were below average (3.7 per cent), mainly as a result of the behavior of West Germany and Italy. It should be borne in mind that 1986 was an atypical year, but there are other indications (which are confirmed by the figures on reinvestments already presented) that most foreign firms in Brazil, notably those from the EEC, reinvest a substantial fraction of their profits in the country. In spite of this, the annual remittances of profits and dividends to EEC countries are equivalent to a far from negligible fraction of the trade surplus of Brazil with the area, and the commercial advantage of the country is partially compensated by a deficit in the services account.

In conclusion, if the trends is post-war foreign direct investment are considered in a longer-term perspective, there was a significant increase in the real stock of foreign capital in Brazil (in 1985 prices, the stock increased fivefold from 1966 to 1985 and almost fourfold from 1970 to 1985).[63] The contribution of EEC countries to this increase was decisive, as their share in total foreign direct investment has been expanding and now represents one-third of the total. It is hoped that new investment inflows, which have been severely curtailed as a result of the debt crisis, may soon resume.

Immigration and capital movements

In the post-war period, the relative contribution of capital movements to the Brazilian economy seems to have been more significant than that of immigration. In fact mass immigration clearly ceased and therefore its previous important impact in terms of expansion of the domestic market and of the labour force was considerably reduced. From a qualitative point of view, however, the available data on more recent years suggest that immigration has become increasingly selective, involving persons with a level of education which is well above the Brazilian average. Also, there is evidence of entry into Brazil of persons with managerial skills, a movement which is certainly associated with the increase in the number of foreign firms in the country.[64] Thus, while in the pre-war period movements of capital and of persons were independent, in more recent years there seems to be a correlation between capital inflows and immigration from specific countries.

The number of immigrants involved, however, is very small. In fact, while from 1946 to 1960 (when the country reached 70.1 million inhabitants) 736,000 immigrants came to Brazil, arrivals decreased to 164,000 from 1961 to 1970 and 78,000 from 1971 to 1980 (by then Brazil had 119 million inhabitants). From 1981 to 1984, only 12,000 persons asked for permanent residence in Brazil (see Table 2.18).

In the whole post-war period, the predominance of immigrants from the Iberian and Mediterranean countries of the EEC remained very clear. Considering the period 1946–84 as a whole, the contribution of Portugal was most important, with 39.4 per cent of the total number of immigrants, followed by Spain with 13.32 per cent, Italy with 12.98 per cent, Japan with

Table 2.18 Number of permanent immigrants from selected countries, 1946–84

Periods	West Germany	Spain	Italy	Portugal	Subtotal	Japan	Total (all countries)
1946–50							
Number	7,891	7,826	22,474	39,533	77,724	45	112,696
(%)	7.00	6.95	19.94	35.08	68.97	0.04	100.00
1951–55							
Number	10,601	60,287	61,388	156,607	288,883	9,369	358,400
(%)	2.96	16.82	17.13	43.69	80.60	2.61	100.00
1956–60							
Number	4,353	35,743	25,749	88,652	154,497	32,514	233,285
(%)	1.87	15.32	11.04	38.00	66.23	13.94	100.00
1961–65							
Number	2,643	18,383	6,378	48,628	76,032	14,246	118,419
(%)	2.23	15.52	5.39	41.06	64.20	12.03	100.00
1966–70							
Number	2,709	2,898	2,962	14,169	22,738	5,535	45,548
(%)	5.95	6.36	6.50	31.11	49.92	7.76	100.00
1971–75							
Number	3,282	1,630	3,025	3,868	11,805	943	39,408
(%)	8.33	4.14	7.68	9.81	29.96	2.39	100.00
1976–80							
Number	487	614	1,064	23,046	25,211	1,702	38,683
(%)	1.26	1.59	2.75	59.57	65.17	4.40	100.00
1981–84							
Number	214	234	409	3,438	4,315	1,043	11,976
(%)	1.79	1.95	3.41	28.71	36.03	8.71	100.00
Total							
Number	32,180	127,615	124,449	377,941	662,885	63,397	958,415
(%)	3.36	13.32	12.98	39.43	69.09	6.61	100.00

Sources: IBGE, *Anuário Estático do Brasil*, 1980–85; IBGE, *Séries Estatísticas Retrospectivas*, 1977.

6.61 per cent and West Germany with 3.36 per cent (see Table 2.18). The four EEC countries taken together accounted for 69.09 per cent of the total.

Statistics are not as detailed for countries which contributed a small number of immigrants, but there were arrivals from all the countries of the EEC.[65] It is to be expected that when economic conditions improve on a more permanent basis, annual inflows will recover somewhat, but immigration will probably continue to be rather selective.

THE EXTERNAL DEBT

As a result of significant reductions in interest rates obtained in the 1930s and of the renegotiation of the principal and interest of the sterling and dollar government debt in 1943, Brazil entered the immediate post-war with a declining debt burden and with significant foreign exchange reserves accumulated during the war. According to official figures, the external debt fell from a maximum of £276.0 million in 1931 to £226.2 million in 1943, declining to £186.8 million in the following mainly as a result of renegotiation.[66]

An agreement with French bondholders was also reached in 1946 and soon afterwards Brazil was 'negotiating with the Dutch government for the retirement' of a debt of the state of São Paulo from 1921.[67] The debt in circulation at the end of 1947 still consisted of at least five currencies $198.2 million; £98.8 million; 229.2 million gold francs; 519.2 million paper francs and 6.4 million Dutch guilders) and amounted to approximately $670 million.[68]

As an American author mentioned in the late 1940s, referring to the renegotiation of 1943, 'although creditors tend to be forgetful. It will not be easy in the future to place Brazilian bonds among private investors abroad'.[69] In fact Brazilian access to long-term private lending in any substantial amounts ceased for at least two decades.

For the mid-1950s there exists a World Bank estimate of Brazil's total external public and private debt. This amounted to $1202.9 million on 31 December 1953, of which $981.2 million corresponded to the external public debt and US$221.7 million (18.4 per cent) to the 'reported' external private debt.[70] By that time, Brazil had developed commercial arrears with some trade partners, and trade agreements had been concluded, notably with West Germany (but also with France and Argentina) to transform commercial debt into suppliers' credits. Brazil had also obtained US government loans, through the Eximbank, and substantial funds from the World Bank.

In the late 1950s, Brazil entered negotiations with the IMF but did not reach an agreement as it was thought that the resulting policies would interfere in the process of economic growth and industrial diversification through which the country was passing.[7] As we have seen, in the second half of the 1950s significant capital inflows arrived in the country, but in the form of direct investments.

After 1955, however, Europe's contribution to long-term loans to Latin America increased, as a 'significant volume of compensatory credits' was granted to Brazil and other countries, but also as a result of 'the development of a system of medium-term financing of European exports to Latin America guaranteed by government agencies in the exporter countries'.[72]

Thus, considering the main sources of non-compensatory long-term loans, from 1951 to 1960 it seems that Brazil received $593 million, including $432.6 million in 'development loans' (from international agencies and US official agencies) and $160.4 million of other long-term loans, most of which were certainly from European sources.[73]

There are no satisfactory detailed data on the foreign debt in the early 1960s. There are clear indications that short-term debt increased in relative importance and in fact Brazil was constantly trying to renegotiate its overall debt. In 1961, the country obtained a 'total package of more than $2 billion . . . including over $300 million in new financing, along with the consolidation and stretching out of the large burden of short-term debt to United States and European (the Hague Club) banks, as well as international authorities' (Central Bank of Brazil). However, as the domestic economy deteriorated, external conditions did not improve and exports stagnated, so that by mid-1963, according to her Finance Minister, 'Brazil's foreign indebtedness totalled about $3 billion and amortization and interest payments already scheduled for the years 1963-65 would amount to $1.8 billion or about 43% of the expected export revenue for the period'. According to American official estimates, by then European creditors held a larger share of the Brazilian debt than American lenders.[74]

Brazil's medium- and long-term debt, after some renegotiation and consolidation in 1964, reached $3,281 million by 1967. In that year, the share of loans from private sector sources in the total public foreign debt still stood at only 26.9 per cent.

After 1968, Brazil achieved very high rates of economic growth.[75] The country gradually increased its borrowing from international private institutions. Thus, from 1967 to 1973, gross medium- and long-term debt increased at an annual rate of 12.2 per cent, which would have been impossible to sustain only on the basis of official loans. By 1973, as there had also been a significant improvement in the country's trade performance, Brazil had accumulated considerable foreign reserves. Gross foreign debt reached $12,572 million but since reserves totalled $6,416 million, net debt was only $6,156 million. In that same year, the structure of Brazil's public foreign debt already showed a participation of private source loans of 64.1 per cent.

With the oil crisis in 1973–4, Brazil's reliance on loans from commercial banks became more pronounced, even though Brazil was also successful in obtaining loans and suppliers' credits from government agencies and international institutions. Thus, gross medium- and long-term debt increased 28.2 per cent per year from 1972 to 1978. In the latter year, 80.5 per cent of the public foreign debt corresponded to loans from private sources, while the country's increasing private debt also originated basically from bank or intercompany loans. Gross medium- and long-term debt reached $43,511 million and net foreign debt $31,616 million in 1978.

Thus, Brazil initially faced the 'second oil shock' and the 'interest-rate shock' with substantial reserves. However, the country's vulnerability to interest-rate fluctuations (or, in other words, to the economic policies of the United States and other developed countries) had increased significantly. In fact, by 1971, only 16.5 per cent of the public foreign debt consisted of variable-interest loans, and 35.8 per cent of the total were concessional loans. By 1978, these proportions were respectively 56.3 and 5.9 per cent, and, by 1982, 70.2 and 3.2 per cent. As international interest rates rose, so did Brazil's, net interest payments, from $2.4 billion in 1978 to $11.4 billion in 1982. Thus, from 1980 to 1982, net interest payments accounted for as much as 70 per cent of the country's current account deficits.

In that context, Brazilian foreign debt continued to increase and by 1982 gross medium- and long-term debt totalled $70,198 million. Brazilian indebtedness towards Brazilian banks abroad had also grown substantially. By 1981–2, this corresponded to about 10 per cent of the outstanding medium- and long-term (registered) debt. However, the short-term (non-registered) debt had also increased significantly as would become clear after the international crisis triggered by Mexico in the second half of 1982.[76]

A detailed examination of the debt crisis is beyond the scope of this study. Some developments must be mentioned, however, before the present EEC position in regard to Brazilian debt may be examined. By the end of 1982, Brazil had announced its decision to accept loans from the International Monetary Fund and to renegotiate its foreign debt. It received a 'bridge loan' at the end of the year and entered a first rescheduling agreement in the first half of 1983. First, the country received a 'Jumbo loan' from the foreign commercial banks of $4.4 billion (Project I). Principal payments due to the banks in 1983 were transformed in new long-term loans (of eight years with a 2½-year grace period), the so-called Project II. The renewal of short-term commercial bank lending was also guaranteed (Project III). Finally it was established that inter-bank credit lines extended to Brazilian banks abroad (which were often short-term, but were re-lent on a long-term basis to borrowers in Brazil), would be restored to their mid-1982 level (Project IV).

In spite of a significant increase in Brazil's trade surplus in 1983, by the end of the year the country had developed arrears of the order of $2 billion. In March 1984, a new rescheduling agreement was reached, including $6.5 billion of 'new money' from hundreds of commercial banks; and the rescheduling of 1984 amortisations (for final amortisation in nine years, with a 5-year grace period). A formal contract was made for the maintenance, during one year, of the volume of short-term credit outstanding in June 1983. The country also agreed to reschedule loans extended or guaranteed by the governments of industrialised countries in the context of the 'Paris Club'.[77]

No new global agreements were reached in 1985 and 1986. Amortization payments were suspended pending a formal agreement with the commercial

Table 2.19 Sources of Brazil's financing, 31 December 1987 (thousands of US dollars)

Country	Government agencies	Type of lender Other	Total
West Germany	1,975,554	896,072	2,871,626
Belgium	25,085	36,793	61,878
Denmark	1,574	345	1,919
France	1,098,915	1,633,862	2,732,777
Netherlands	17,735	45,898	62,633
Ireland	—	30,467	30,467
Italy	516,112	812,058	1,328,170
Luxembourg	—	11,518	11,518
United Kingdom	443,028	857,135	1,300,163
Subtotal	4,078,003	4,324,148	8,402,151
Spain	119,399	75,059	194,458
Portugal	95,144	8,993	104,137
Total EEC	4,292,546	4,408,200	8,700,746
Canada	837,650	122,207	959,857
Japan	2,170,508	2,589,838	4,760,346
United States	2,582,318	675,743	3,258,061
Sweden	91,725	273,818	365,543
Switzerland	52,463	140,064	192,527
Brazilian banks abroad	—	74,024	74,024
Total	10,224,863	8,428,807	18,653,670

Source: Banco Central do Brasil. These figures were published in *Folha de São Paulo*, 2 September 1987, pp. A19–A21.

banks and a formal agreement with the Paris Club was not reached until early in 1987. Commercial and inter-bank lines were maintained, but in this case no formal agreement existed by mid-1987. Finally, on 23 February 1987 Brazil announced the suspension of interest payments on its medium- and long-term debt towards commercial banks. The payment of obligations towards international institutions and interest payments related to the short-term debt were maintained. By mid-year, as no new loans were extended by 'Paris Club' countries to Brazil, the latter also suspended the payment of amortisations relative to official loans, and tried to enter negotiations with commercial banks independently of an agreement with the IMF.

The involvement of EEC countries in Brazilian debt, both from public and private sources is considerable. The most recent available detailed data refer to the end of 1986. With respect to import financing, the EEC has in recent years been the most important supplier of funds to Brazil. The 12 EEC countries had extended $8.7 billion to Brazil, 46.6 per cent of a total of $18.7 billion. In fact government agencies of EEC countries gave a total of $4.3 billion in loans related to import financing (including a loan from the German KFW to the Brazilian nuclear programme of almost $1.2 billion), while other non-government import financing from EEC countries reached $4.4 billion. Four countries accounted for most of the total EEC import financing (Germany with $2.87 billion, France with $2.73 billion, Italy with $1.33 billion, and the United Kingdom with $1.3 billion). Three other countries outside the EEC extended important import financing lines to Brazil, Japan ($4.76 billion), the United States ($3.26 billion) and Canada ($0.96 billion) — see Table 2.19.

As regards currency loans, including operations of commercial banks abroad with banks located in Brazil (Resolution no 63) and, on a greater scale, direct loans to Brazilian private and public firms (Law 4131), EEC predominance is not as marked. The 12 countries accounted for 29.6 per cent ($19.9 billion) of a total of $67.2 billion, closely followed by the United States with $18.8 billion, and then by Japan with $10.3 billion, and Canada with $4.6 billion. Brazilian banks abroad, as a group, were also quite important, accounting for $7.7 billion in currency loans (see Table 2.20).

Considering individual EEC countries, the United Kingdom ranked first with $7.96 billion, followed by France with $4.76 billion and West Germany with $3.68 billion. Belgium granted loans of the order of $1.17 billion, considerably more than Italy, which limited its currency loans to only $380 million, much less, for instance, than Luxembourg ($678 million) and the Netherlands ($667 million). It is clear then that the relative commitment of EEC countries to banking debt differs from the distribution of obligations resulting from import financing.

On the other hand, with respect to bonds issued by the federal government and other Brazilian government entities, only West Germany held a significant share (about 32 per cent of the total of about $1.9 billion outstanding at the end of 1986).[78]

In spite of different degrees of EEC member-state participation in the various forms of Brazilian foreign debt, of the overall medium- and long-term debt of the country $101.8 billion as at the end of 1986, the 12 countries as a group are owed the greatest share $29.2 billion or 28.7 per cent of the total, followed by the United States with 22.2 per cent, Japan with 15.8 per cent and Canada with 5.5 per cent, while Brazilian banks abroad were owed 7.6 per cent of the total. The total of $29.2 billion of medium- and long-term debt does not include the fraction of the non-registered debt held by banks of EEC countries. Total non-registered debt

Table 2.20 Currency loans and total medium- and long-term debt, 31 December 1986 (thousands of US dollars)

	Resolution no. 63	Instruction no. 289	Currency loans Law 4131	Com. FIRCE 20	Total	Total debt US$ 1000	%
West Grmany	93,599	814	3,582,876	6,578	3,683,867	7,166,217	7.04
Belgium	79,986	95	1,064,779	25,966	1,170,826	1,232,704	1.21
Denmark	5,961	–	32,247	–	38,208	40,127	0.04
France	298,506	117	4,453,219	8,919	4,760,761	7,493,538	7.36
Netherlands	43,885	397	618,932	3,530	666,744	730,377	0.72
Ireland	1,960	–	34,409	–	36,369	66,836	0.07
Italy	33,441	361	345,855	67	379,724	1,707,894	1.68
Luxembourg	71,311	–	601,277	5,689	678,277	689,795	0.68
United Kingdom	1,463,044	1,592	6,441,366	49,567	7,955,569	9,256,030	9.10
Greece	–	–	2,000	–	2,000	2,000	0.00
Subtotal	2,091,693	3,376	17,176,960	100,316	19,372,345	28,386,018	27.90
Spain	92,316	–	274,391	3,900	370,607	565,065	0.56
Portugal	32,745	–	131,352	–	164,097	268,234	0.26
Total EEC	2,216,754	3,376	17,580,703	104,216	19,907,049	29,219,317	28.72
Japan	592,761	12	0,643,090	79,111	10,314,974	16,047,049	15.77
Canada	324,655	35	4,288,562	167	4,613,419	5,591,143	5.49
USA	3,465,132	2,552	14,883,457	426,631	18,787,772	22,550,220	22.16
Sweden	8,296	218	287,440	793	296,747	662,290	0.65
Switzerland	213,915	669	1,476,075	4,512	1,695,171	2,089,843	2.05
Brazilian banks abroad	1,412,924	–	6,154,314	112,434	7,679,672	7,753,696	7.62
Total debt (including other countries)	8,772,150	7,484	57,623,330	782,386	67,185,350	101,758,680	100.00

Source: as Table 2.19.

Table 2.21   Brazil's estimated total external debt, 31 December 1986

	US$ billion
IMF loans	4.5
Import financing	27.7
World Bank (IBRD)	6.4
Interamerican Development Bank	2.1
International Financial Corporation	0.2
Other	0.4
Government agencies	10.2
Other creditors	8.4
Currency loans	67.2
Resolution no. 63	8.8
Law 4131	58.4
Bonds	1.9
Other (including aid)	0.5
Total medium;- and long-term loans	101.8
Non-registered debt*	9.3
Total debt[†]	111.1

*   Estimate.
†   Provisional.
Source: As Table 2.19; and *Brazil—Economic Program*, vol. 15, June 1987, p. 100.

on 31 December 1986 was estimated at $9,286 million of which $1,508 million (16.2 per cent) was accounted for by loans from four large EEC countries.[79] Even if the remaining EEC countries are included, it is clear that the EEC's share of the non-registered debt is much less important than its share of the medium- and long-term debt.

If this short-term debt is taken into account, it appears that the total indebtedness of Brazil towards EEC countries is at least $30.7 billion, or 27.7 per cent of Brazil's total estimated debt of $111 billion, while the share of the United States would be 24.7 per cent (see Table 2.21).[80]

Finally, as far as the largest creditor banks are concerned, considering only those which individually hold more than $50 million of Brazilian debt, there are 18 located in the United Kingdom, 12 in France, 11 in West Germany, five in Belgium, four in the Netherlands, four in Italy, three in Luxembourg, two in Spain, and one in Portugal. These 56 banks in EEC countries account for $21.1 billion in loans to Brazil.[81]

To summarise, in the last two decades EEC countries have been increasingly involved with the Brazilian external debt, both public and private, and as a group they have become Brazil's main creditor. On the other hand, the burden of the debt, in the form of interest payments has also grown considerably, offsetting the increasing trade surpluses generated by the country. Thus, in 1986, total net interest payments reached $9.1 billion, compared with a trade surplus of $8.3 billion, and interest payments due in 1987 should still reach $9 billion.[82] In view of the data presented in this section, it becomes clear that no solution to the Brazilian debt question of a more permanent character may be envisaged without the active participation of EEC governments and financial institutions.

CONCLUSION

The central objective of this study has been to retrace from a long-term perspective and a quantitative point of view the relative importance of present-day EEC countries in Brazilian external economic relations.

We began by observing that, as a result of Britain's economic pre-eminence in Brazil in the nineteenth century, before World War I the economic presence of EEC countries in the Brazilian economy was overwhelming. They accounted for most of Brazilian trade (in spite of the American share of the export trade), for practically all the foreign direct investment in Brazil and of the external public debt of the country, and the countries of southern Europe contributed the majority of the immigrants who entered Brazil.

After World War I and in the inter-war period, the role of the United States in the Brazilian economy gradually became increased in importance as Britain's pre-eminence eroded. However, as a group the EEC retained its dominating position in trade, investment and debt, as well as in immigration. During World War II and in the immediate post-war period, the American presence in all areas of economic activity was considerably strengthened, but after the mid-1950s EEC countries showed an increasing pariticpation in Brazilian trade, while their relative importance in total foreign direct investment and in the external debt also showed a significant increase.

In the 1980s, the EEC lost its dominant position in trade which it had gained and held during the 1970s. However, its participation remains at a level close to that of the United States and its dominant position may well be restored. As regards direct investments, the available data suggest a slight advantage to the EEC, but again American participation is very important. As far as the external debt is concerned, EEC countries also hold the largest share of the total. Finally, though immigration declined significantly in the post-war period, and especially after the 1960s, the EEC and especially the Portuguese contingent remained predominant.

The evidence presented in this study, therefore, confirms that the EEC has played and should continue to play a role of the utmost importance in Brazilian external economic relations. In the immediate future, by engaging themselves actively in the process of renegotiation of the external debt, by relaxing their restrictions on certain areas of trade and by maintaining direct investment flows to Brazil, EEC member countries could make a fundamental contribution to guaranteeing Brazil's sustained economic development.

NOTES

1. See Chapters 3, 5 and 7 respectively.
2. See IBGE, *Anuário Estatístico do Brasil, 1939–40*, Rio de Janeiro, 1940, Appendix, p. 1307. Net immigration accounted for 13.5 per cent of the total increase in population between 1872 and 1890 and for 23.4 per cent of the increase between 1891 and 1900. Total population, according to census figures increased from 10.1 million in 1872 to 14.3 million in 1890 and 17.3 million in 1900. In that year, foreigners (not including naturalised foreign-born persons accounted for 6.2 per cent of the total population.
3. See Marcelo de Paiva Abreu, 'A Dívida Pública Externa do Brasil, 1824–1931', Discussion paper no 83, Departmento de Economia, Pontifícia Universidade Católica, Rio de Janeiro, 1985, pp. 4–5. According to that author direct investments and private portfolio investments were £255.9 million in 1913 and £242.4 million in 1930, and the British share of the total respectively 52.9 and 48.9 per cent. According to his calculations, public debt reached £252.9 million, of which 64.4 per cent was held by Britain, 30.3 per cent by the United States and only 5.2 per cent by other countries. Thus, by 1930, total foreign investment reached £495.3 million, of which 56.9 per cent was held by Britain.
4. Total immigration from 1920 to 1929 was 846,000. Immigration to São Paulo was 487,300, of whom 23.3 per cent were Portuguese, 15.3 per cent Italian, 13.1 per cent Spanish and 11.7 per cent Japanese. The total population reached 30.6 million in 1920. See IBGE, *Anuário Estatístico do Brasil, 1939–40*, p. 1307.
5. The most recent estimates on the growth of total real product and the real product of agriculture and industry are as follows:

	1921–29	1930–39	1940–45
Agriculture	4.0	2.0	1.6
Industry	5.3	7.6	4.6
Total real product*	5.2	4.5	3.1

* Includes transport, communications and commerce.

See R.M. Zerkowski and M.A. de G. Veloso, 'Seis Décades de Economia Brasileira através do PIB', *Revista Brasileira de Economia*, July–September 1982.
6. See Marcelo de Paiva Abreu, 'Anglo-Brazilian Economic Relations and the Consolidation of American Pre-eminence in Brazil, 1930–1945', Discussion Paper no 30, Departamento de Economia, Pontifícia Universidade Católico, Rio de Janeiro, July 1982, p. 11.
7. League of Nations, *The Network of World Trade*, Geneva, 1942, Table IIA3,

quoted by N.S. Buchanan and F.A. Lutz, *Rebuilding the World Economy*, Twentieth Century Fund, New York, 1947, p. 45.

8. See IBGE, *Anuário Estatístico, 1939–40*, p. 1307.
9. These data, based on Cleona Lewis, *United States and the Foreign Investment Problem*, are quoted in J.P. Almeida Magalhães, *Crescimento Econômico da Américo Latina: Contribuição dos Investimentos Estrangeiros*, Rio de Janeiro, 1953, p. 33. According to another source, of the $2 billion, $0.7 billion were direct investments and $1.3 billion were portfolio investments. See Buchanan and Lutz, *Rebuilding the World Economy*, p. 157.
10. There are slight variations between publications. For these figures, see Gustavo H.Barroso Franco, 'Estatísticas Históricas Relativas ao Setor Externo', Departamento de Economia, Pontifícia Universidade Católica, Rio de Janeiro, 1986. These are revised figures to be included in the republication of *Annuário Estatístico do Brasil, 1939–40*, with updated series.
11. See United Nations, *Foreign Capital in Latin American, Part II—Country Studies*, Washington DC, 1955, pp. 49–50. This publication presents the following figures for total debt:

1930	£267.2 million
1931	£277.0 million
1935	£259.8 million
1940	£242.3 million

12. On the Aranha Plan, enforced by Minister Oswaldo Aranha (Finance Minister from 1931 to 1934) and debt renegotiation from 1931 to 1934, see Marcelo de Paiva Abreu, 'A Dívida Pública Externa do Brasil 1931–1943', *Pesquisa e Planejamento Econômico*, Rio de Janeiro.
13. See marcelo de Paiva Abreu, 'Anglo-Brazilian Sterling Balances: 1940–1952', Discussion paper no 56, Pontifícia Universidade Católica, Rio de Janeiro, September 1983.
14. See George Wythe, Royce A. Wight and Harold M. Midkiff, *Brazil: An Expanding Economy*, Twentieth Century Fund, New York, 1949, p. 173. However, the rate of growth of industrial production declined compared with 1930s levels. See note 5.
15. See Abreu, 'Anglo Brazilian Economic Relations', p. 20.
16. US Department of Commerce data, in United Nations, ECLA, *External Financing in Latin America*, New York, 1965, p. 32.
17. United Nations, *Foreign Capital in Latin American*, p. 50 and ECLA, *External Financing in Latin America*, p. 27. 'Brazil offered its dollar and sterling creditors the choice between reduction in the rate of interest and postponement of redemption without reduction of the principal (Plan A) and a reduction of the principal with partial payment in cash (Plan B).' The United Kingdom and United States associations of Creditors agreed to these arrangements,'although more reluctantly' (p. 30).
18. See Zerkovski and Veloso, 'Seis Décadas) pp. 335/-/6 for indexes of real production. On Brazilian development from 1945 to 1976, see Werner Baer, *The Brazilian Economy: Its Growth and Development*, Grid, Columbus, OH, 1979.
19. The evolution of imports as a percentage of total supply from 1949 to 1964 was as shown in the table below.
    See Joel Bergsman, *Brazil: Industrialization and Trade Policies*, Oxford University Press, London, 1970, p. 92.

	Consumer goods		Intermediate goods	Capital goods	All manufactured goods
	Durable	Non-durable			
1949	64.5	3.7	25.9	63.7	19.0
1955	10.0	2.2	17.9	43.2	11.0
1959	6.3	1.1	11.7	32.9	9.7
1964	1.6	1.2	6.6	9.8*	4.2*

20. The average annual rates of increase shown by the Consumer Price Index of Rio de Janeiro from 1945 to 1964 were as follows:

1945	16.4	1950	9.4	1955	23.3	1960	29.3
1946	17.0	1951	12.4	1956	20.7	1961	33.2
1947	21.9	1952	17.3	1957	16.4	1962	51.5
1948	3.4	1953	14.0	1958	14.7	1964	70.8
1949	4.2	1954	22.5	1959	39.1	1964	91.4

Source: Fundação Getulio Vargas.

21. See '25 Anos de Política Cambial', *Conjuntura Econômica*, November 1972, pp. 77–81. A new tariff was adopted in 1957.
22. According Zerkovski and Veloso, 'Seis Décadas', pp. 337–8, using figures from the Fundação Getulio Vargas, real growth rates in the 1960s were as follows:

1961	7.7	1966	5.4
1962	6.6	1967	4.7
1963	1.1	1968	11.0
1964	2.6	1969	10.2
1965	2.1	1970	8.3

The revised official figures for growth on real GDP in the 1970s and 1980s are as follows:

1971	11.3	1975	5.2	1979	7.2	1983	−2.5
1972	12.1	1976	9.8	1980	9.1	1984	5.7
1973	14.0	1977	4.6	1981	−3.3	1985	8.3
1974	9.0	1978	4.8	1982	0.9	1986	8.2

These figures are reproduced in IBGE, *Contas Nacionais do Brasil, 1970–1985*, Rio de Janeiro, May 1987.

23. The rate of inflation, after a period of comparative stability in the late 1960s and early 1970s began to increase as a result of the first 'oil shock'. In 1986, a change in the monetary standard was accompanied by a price freeze which was successful for a number of months, and which explains the deceleration of inflation in that year. The annual rates of increase of the Consumer Price Index

of Rio de Janeiro, from 1965 to 1986, were as follows:

1965	65.9	1970	22.7	1976	41.9	1982	98.0
1966	41.3	1971	20.2	1977	43.7	1983	142.0
1967	30.5	1972	16.4	1978	38.7	1984	196.7
1968	22.3	1973	12.6	1979	52.7	1985	227.0
1969	22.0	1974	27.7	1980	82.8	1986	143.8
		1975	29.0	1981	105.6		

24. The geographical distribution of Brazil's foreign trade (FOB), in 1985–6 (in US$ million) was as follows:

	1985			1986		
	Exports	Imports	Balance	Exports	Imports	Balance
Total	25,639	13,153	12,486	22,393	14,044	8,349
EETA	661	397	264	648	644	4
IAFTA*	1,816	1,350	466	2,049	1,710	339
EEC	6,896	1,937	4,959	5,881	3,174	2,707
Comecon	1,032	334	698	863	400	463
USA	6,956	2,602	4,354	6,315	3,228	3,087
Japan	1,398	550	848	1,515	882	633
OPEC	2,636	4,673	−2,037	1,804	2,511	−707
Other	3,816	912	2,904	2,881	1,061	1,820

* Venezuela and Ecuador are included in OPEC.

Source: Banco Central do Brasil, Brazil–Economic Program, vol. 15, June 1987, p. 93.

25. Export and import coefficients (exports/imports of goods and services divided GDP), have evolved as follows:

Years	Coefficients		Years	Coefficients	
	Export	Import		Export	Import
1947–50	11.09	11.07	1981–85	10.84	8.44
1951–55	7.97	8.80			
1956–60	6.41	6.94	1981	9.34	9.72
1961–65	7.59	7.39	1982	7.99	8.69
1966–70	7.15	7.20	1983	11.33	8.94
1971–75	7.49	10.36	1984	13.48	7.89
1976–80	7.40	9.11	1985	12.04	6.98

CCN/IBRE/FGV, Sistema de Contas Nacionais, November 1973; and Conjuntura Econômica, May 1987.

26. See Franco, Estatísticas Históricas'.
27. See Chapter 3.
28. The agreement was negotiated on the Brazilian side by Ambassador Antonio Corrêa do Lago, who also signed it on 19 December 1973. Mr Wolfgang Ernst,

Director General of the Directoure of Foreign Relations of the EEC, was the principal negotiator for the Community, and signed the agreement together with Mr Niels Ersboll, President of the Committee of Permanent Representatives and Danish Ambassador. The agreement secured for Brazil lower tariffs on soluble coffee and cocoa butter; the principle of co-operation, to facilitate exports of Brazilian beef to the EEC under conditions identical to those accepted in the agreements with Argentina and Uruguay, was established; other topics included the study of reductions of non-tariff restrictions and the inclusion of Brazil in the System of General Preferences in the case of cotton textiles. Brazil did not make concessions which were expected with regard to shipping, as the proportion of imports and exports carried in Brazilian ships was not affected, but the agreement included a declaration on the general principles which were to regulate EEC investments in Brazil. For greater details see Antonio Corrêa do Lago, *Acordo Comercial entre o Brasil e a Comunidade Econômica Européia*, Ministry of Foreign Affairs, March 1974 and 'Brazil: Labour of Hercules', *Latin America*, 14 December 1973, p. 394 (which, however, contains certain errors of detail). 'See Annex 3 for the text of the agreement.)

29. See Chapter 7.
30. On this question, see for instance IPEA/CEPAL (ECLA of the United Nations), *Protecionismo das Comunidades Européias contra as Exportações Brasileiras*, Brasília, 1985, pp. 21–2. On the fluctuations in the real and effective exchange rates of the Brazilian currency in more recent years, see CEMEI/IBRE/FGV, 'Banco de Dados Financeiros Nacionais e Internacionais', mimeo, various issues.
31. See IPEA/CEPAL, *Protecionismo*, pp. 25 and 31. The classification used is that of the Commodity Trade Statistics of the United Nations.
32. EEC imports (in US$ billion) in the years 1980–6 were as follows:

	1980	1981	1982	1983	1984	1985	1986
From world	772.5	686.8	656.0	627.7	636.6	664.1	781.7
From EEC	381.3	333.0	328.3	323.1	325.7	349.7	445.5
World ex-EEC*	391.2	353.8	327.7	304.6	310.9	314.4	336.2
Brazil	6.63	6.41	6.48	6.77	7.40	7.96	7.22
Brazil/total (%)*	0.86	0.93	0.99	1.08	1.16	1.20	0.92
Brazil/total ex-EEC (%)*	1.69	1.81	1.98	2.22	2.38	2.53	2.15

* Computed from data in International Monetary Fund, *Direction of Trade Statistics Yearbook 1987*, Washington DC, pp. 56, 58 and 60.

33. See IPEA/CEPAL, *Protecionismo*.
34. For more detailed data, see ibid., pp. 26 and 31. The diversification of manufactured products imported from Brazil by the EEC is suggested by the following data for 'the Ten' during the period 1980–1983 reproduced in that source. The share of selected groups of manufactured products in total imports of manufactures from Brazil by the EEC was as follows:

SITC	65	Textiles	17.3%
SITC	78	Transportation equipment	16.2%
SITC	71	Equipment for energy generation	9.6%
SITC	61	Leather, leather products	5.5%
SITC	85	Footwear, etc.	5.0%

35. See 'Balanço de Pagamentos—1947 a 1971', *Conjuntura Econômica*, November 1972, p. 84.
36. The share of fuels in the total value of Brazilian imports increased from 13.6 per cent in 1968–73, to 29.7 per cent in 1974–8 and to 43.6 per cent in 1979–81. The share of manufactured products fell from 71.1 per cent in 1968–73, to 43.6 per cent in 1978–81. Since manufactures constitute the main exports of the EEC to Brazil, a decline in the relative importance of this group of countries in Brazilian trade should be expected. See International Monetary Fund, *International Financial Statistics*, Supplement on Trade Statistics, Supplement Series no. 4, IMF, Washington DC, p. 63. See also note 39 below.
37. See Luiz Aranha Corrêa do Lago, Fernando Lopes de Almeida, Beatriz M.F. de Lima, *A Indústria Brasileira de Bens de Capital: Origens, Situação Recente e Perspectivas*, Editora da Fundação Getulio Vargas, Rio de Janeiro, 1979.
38. From 1984 to 1986, Brazilian oil production increased from 474,000 thousand barrels a day to 593,000. The share of domestic production in total apparent consumption averaged 53.7 per cent from 1984 to 1986, having been negligible in the late 1970s. See Banco Central do Brasil, *Brazil—Economic Program*, vol. 15, June 1987, p. 92.
39. The evolution of the percentage share of oil and derivatives in total imports since 1978 was as follows:

1978	30.7	1981	49.8	1984	49.3
1979	35.6	1982	52.2	1095	43.3
1980	42.9	1983	53.0	1986	21.5

See Banco Central do Brasil, *Brazil—Economic Program*, vol. 5, October 1983, p. 58; vol. 5, November 1984, p. 78; vol. 9, November 1985, p. 66; vol. 13, November 1986, p. 88; vol. 15, June 1987, p. 91.
40. IPEA/CEPAL, *Protecionismo*, pp. 21 and 30. The United States tend to be less affected by these factors, since in the early 1980s, manufactures only accounted for around 70% of Brazilian imports from that country. See IPEA/CEPAL, *Relações Comerciais entre Brasil e os Estados Unidos*, Brasília, 1985, p. 99.
41. EEC exports ($ billion) in the years 1980–6 were as follows:

	1980	1981	1982	1983	1984	1985	1986
World	691.2	636.9	614.7	598.7	613.4	649.8	796.4
Within EEC	385.2	335.8	331.4	325.8	330.7	353.1	451.3
World ex-EEC*	306.0	301.1	283.3	272.9	282.7	296.7	345.1
Brazil	3.76	2.96	2.58	2.00	2.34	2.05	3.51
Brazil/World (%)*	0.54	0.46	0.42	0.33	0.38	0.32	0.44
Brazil/World ex-EEC (%)*	1.23	0.98	0.91	0.73	0.83	0.69	1.02

Computed from data in International Monetary Fund, *Direction of Trade Statistics Yearbook 1987*, pp. 56, 58 and 60.

42. It may be noted that the comparison is between exports EOB, and imports CIF. If imports FOB had been considered there would be some differences in specific years.

43. Direct investment may be defined as 'the establishment or purchase by residents of one country of a substantial ownership and management share— which is deemed to constitute 'an effective voice in management'—of a business enterprise or real property in another country, or an increases in the amount of an already existing investment'. See US Department of Commerce, *International Direct Investment, Global Trends and U.S. Role*, Washington DC, August 1984, p. 1. 'Other forms of international investment include portfolio investment, commercial bank lending, or international holdings of official government reserves.' Only direct investment is considered in this section. It should be stressed that Brazilian statistics consider inter-company loans as *debt*, not as investment, while the opposite is true in the case of American data.

44. On this question see Luiz Aranha Corrêa do Lago, 'Investimentos Direstos no Brasil e a Conversão de Empréstimos em Capital de Risco', Discussion Paper no. 161, Departamento de Economia, PUC/RJ, May 1987. The accounting of each investment at the Central Bank is in the original currency, a fact which clearly creates a problem for inter-temporal comparisons of the total stock measured in US dollars, in view of international exchange-rate fluctuations. Thus, the difference in US dollars between the total stocks of two successive years does not correspond exactly to the flows of investment and reinvestment in US dollars *during* the intervening year. Also, the distribution of the total capital stock in US dollars according to periods in which the investments took place also changes at each publication.

45. The figure of £85 million is from the *South American Journal* (London). See Wythe, Wight and Midkiff, *Brazil: An Expanding Economy*, pp. 301–2. See also ECLA, *External Financing in Latin America*, p. 32. In 1948, the Argentinian government similarly 'bought the railways owned by United Kingdom firms for £150 million'. Another source puts the total purchase of British-owned railways between 1945–52 to £22 million. See Abreu, 'Anglo-Brazilian Economic Relations', p. 32, note 24. On the nationalisation of various public utilities and other firms from 1940 to 1948, see Whythe, Wight and Midkiff, *Brazil*, pp. 298–9.

46. Their distribution by type of business was as follows (in US$ million):

Manufacturing	66.4	Agriculture	10.1
Mining and smelting	2.5	Trade	29.7
Petroleum distribution	30.2	Finance	3.5
Public utilities and		Miscellaneous	3.1
transportation	87.8	Non-profit organisations	3.5

These figures do not include holdings of securities, which included $49.7 million of government bonds and $2.9 million of corporate bonds and shares, at market value (the par value of the government bonds was $119 million!). See Whyte, Wight, Midkiff, *Brazil*, pp. 300–1.

47. See ibid., pp. 154 and 303, and H.W. Spiegel, *The Brazilian Economy: Chronic Inflation and Sporadic Industrialization*, Blackiston, Philadelphia, 1949, pp. 148–9.

48. On French investments in Brazil, see Frédéric Mauro, 'Les Investissements Français au Brésil (XIXe et XXe Siècles)' in *La Préindustrialisation du Brésil*, CNRS, Paris, 1984, pp. 151–3. According to Ambassador Couty, in 1922 French investments in Brazil reached 4,050 million francs, of which 2,500 million were in government loans, 170 million in banks, 1250 million in

railways, and 130 million in industry. The total was reduced to 3,500 million when the Brazilian government decided to purchase certain French companies. By 1938, total investments had shrunk to 3,357 million francs, of which 2,357 million were in government loans. In 1943 according to the US Office of Strategic Services, French investments reached 3,186 million francs, 'but the value of the franc had been substantially reduced'. On the other hand, the share of *direct* investments was not significant.

49. See United Nations, *Foreign Capital in Latin America*, p. 53. 'Much of the German manufacturing capital was scattered in small amounts; the most important products included chemicals, beer and pencils.' Before 1939, Italy was represented by a large company producing cables, tyres and other rubber products. (After the war, it returned to Brazil).

50. Wythe, Wight and Midkiff, *Brazil*, pp. 148, 165 and 218.

51. See Spiegel, *Brazilian Economy*, pp. 144–5. This author notes that not all of the capital stock was held abroad and that in certain cases subsidiary corporations had been formed in Brazil and had sold their issues locally. Data on 3,863 stock companies in 1946 showed a total capital of 27.6 billion cruzeiros. Only 197 companies were considered foreign, with a capital of 3,601 million cruzeiros (about $180 million). See Wythe, Wight and Midkiff, *Brazil*, pp. 280 and 291. It must be stressed that several foreign companies were not corporations but limited liability companies. The four leading foreign banks held only 7.9 per cent of the total deposits in the 30 leading banks on 31 December, 1946.

52. Banco do Brasil, *Relatório 1950*, Rio de Janeiro, 1951, p. 162.

53. ECLA, *External Financing in Latin America*, p. 32. These are revised figures.

54. On all these questions, see L. Gordon and E.L. Grommers, *United States Manufacturing Investment in Brazil: The Impact of Brazilian Government Policies, 1946–1960*, Graduate School of Business Administration, Harvard University, Boston, 1962. See also, Corrêa do Lago *et al.* *A Indústria Brasileira*, pp. 97–118.

55. Brazil was followed by the United States with 13.2 per cent of the total, Switzerland with 12 per cent, Canada with 9.1 per cent and France with 5.2 per cent. These official figures are quoted in Mem de Sá, *O Problema da Remessa de Lucros*, Associação Comercial da Guanabara, Rio de Janeiro, 1962, pp. 45–6.

56. See Gordon and Grommers, *US Manufacturing Investment*, p. 7.

57. See F. Brandenburg, *The Development of Latin American Private Enterprise*, National Planning Association, Washington DC, 1964, p. 55.

58. According to official American data, total direct investment in Brazil was only $882 million in 1966, less than in 1960, but increased thereafter to $5,695 million in 1977 and $9,081 million in 1982. See US Department of Commerce, *International Direct Investment*, p. 49.

59. For greater details, see Corrêa do Lago, 'Investimentos Diretos no Brasil e a Conversão de Empréstimos em Capital de Risco'.

60. Thus, it has been calculated that from 1951 to 1960, undisbursed earnings of United States subsidiaries accounted for 49 per cent of net United States private direct investment inflows in Brazil in the period. See ECLA, *External Financing in Latin America*, p. 142.

61. On Brazilian industrial policies, see Luiz Aranha Corêa do Lago, 'Brazilian Industrial Policy and International Restructuring of Industry' in Robert E. Driscoll and Jack N. Behrman, (eds), *National Industrial Policies*, O.G & H, Cambridge, MA., 1984, pp. 25–39.

62. The source is *Exame* and the data are reproduced in *Veja*, September 16, 1987, pp. 90–1.

63. See Corrêa do Lago, 'Investimentos Diretos', p. 3. According to the figures in Table 2.13 above, at 1971 prices, the increase from 1971 to 1986 was of the order of 264 per cent.
64. On the personal characteristics of the immigrants in the last two decades, see IBGE, *Anuário Estatístico do Brasil*, various years. The fact that, between 1961 and 1975, 14,767 Americans migrated to Brazil, accounting for 7.3 per cent of the total in the period, is certainly associated with the increase in American firms in the country. From 1971 to 1975, the Americans were the most important group of immigrants, accounting for 12.8 per cent of the total, as immigration from Portugal was temporarily reduced. In more recent years, many nationalities, including several Latin American countries, have increased their participation. In the last decade, several professionals have migrated to Brazil for political reasons and in view of the deterioration of the economic situation in certain Latin American countries.
65. Thus, from 1971 to 1975, 15,362 immigrants from the EEC arrived in Brazil. The distribution by country was as follows:

West Germany	3,282	Netherlands	637
Belgium–Luxembourg	439	United Kingdom	1,652
Denmark	194	Ireland	39
Spain	1,630	Italy	3,025
France	528	Portugal	3,868
Greece	68		

Source: Anuário Estatístico do Brasil, various years.

66. Franco, 'Estatísticas Históricas', p. 000.
67. Wythe, Wight and Midkiff, *Brazil*, pp. 296–7. The amount spent on the redemption of the French debt was about $19 million. See also Spiegel, *Brazilian Economy*, pp. 143–4.
68. Wythe, Wight and Midkiff, *Brazil*, p. 297.
69. Spiegel, *Brazilian Economy*, p. 143.
70. The composition of the external public debt and reported external private debt were (in US$ millions, as at 31 December 1953) as follows:

	Total debt	External public debt	Reported external private debt
Total	1,202.9	981.2	221.7
Disbursed, still outstanding	970.0	868.1	101.9
Undisbursed	232.9	113.1	119.8
Currency composition:			
US dollars	931.0	717.2	213.8
of which US Government loans	609.9	433.5	176.4
IBRD	150.4	150.4	
Canadian dollars	22.8	22.8	
Swiss francs	5.2	0.9	4.3
Pounds sterling	222.9	221.9	1.0
of which IBRD	(1.7)	(1.7)	
Belgian francs	2.7	0.1	2.6
French francs	16.9	16.9	
Deutschmarks	1.4	1,4	

Source: International Bank for Reconstruction and Development, *Current Economic Conditions and Prospects of Brazil*, April 1954, Table I, p. 42.

According to data from Banco Central do Brasil, the consolidated public external debt of Brazil, with the United Kingdom as the only creditor, still reached $298,000 on 31 December 1986. See *Folha de São Paulo*, 2 September 1987, pp. A19–A21.

71. On the political climate in which these negotiations took place see, for instance, Thomas E. Skidmore, *Politics in Brazil*, Oxford University Press, London, 1967, p. 181.
72. ECLA, *External Financing in Latin America*, New York, 1965, p. 128.
73. Ibid., Table 121, p. 137.
74. Skidmore, *Politics in Brazil*, pp. 195, 257 and 324. Unfortunately no disaggregation to identify the share of EEC countries is available.
75. See note 22.
76. For the various data from 1967 to 1982 quoted above, see Paulo Nogueira Batista Jr., 'International Financial Flows to Brazil since the Late 1960s: An Analysis of Debt Expansion and Current Payments Problems', mimeo, October 1984, pp. 8, 25, 28, 42, 46, 49, 55.
77. On debt rescheduling in 1982–4, see, for instance, ibid., pp. 69–71. For greater details, see Luiz Aranha Corrêa do Lago, 'A Dívida Externa Brasileiro e o Endivedamento Global dos Países em Desenvolvimento: Experiência Recente e Perspectivas de Reescalonamento', FGV/IBRE/CEMEI, mimeo, 1984.
78. According to data from Banco Central do Brasil, the percentage share of the countries which held bonds of the federal government or of Brazilian public companies, totalling $1,900,749,000 on 31 December 1986, was as follows:

Switzerland	10.64	United States	2.77
Japan	51.12	Kuwait	3.31
West Germany	32.16		

79. The distribution of the external bank debt of Brazil in December 1986, was as follows (in US$ million):

	Medium- and long-term debt	Short-term debt*	Total
Total	68,921	9,286	78,207
Foreign banks	61,217	8,735	69,952
United States	18,749	4,857	23,006
Japan	9,484	1,334	10,818
United Kingdom	8,739	738	9,477
France	6,348	402	6,750
Canada	4,718	229	4,947
Germany	4,072	258	4,330
Switzerland	1,620	201	1,821
Belgium	1,190	110	1,300
Other	6,297	606	6,903
Brazilian banks abroad	7,704	551	8,255

* Country distribution is estimated.

Source: Banco Central do Brasil, DEPEC/DIBAP.

80   Total debt, including $101,758 million of medium- and long-term debt and
     $9,286 million of non-registered debt, would have reached $111,044 million in
     December 1986, of which at least $30,727 million was held by EEC countries.
81. The distribution of these loans was as follows:

	No. of banks	Loans in US$ millions
Germany	11	3,891.9
Belgium	5	1,151.2
Spain	2	199.9
France	12	5,998.5
Italy	4	789.4
Luxembourg	3	491.1
Portugal	1	60.9
United Kingdom	18	8,517.1
Total	56	21,100.0

Source: as Table 2.19.

82. See Banco Central do Brasil, *Brazil—Economic Program*, vol. 15, June 1987.

PART 2: TRADE BETWEEN THE EEC AND BRAZIL

3

Brazil–EEC trade trends and the Uruguay Round

Marcelo de Paiva Abreu[1]

This chapter examines the prospects of Brazil–EEC trade in the light of past structural trends and of the present multilateral trade negotiations in the context of the Uruguay Round.

The first section is concerned with the declining commercial role of the EEC in the Brazilian market both as a market for Brazilian products and as a supplier to Brazil. The second section examines in detail the more relevant obstacles to Brazilian exports in the EEC market. The third section considers the pending trade questions in a global context, taking into account the specifics of the Brazilian position as a heavily indebted economy facing extremely complex problems in relation to price stablity, investment finance, fiscal disequilibria and social imbalances. The final section briefly considers common Brazil–EEC interest in relation to the main trade and financial problems faced by the world economy.

TRENDS IN BRAZIL–EEC TRADE

The share of Brazilian exports absorbed by the EEC has been steadily declining since the early 1970s as Brazilian exports to developing countries increased significantly, partly in response to the increased importance of oil imports which were supplied by those countries. Export shares of all developed areas in the mid–1980s, with the exception of Japan, were below their level in the late 1960s. New markets were found in Africa, Asia and the Middle East, and, until the early 1980s debt crisis, in Latin America. The US market share recovered quite dramatically in recent years as Brazil benefited from the sharp improvement in US growth performance (see Table 3.1).

As the share of oil imports in total Brazilian imports rose significantly after the oil shocks—to reach more than 50 per cent in the mid-1980s—developed countries lost their market shares. The share of imports

Table 3.1   Direction of Brazilian trade, selected years, 1960–84 (percentage of total)

	1960	1964	1967	1970	1973	1979	1982	1984
Total exports								
United States	44.4	37.2	33.1	24.7	18.1	19.3	20.5	28.5
EEC (of 9)	26.7	32.9	33.4	34.9	37.0	29.5	26.6	22.5
West Germany	7.1	9.3	8.1	8.6	8.9	7.3	5.8	4.7
France	3.4	3.6	3.5	4.0	3.4	3.9	4.3	3.1
UK	5.1	4.4	3.7	4.7	5.0	4.6	3.3	2.6
Italy	3.1	4.7	6.6	7.2	5.7	4.6	4.9	4.1
Benelux	6.1	8.4	8.8	7.6	12.5	8.1	7.6	7.4
Japan	2.4	2.0	3.4	5.3	6.9	5.8	6.5	5.6
Other developed countries	15.9	18.0	17.3	18.1	18.4	15.2	12.8	12.7
Developing countries	10.6	9.9	12.8	17.0	19.6	30.2	33.7	30.7
Total imports								
United States	30.3	34.5	34.3	32.3	28.7	18.3	15.0	16.6
EEC	25.6	21.1	23.4	28.6	27.6	18.0	12.6	12.3
West Germany	9.3	8.2	10.1	12.6	12.6	17.4	4.4	4.5
France	4.7	4.1	2.6	3.1	3.5	3.2	2.8	2.6
UK	3.5	3.0	3.4	5.6	3.8	1.9	1.3	2.0
Italy	2.6	2.1	3.1	3.1	3.1	1.7	2.5	1.4
Benelux	3.5	2.4	3.3	3.3	4.0	1.8	1.4	1.6
Japan	2.6	2.7	3.0	6.3	7.9	6.0	4.6	4.0
Other developed countries	15.7	13.0	15.8	11.9	11.9	10.1	9.1	10.1
Developing countries	25.8	28.7	23.5	20.9	23.9	47.6	58.7	57.0

Source: United Nations, *Yearbook of International Trade Statistics*, various issues.

originating in the EEC, however, fell more than the shares of other developed suppliers such as Japan and the United States (see Table 3.1).

The contraction of Brazilian exports to the EEC cannot be attributed to the laggard growth of EEC imports if compared to other developed markets. Indeed, as shown in Table 3.2, the EEC's import volume rate of growth, while lower than the Japanese before the first oil shock and lower than the American since then, has remained reasonably steady if normalized by the rate of growth of GDP: the relevant elasticities are also presented in Table 3.2. This probably cannot be attributed to the higher rate of growth of intra-EEC trade: the value of aggregate intra-EEC imports since the early 1960s increased only marginally more than that of EEC total imports: 12.5 per cent per year against 11.4 per cent.[2]

Market trends in manufactured exports underline what was mentioned in relation to total exports. The United States is now by far the main market for Brazilian manufactures. It absorbed in 1985 more than 85 per

Table 3.2   Import volume growth and elasticities, EEC, Japan and USA, 1960–85 (per cent)

	1960–68	1968–73	1973–79	1979–85
Import volume growth				
EEC	8.3	11.1	4.0	1.9
Japan	13.9	15.0	1.8	0.5
US	9.5	7.2	4.3	5.1
GDP growth				
EEC	4.6	4.9	2.4	1.4
Japan	10.4	8.4	3.6	4.0
US	4.4	3.2	2.4	1.4
Import volume elasticities				
EEC	1.80	2.27	1.67	1.36
Japan	1.34	1.79	0.50	0.13
US	2.16	2.25	1.79	2.04

Source: Elaboration of basic data from OECD (1987).

Table 3.3   Destination of Brazilian manufactured exports, 1971–84 (percentage of total)

	1971	1973	1975	1977	1979	1981	1984
Manufactured exports							
United States	33.4	29.5	20.7	26.9	22.8	20.8	38.0
EEC*	17.2	27.1	18.6	22.0	20.9	17.8	15.5
Japan	1.7	4.2	2.9	2.4	2.5	2.3	
Developing countries	34.5	30.6	47.4	38.9	46.6	52.8	39.9
Other developed countries	13.2	8.6	10.4	9.8	7.2	6.3	6.6

*   Membership varies with year.
Source of raw data: Ministério da Fazenda and Cacex.

cent of footwear exports, 28 per cent of steel products (1984), 41 per cent of non-electric machinery and 18.9 per cent of transport equipment exports. The EEC is a much less important market which has been shrinking: it absorbed less than 4 per cent of steel exports (1984), 6.6 per cent of footwear exports, 18 per cent of electrical machinery and 14.5 per cent of transport equipment. Developing countries imported almost 30 per cent of non-electric machinery exports (22 per cent of the total was taken by Latin American countries), and 60 per cent of transport equipment exports was evenly distributed between Africa, Latin America and the

Middle East. Foreign debt difficulties in other developing countries which reduced their rate of growth and made them curtail imports affected Brazilian exports after 1982 (see Table 3.3).

THE IMPACT OF EEC PROTECTIONISM ON BRAZILIAN EXPORTS[3]

This section will deal with the more relevant Brazil–EEC trade issues: trade preferences; tariff escalation; agricultural protectionism; textile and clothing quotas; anti-dumping procedures, subsidy countervailing duties and voluntary export restraints; and services.

Significant non-tariff obstacles in the markets of developed countries reduce the value of Brazilian exports to these markets. In the early 1980s about one-fifth of the value of Brazilian exports to developed countries was affected—roughly the same proportion as in 1986. This was similar to the coverage for all countries but above the level of developing countries and would seem to be explained mainly by the diversification of Brazil's export structure which resulted in a larger share of manufactured products in total exports.[4] Market-access problems for Brazilian products are concentrated in the United States and the EEC. While still remaining marginally below US levels, coverage ratios against Brazil have increased significantly in the EEC while they have remained roughly constant for Latin American countries as a whole as well as for all developing countries (see Table 3.4).

Table 3.4   Non-tariff measures coverage ratios in developed countries, 1981–86

Markets	Brazil		Latin America		All developing countries		All countries	
	1981	1986	1981	1986	1981	1986	1981	1986
USA	29.1	24.4	56.2	9.7	66.5	10.5	45.9	17.6
EEC	15.3	20.4	22.1	3.8	27.9	28.7	22.6	25.1
Japan	7.2	7.3	9.4	9.3	7.0	6.9	16.1	15.9

Source: UNCTAD inventory, Gonçalves (1987).

The Generalised System of Preferences and other preferential agreements

Some Brazilian exports enjoy tariff preferences in the EEC under the Generalised System of Preferences (GSP). The graduation of Brazilian exports, that is, the unilateral removal of tariff preferences, is obviously undesirable from the point of view of Brazil as it would reduce the value of

Brazilian exports through both trade contraction and trade diversion. Brazil is one of the countries most affected by exclusions but losses are unlikely to be very significant: it has been suggested that trade losses entailed by complete US graduation of Brazil are unlikely to exceed $200 million.[5] This is roughly in line with the Karsenty and Laird (1986) estimate that Brazil's GSP gains under all schemes are of the order of $303 million, that is, slightly more than 1 per cent of total Brazilian exports. The EEC share of such gains or losses is unlikely to be much above $70 million.

While aggregate losses are not very substantial, trade in specific products can be significantly reduced by the withdrawal of preferences. In spite of this, it does not seem that even comprehensive GSP graduation constitutes a major trade issue from the point of view of Brazil. Doubts have been accumulating in Brazil and in other countries which are successful exporters of manufactures as to whether it is convenient to insist on the continuation of GSP and to pay the costs entailed by allowing the developed countries, following the so called 'new recoprocity' policies, to use this modest provision of special and differential treatment to developing countries as a bargaining element in the negotiations of more important issues such as safeguards.[6]

The Lomé Convention preferences granted by the EEC also unfavourably affect Brazilian exports but the damage is mitigated by the well-known supply difficulties of the less advanced developing countries. But to press for the elimination of this unknown economic cost would involve large political costs as it would undermine the much battered long-standing coalition of all developing countries in the Group of 77.

Tariff escalation

Brazil, as a large exporter of raw materials not facing the supply constraints which are typical of small primary producing countries, has a special interest in tariff escalation, that is, the tendency of the tariff schedules of developed countries to show high effective protection rates in the final stages of raw material processing as nominal tariff structures tend to increase with the degree of raw materials fabrication.

Inspection of processing chains in Brazilian exports reveals a dominating influence of raw and processed coffee, cocoa and oil seeds among agricultural products, and of iron ore and products within the metals group. Unprocessed materials along these four chains account for around two-thirds of all Brazilian exports of primary and semi-manufactured products. However, the structure of protection against seed oil and iron and steel imports in developed countries is to a large extent based on quantitative restrictions, which are discussed below.

Evidence shows that EEC's tariff structure allows substantial preferences to third suppliers, thus discriminating against Brazil: typically,

Brazilian processed coffee and cocoa pay duties of between 12 and 18 per cent while ACP goods enter the EEC duty-free (UNCTAD 1984b; and 1984c). Resistance to reform by ACP countries is also to be expected.

Agricultural protectionism

Brazil is significantly affected by the Common Agricultural Policy (CAP) as its impact on world prices and output influences both Brazilian agricultural imports and exports. It is not a priori clear whether this impact is favourable or unfavourable.

Traditional exports such as sugar and beef would increase as the removal of protectionist barriers would result in higher international prices and— if domestic prices reflect changes in international prices—imply lower domestic consumption and greater production (see Australia Bureau of Agricultural Economics 1985, pp. 335–7). Zietz and Valdés (1986, p. 47) estimate that Brazilian foreign exchange gains resulting from agricultural trade liberalisation in developed countries in 1979–81 would be on average $617 million for sugar exports and $1,370 million for beef exports.[7] Average sugar exports were, however, much greater in 1979–81 than more recently: sugar exports fell from $904.6 million in 1979–81 to $492.3 million in 1983–5. Part of the domestic output is heavily subsidised and the above estimates do not take this into account. Beef exports, on the other hand, doubled from $267.7 million to $520.9 million. Recent massive imports were mainly due to a temporary surge in demand unlikely to recur.

Brazilian exports of soya beans and derived products, on the other hand, would be unfavourably affected by the reduction in agricultural protectionism as this would entail cut in dairy and meat output in the EEC, which is by far the most important consumer of Brazilian soya exports. Soya beans and bran, exports of which amount to about $2 billion per year, are basically absorbed by the EEC. With a complete overhaul of the CAP it is expected that domestic output of milk and meat would fall sharply. Much of the diverted output would not rely on soya feedstuff imports. Koester (1982, p. 37) has suggested that supply contraction in the United States and Brazil would result in the price of soya remaining more or less stable. Supposing that one-third of soya exports to the EEC are used to produce beef and milk and the rest to produce poultry, eggs and pork, it is unlikely that foregone exports would exceed $300–400 million. Agricultural land released by a contraction of soya output could be used to grow alternative export crops so that the adverse net balance-of-payments effect of the elimination of agricultural protectionism in the developed countries would be still less marked.

As a major importer of wheat in normal years, Brazil would, on the other hand, be unfavourably affected by a more liberal agricultural policy in the developed countries including the EEC, as a reduction in protectionism would induce a rise in world wheat prices. In 1980, Brazil imported 4.3 million tonnes of wheat, a volume identical to the 1981–5 average. Total liberalisation in developed countries would result in price inceases of 20 per cent over 1980 levels.[8] Available demand and supply elasticities suggest a modest impact on demand—a contraction of the order of 8 per cent in a total consumption of 6.5 million tonnes in 1980—but a significant supply response in the short run of more than 20 per cent on a level of production of 2.6 million tonnes. In the long run there would be a strong incentive to import substitution in wheat production with imports almost disappearing.[9] Foreign exchange losses in the short run would not, *ceteris paribus*, exceed $50 million in 1980; in the long run they would be reversed. These estimates are fragile as the wheat market in Brazil is totally controlled by the government, which has adopted in the past policies which subsidise consumption as well as domestic production.

Brazilian exports would have increased by about $1.5 billion in the early 1980s with the abolition of agricultural protectionism in developed countries. Computations based on more recent data are likely to reduce this estimate but not change its sign.

Textile and clothing quotas

The EEC is the main developed market for Brazilian manufactured textile and clothing exports (see Table 3.5) but its importance is declining as US imports have trebled in value between 1973 and 1983 while EEC imports have doubled. In the EEC textile market Brazil's share, which was insignificant in 1963, rose to 3.1 per cent in 1973, fell to 2.5 per cent in 1978, and recovered to 3.1 per cent in 1982 (intra-EEC trade excluded). Brazil was not a significant supplier of clothing to the EEC (GATT 1984, vol. 1, pp. 46 and 48; vol. 2, p. 11).

Table 3.6 shows the extent to which Brazilian textile and clothing manufactured exports are affected by NTMs in the main developed markets. The EEC market is considerably more protected than either the American or the Japanese markets in the case of both textiles and clothing. Brazilian quotas have been growing in the most recent bilateral agreements—the last of which was reached in 1986—roughly in line with other members of quite well developed Third World textile producers, such as India, Malaysia, Singapore, the Philippines and Pakistan, but little is known on the actual impact of further impediments to trade expansion such as the 'basket extractor mechanism' or the 'anti-surge clause'.[10]

Specific sectors of the Brazilian textile and clothing industries could possibly benefit from the liberalisation of textile and clothing trade but, on the whole, it is unlikely that the dismantling of the MFA would have any significant economic advantage from a Brazilian point of view. Limited data available on cost structures and the industries' structural characteristics

Table 3.5 Brazilian textile and clothing exports, 1973 and 1983 (US$ million)

	USA		EEC		Japan		Total	
	1973	1983	1973	1983	1973	1983	1973	1983
Man-made fibres, continuous	0.8	3.3	1.6	7.7	–	–	25.1	37.0
Cotton yarn	3.8	8.9	31.4	74.1	0.48.4	45.0	196.7	
Cotton fabric	8.4	25.4	22.6	51.3	5.1	–	52.6	143.2
Man-made fibres, discontinuous	1.8	16.9	2.8	5.8	0.9	0.1	24.0	87.8
Carpets, mats, etc.	0.2	2.7	0.7	1.7	0.1	–	3.3	16.8
Wadding and felt, twine, cordage, etc.	6.7	37.0	1.5	5.6	0.2	–	10.9	64.3
Knitted goods	6.0	9.2	15.6	13.1	–	–	40.0	43.8
Apparel and clothing	10.8	19.3	7.4	9.4	0.4	–	41.6	43.7
Other made-up textile articles	3.4	5.8	12.1	24.9	0.4	–	21.6	69.3
Old clothing and rags	–	0.1	–	–	–	–	–	0.1
Total	41.9	128.6	95.7	193.6	7.5	8.5	264.1	702.7

Source: CACEX

Table 3.6 Brazilian exports: NTM coverage ratio by product in the main developed countries, 1986 (per cent)

	United States				EEC				Japan
	A	B	C	D	A	B	C	D	A
Food products	27.8	0.0	0.0	8.5	15.5	0.1	0.0	0.0	13.5
Agricultural raw materials	0.0	0.0	0.0	0.0	1.3	0.0	0.0	0.0	7.9
Minerals and metals	62.7	44.6	0.0	58.1	8.2	3.4	0.0	5.1	1.2
Iron and steel	75.5	65.1	0.0	68.7	98.3	41.6	0.0	61.8	0.0
Fuels	0.0	0.0	0.0	0.0	91.1	0.0	0.0	0.0	0.0
Chemical products	14.0	0.0	0.0	14.0	1.3	0.0	0.0	0.1	44.0
Manufactures	12.9	0.4	4.7	8.4	52.1	0.0	22.5	9.1	3.8
Leather	0.0	0.0	0.0	0.0	18.1	0.0	0.0	0.0	0.0
Textile	50.5	0.0	50.5	4.0	95.5	0.0	90.9	4.4	35.9
Clothing	68.3	0.0	57.0	11.3	77.2	0.0	77.1	0.0	0.0
Footwear	0.0	0.0	0.0	0.0	100.0	0.0	0.0	87.7	98.7

A = All non-tariff measures
B = Voluntary export restrictions
C = Multi-Fibre Arrangement (MFA) quotas and other textile restrictions
D = AD/CVD actions
All figures for Japan in columns B–D are zero.

Source: UNCTAD inventory, Gonçalves (1987).

suggest that Brazilian goods would be probably displaced in world markets in the event of a textile and clothing trade liberalisation.[11]

Anti-dumping procedures, subsidy countervailing duties and voluntary export restraints

These are vital issues from the point of view of Brazilian interests because of the damage entailed by past actions by developed countries and also because of the risk of further damage if developed countries are not retrained. More recently, the bulk of protectionist initiatives by developed countries took the form of anti-dumping (AD) and countervailing duty (CVD) initiatives which in many cases, such as those of steel products, have served as instruments to obtain aggreement on Voluntary Export Restrictions (VERs) both in the EEC and the United States. VERs also affect other less important products such as cassava in the EEC. Data presented in Table 3.6 on NTM coverage ratios show the relative importance of VERs and/or AD/CVDs in the case of iron and steel products, chemicals, shoes and manufactured exports generally.

Brazil has since 1980 traditionally led the table of countries facing countervailing subsidy initiations. After Mexico and Spain it also leads the list of affected countries in the case of provisional measures and definitive duties. Similarly, with the exception of initiations—in relation to which it has suffered marginally less than South Korea—Brazil is the developing nation which leads the table of countries subject to AD actions concerning the imposition of provisional measures and definitive duties as well as price undetaking.[12]

The EEC has traditionally relied on AD protective measures rather than on anti-subsidy actions. Such actions affected at different moments in the EEC market a wide range of Brazilian exports such as plywood, sisal, soya cake and oil (anti-subsidy), iron and steel products, finished leather, compressors, hand tools, oxalic acid and women's footwear (anti-subsidy).[13]

Taking a prospective stance, Brazil is likely to be especially concerned if the EEC insists once again on the inclusion of the possibility of selective action in relation to safeguards making legal under GATT rules the negotiation of bilateral trade-restraint agreements.[14] Quantitative assessment of the losses entailed by such duties depends on new research into the subject, especially so as the actual position concerning the application of these impediments is volatile and the dissuasive impact of initiations— almost impossible to treat empirically—is likely to be more important than the price effects. These price effects can be estimated using the conventional methodology for assessing the impact of both trade diversion and trade contraction.[15] For instance, Brazilian export contraction due to AD/CVD duties or export taxes can be roughly estimated at $8 million for footwear in the EEC. In 1984 AD/CVD duties and import taxes affected $1,255 million in the United States and $1,220 million in the EEC but these values were inflated in both cases by the inclusion of steel and iron products—since then regulated by VERs—and especially so in the EEC by the inclusion of soya products which corresponded to about $900 million.

VERs in exchange for the suspension of AD/CVD duties usually result from bilateral negotiations. In the case of Brazil–EEC trade they mainly affect exports of steel and iron products which are limited to 150,000 tonnes/year. It is possible to compute the impact of VERs on export values taking into account both volume contraction and price increases entailed by their introduction.[16] Rough estimates indicate that such arrangements result in only a slight contraction of steel exports to the EEC.

New themes: services

It is impossible to exaggerate the extent of the ignorance on the real issues at stake in the negotiation of the so-called new themes included in the Punta del Este compromise concerning the Uruguay Round agenda. Even the rigid stance of the US government in favour of the inclusion of such themes seem to have been based on intuition rather on firm evidence demonstrating the real importance of such themes.

Data on Brazilian trade in services are presented in Table 3.7. It is apparent that the recent reduction of the deficit in the trade in services is, as in the case of goods, basically due to a contraction of imports—particularly in transport and 'other' services—rather than to any improvement in exports. This contraction since the early 1980s is explained by the fall in the level of imports of goods and of economic activity generally, as the major subitems of other services are leasing of equipment, communications, and specialised technical services as well as reduce in commodity exchanges. Other service payments—that is, excluding interest, travel, transport, insurance and government—are highly concentrated geographically: about 60 per cent are made to the United States and much of the rest to other developed countries (1983 data). Exports of non-factor services are similarly concentrated in developed markets but an increasingly important role is being played by Middle-Eastern markets such as Iraq.

From the viewpoint of GATT negotiations—or, to be more precise, Uruguay Round negotiations outside GATT using GATT machinery—these are the crucial discussion items which are recorded by present balance-of-payments accounting procedures. There is, however, no publicly available long-term information on profit remittances and reinvestment of foreign firms which provide services in Brazil and are certainly relevant in any overall discussion of the issues of trade in services. In 1986, of total profit remittances of $1,133.1 million, remittances related to foreign

Table 3.7 Brazilian trade in non-factor services, 1980–85 (US$ million)

	1980	1981	1982	1983	1984	1985
Exports	1,765	2,287	1,819	1,729	1,955	2,092
Travel	126	243	65	39	65	66
Transport	814	1,087	998	1,106	1,295	1,490
Insurance	138	109	84	39	37	32
Government	59	73	62	55	74	69
Other services	628	775	610	490	484	435
Imports	4,884	5,150	5,407	4,137	3,669	3,794
Travel	367	408	911	431	218	441
Transport	2,750	2,779	2,454	2,019	2,055	1,860
Insurance	52	65	102	82	151	135
Government	171	172	184	166	194	247
Other services	1,544	1,726	1,756	1,439	1,081	1,111
Balance	−3,119	−2,863	−3,558	−2,408	−1,744	−1,702
Travel	−214	−165	−846	−392	−153	−375
Transport	−1,936	−1,692	−1,456	−913	−760	−370
Insurance	86	44	−18	−43	−114	−103
Government	−112	−99	−122	−111	−120	−178
Other services	−916	−951	−1,146	−949	−597	−676

Source: Banco Central do Brasil, *Relátorio*, various issues; and *Boletim*, various issues.

investment in the services sector amounted to $188 million. Of this total, $129.8 million corresponded to non-commercial services, of which only $25.1 million was directed to the United States and more than $41 million to the EEC. To put numbers into perspective, profit remittances originating in the largest industrial sector, basic chemicals, amounted to $138.6 million.

The resistance of developing countries in Punta del Este concerning the inclusion of 'new themes'—that is, services, intellectual property and trade-related investment—was rooted in a diversified set of arguments. Too little was, and is, known in terms of hard economic evidence on 'new themes' included in the agenda of the Uruguay Round. Such a state of knowledge—or rather the lack of it—lent strength to the decision of the Group of Ten (G-10), in which Brazil and India have played a particularly active role, to back the position to resist consideration of such issues before pending business was discussed and dealt with.[7] The G-10 (GATT) stance also relied on the fact that the discussion was bound to raise questions such as right of establishment, national treatment and other issues concerning the general conditions faced by developed countries' firms operating in developing countries which are complex and politically sensitive.

The outcome of the Punta del Este meeting concerning 'new themes' involved the segregation of the service negotiations formally outside

GATT. Part 1 of the declaration launching the new round included intellectual property matters (such as countefeited goods) and trade-related investment questions which refer, for instance, to requirements of domestic purchase of inputs or of export performance as preconditions to foreign investment. It does not seem likely that the EEC, in spite of having supported the United States in her insistence on the inclusion of the new themes in the agenda, will be very sanguine on trade liberalisation in services as there are serious doubts about the EEC's competitive capability as compared to the United States and Japan.[18]

BRAZIL–EEC ECONOMIC PROBLEMS IN A LARGER PERSPECTIVE: THE TRADE–DEBT LINK

Possible gains from trade liberalisation must not be exaggerated. Brazilian gains from the total liberalisation of tariffs and non-tariff barriers would correspond in 1986 to exports of $3 billion.[19] Brazilian foreign debt interest payments in 1986 stood at $9.1 billion. Brazil has since 1982 been a net exporter of resources: her net transfer—that is, her aggregate balance of trade and non-factor services—rose from 2.0 per cent of GDP in 1983 to 5.4 per cent in 1984, falling back to 2.3 per cent of GDP in 1986. An interest-rate fall of 1 per cent would result in a reduction of interest-rate transfers—if and when default is abandoned—of around $1 billion. For each 1 per cent additional growth in OECD economies, on the other hand, exports should increase, *ceteris paribus*, by about $500 million.

It is apparent that developing countries such as Brazil are extremely vulnerable to macroeconomic policies adopted by developed countries. It is easy to think of a combination of interest rates, rates of growth and commodity prices whose impact on trade values would vastly exceed the advantages of a radical liberalisation of world trade. It is obviously impossible for a heavily indebted country such as Brazil to envisage the maintenance of its foreign debt payments in the long run without either a renewal of capital flows or generating substantial overall trade surpluses, especially with developed countries as developing markets tend to be similarly constained by payments difficulties. It should be noted, however, that this second option is difficult to maintain in the long run, as shown by the Brazilian default, as it is politically impossible to sustain an austerity programme with a duration compatible with debt repayment.

The EEC's role as a source of trade surpluses in the recent past has been of vital importance in making possible the generation of sizeable commercial surpluses. The EEC's trade deficit with Brazil increased from $4.4 billion in 1983 to $5.0 billion in 1984 and 1985; it fell in 1986 to $3.8 billion due both to the import boom and the export contraction prompted by the Cruzado Plan. Brazil–EEC export–import ratios in the recent past (1986 excepted) were always above 3.0, while overall ratios were below 1.94. As opposed to what happened in the United States, EEC government circles and public opinion are aware of the obvious links between trade and debt, so that in spite of the decline of EEC–Brazil trade flows trade with the EEC remains of paramount importance for Brazil.

Besides this trade–debt link associating exports to debt payments there is a trade–debt link which limits the possibility of introducing an import liberalisation programme—whose beneficial impact in the long term is not in doubt—without a tied financial package as the short- and medium-term impact of such a programme is likely to worsen the trade-balance position.

COMMON BRAZIL–EEC ECONOMIC INTERESTS

Major Brazilian trade interests are: the reduction of protective barriers which mainly affect its exports of manufactured goods by means of CVD, AD and safeguard actions; the reduction of agricultural protectionism which has a damaging impact on its net agricultural exports; and reduction of tariffs on processed primary goods.

In the case of AD, CVD and safeguard actions the main issue is how the application of such devices can be limited. Average-cost should be abandoned in favour of marginal-cost criteria. The notion of injury should be based on injury to competition rather than on injury to domestic producers. The old issue of payment of financial compensation to injured parties should be reconsidered.[20]

The position concerning agricultural protectionism is straightfoward: Brazil should make its best efforts to dismantle the protectionist agricultural policies of developed countries. This provides solid ground for the coalition of agricultural exporters. On the other hand, the majority of Group of 77 members, being net food importers, are favoured by the depression of agricultural prices entailed by policies such as the CAP and should be compensated in the event of a reduction of protectionism in agriculture.

While it would be beneficial for Brazilian interests to reduce tariff escalation on processed tropical products, such a move would damage ACP exports, with an important political impact on the political cohesion of the Group of 77. Recent EEC proposals in the GATT of a comprehensive dismantlement of tariff barriers affecting tropical goods constitute an important initiative from the point of view of primary commodities exporters, including Brazil.

On the whole, however, there seems to be limited scope for close Brazil–EEC co-operation in relation to active trade issues. On the defensive side, there is apparently more room for co-operation in the case of both services and textile and clothing protectionism.

From the limited available evidence it would seem that Brazilian national interests will be best served in the case of 'new themes' by a strategy of trying to reduce the speed of liberalisation of trade while stressing the need for special consideration—not necessarily through special and differentiated treatment—of the services sector in developing countries. Interest in reducing the speed of liberalisation of trade in services is common to a limited number of developing countries, among which are Brazil and India. It is also important to recognise that the stance of developed countries on the 'new themes' is far from homogeneous and can provide a basis for co-operation of a North–South type.

Brazil's permanent interest in the dismantlement of the MFA can only be explained by a principled stand against protectionism or, more under-standably, by a concerted overall action with countries such as India or (less likely) China, which would gain from the repeal of MFA and could support Brazil in other issues such as AD/CVD/VERs in which they are not so interested. There should be very limited Brazilian interest in rapid dismantlement of MFA and some convergence with the EEC stand on the issue.

The problems raised by foreign debt payments provide a powerful incentive for coalition formation among heavily indebted countries. This affects most of Latin America and other more advanced developing countries such as the Philippines and Turkey and even South Korea, whose foreign debt position can deteriorate markedly with a slowing down of US growth and a rise in interest rates. As far as the EEC is also unfavourably affected by the consequences of US macroeconomic policy, there is a common ground with the indebted group of countries of which Brazil is a prominent member.

NOTES

1. The author thanks Eduardo Loyo and Luciana Sá for research assistance.
2. See GATT (1986, Table A13). Price effects probably make these differences more significant.
3. This section makes use of Abreu and Fritsch (1987) which is a much more general paper on the problems faced by Brazilian commercial policy and the Uruguay Round.
4. Currently used measures of incidence of non-tariff measures (NTMs) are notoriously fragile, but the available evidence on tariff equivalents is too limited to allow a comprehensive perspective of protection entailed by NTMs.
5. See Abreu and Fritsch (1987). The methodology used is *ex ante*, assessing losses due to both trade contraction and trade diversion.
6. See Blackhurst (1986, p. 5) for the point of view of a high-ranking GATT official on this matter.
7. While these estimates relate to overall trade liberalisation and not only to the abolition of the CAP, agricultural trade liberalisation restricted to the EEC without similar moves in the United States and Japan is an impossible scenario.
8. Anderson and Tyers (1984).
9. See Modiano (1983) for wheat demand and supply elasticities.

10. Agreement between the EC Commission and Brazil on Trade in Textile Products, Brussels, 1986; Teunissen and Blokker (1985).
11. Cable (1986, pp. 29–30) and International Textiles Manufacturers Association (1985).
12. GATT, General set of tables, Committee on Subsidies and Countervailing Measures and Committee on Anti-Dumping Practices.
13. UNCTAD NTM inventory, IPEA/CEPAL (1985) and Beseler and Williams (1986).
14. EEC, 1986, pp. 7–8. See Bourgeois (1986, pp. 593/-/4) for the problems raised by selective complaints.
15. See Abreu and Fritsch (1987) for a similar use in the evaluation of the impact of GSP graduation.
16. See Greenaway and Hindley (1985, passim).
17. See Batista (1987, p. 1).
18. See, for instance OECD (1985, pp. 22–5) and English (1984) on the lack of competitiveness of European high-technology industry which is bound to reflect on its competitive margin in the provision of services.
19. Estimates based on 1980 trade values: see Laird and Yeats (1986, p. 18) and UNCTAD (1984a).
20. See Oum (1986, pp. 17–8) and Dam (1970, pp. 368/-/9).

BIBLIOGRAPHY

Abreu, M. de P. and W. Fritsch (1987). 'Brazil, Latin America and the Caribbean' in J. Whalley (ed.), *Dealing with the North. Developing Countries and the Global Trading System*, CSIER/University of Western Ontario, London (Ontario).
Abreu, M. de P. and W. Fritsch (1987). 'GSP Graduation: Impact of Major Latin American Beneficiaries', Discussion Paper no. 150, Departamento de Econõmia, Pontifícia Universidade Católica, Rio de Janeiro, *Agreement between the European Economic Community and the Federal Republic of Brazil on Trade in Textile Products*, Brussels, 12 September 1987.
Anderson, K. and Tyers, R. (1984). 'European Community Grain and Meat Policies: Effects on International Prices, Trade and Welfare', *European Review of Agricultural Economics*, vol. 2, no. 4.
Australia Bureau of Agricultural Economies (1985). *Agricultural Policies in the European Community. Their Origins, Nature and Effects on Production and Trade*, Australian Government Printing Office, Canberra.
Batista, P.N. (1982). 'Trade in Services: Brazilian View of the Negotiating Process', Statement Made at the General Debate in the Group of Negotiations on Services, Geneva.
Beseler, J.F. and Williams, A.N. (1986). *The European Communities Anti-Dumping and Anti-Subsidy Law*, Sweet & Maxwell, London.
Blackhurst, R. (1986). 'The New Round of GATT Negotiations. Rejuvenating the Trading System', *EFTA Bulletin*, vol. 27, October–December.
Bourgeois, J.H.J. (1986). 'EC Antidumping Enforcement—Selected Second Generation Issues' in *The Annual Proceedings of Fordham Corporate Law Instittute*, New York, Matthew Bender, Chapter 27.
Cable, V. (1986). 'Textiles and Clothing in a New Trade Round', paper prepared for the Commonwealth Secretariat.
Dam, K.W. (1970) *The GATT: Law and the International Economic Organization*, Chicago, University of Chicago Press.

EEC, 'The Overall Approach: New Round of Trade Negotiations', in *Defence of Open Multilateral Trade*.

English, M. (1984). 'The European Information Technology Industry' in A. Jacquemin (ed.), *European Industry: Public Policy and Corporate Strategy*, Oxford, Clarendon Press.

GATT (1984). 'Textiles and Clothing in the World Economy', Background study prepared by the GATT Secretariat to assist work undertaken by the Contracting Parties in pursuance of the Decision of Textiles and Clothing taken at the November 1982 Ministerial meeting, 2 volumes, Geneva.

GATT (1986). *International Trade 1985–86*, Geneva.

Gonçalves, R. (1987). 'Medidas Não-Tarifárias Aplicadas por Países Desenvolvidos contra as Exportações Brasileiras', mimeo.

Greenaway, D. and Hindley, B. (1985) *What Britain Pays for Voluntary Export Restraints*, London, Trade Policy Research Centre.

International Textile Manufacturers Federation (1985). *1985 International Production Cost Comparison. Spinning and Weaving*, Zurich.

IPEA/CEPAL (1985). *Protecionismo das Comunidades Européias contra as Exportações Brasileiras*, Brasilia.

Karsenty, G. and S. Laird (1986). 'The Generalized System of Preferences. A quantitative assessment of direct trade effects and policy options', Discussion Paper no. 18, UNCTAD, Geneva.

Loester, U. (1982). 'Policy Options for the Grain Economy of the European Community: Implications for Developing Countries'. International Food Policy Research Institute, research Report 35, Washington DC.

Laird, S. and Yeats, A. (1986). 'On the Potential Contribution of Trade Policy Initiatives for Alleviating the International Debt Crisis', mimeo.

Modiano, E. (1983). *Energia e Economia: um Modelo Integrado*, PNPE, Rio de Janeiro.

OECD (1985). *OECD Economic Outlook*, 38, December.

OECD (1987). *Historical Statistics 1960–1985*, Paris.

Oum, B. (1986). 'Dumping, Subsidies and Countermeasures', paper prepared for the First Pacific Trade Policy Forum, 20–22 march, San Francisco.

Teunissen, H. and N. Blokker (1985). 'Textile Protectionism in the 1980s: the MFA and EEC's Bilateral Textile Agreements with Developing Countries' in C. Stevens and J.V van Theemat, *Pressure Groups, Policies and Development. The Private Sector and EEC–Third World Policy*, London, Hodder and Stoughton.

UNCTAD (1984a). *Review of Trends, Developments and Restrictions in Trade in Manufactures and Semi-Manufactures, Including Areas of Special Interest to Developing Countries, and of Developments Arising from the Implementation of the Results of the Multilateral Trade negotiations, International Trade in Textiles, with Special Reference to the Problems Faced by Developing Countries*, TD/B/C.2/215, Geneva.

UNCTAD (1984b). *Studies in the Processing, Marketing and Distribution of Commodities. The Processing and Marketing of Coffee: Areas for International Cooperation*, TD/B/C.1/PSC/31/ Rev.1, UNCTAD, Geneva.

UNCTAD (1984c). *Studies in the Processing, Marketing and Distribution of Commodities. The Processing before Export of Cocoa: Areas for International Cooperation*, TD/B/C.1/PSC/ 18/Rev. 1, UNCTAD, Geneva.

Zietz, J. and Valdés, A. (1986). 'The Costs of Protectionism to Developing Countries. An Analysis for Selected Agricultural Products', World Bank Staff Working Papers 769, Washington DC.

4

Trade relations between Brazil and the European Community

Philippe Pochet and Peter Praet

In essence, this chapter shows that in spite of important diversification efforts, Brazil's foreign trade with the European Community remains highly vulnerable to policy changes.

In the first part, the striking features of Brazil–EEC trade are presented from both a European and a Brazilian perspective. The second part of the paper deals with policy issues. The two main questions which underlie the discussion are the extent to which newly industrialised countries (NICs) deserve special trade treatment, and the extent to which mature industrial countries can postpone necessary adjustments by the means of trade policy.

THE OVERALL PERSPECTIVE

Brazil in EEC external trade

EC imports from Brazil represented in 1985 2.4 per cent of its total imports (excluding intra-EC trade[1]), 6.2 per cent of its imports from LDCs and more than one-third of its imports from Latin America. The importance of Brazil in EEC exports is much smaller: less than 1 per cent of the total.

Figure 4.1 shows the geographical structure of EEC foreign trade according to the trade regimes applied for imports, it reflects the fact that, more than other developed countries, the EEC countries have organised their foreign trade on a principle of differentiation. Notwithstanding the fact that about 50 per cent of EEC foreign trade is directed towards the internal market (which is exempt from tariffs and quotas) only one-third of EEC imports from non-member states is under the Most Favoured Nation

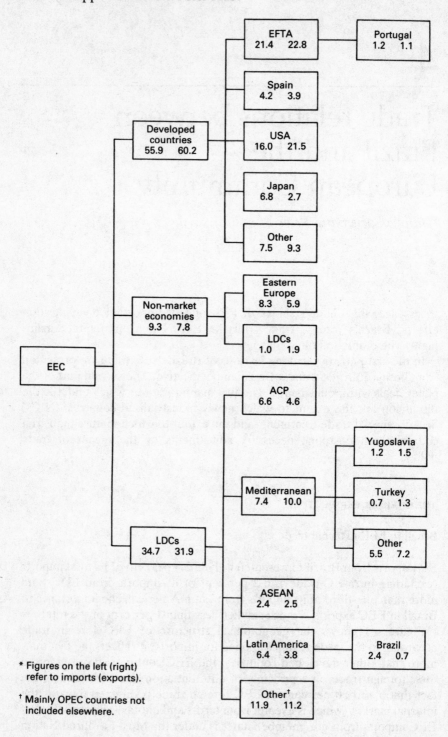

* Figures on the left (right)
  refer to imports (exports).

† Mainly OPEC countries not
  included elsewhere.

(MFN) regime. A major share of imports from the European Free Trade Association (EFTA) and a smaller share of imports from LDCs benefit from a preferential, but differentiated, status. With LDCs, the EEC has signed over 20 bilateral or multilateral agreements, forming a 'pyramid of privileges' (Stevens 1981). The 66 members of the African, Caribbean and Pacific (ACP) group benefit from preferences not only over the developed MFN countries but also over other LDCs. They are followed in the hierarchy by the Mediterranean countries. These two groups of countries represent about 40 per cent of EEC imports from LDCs. Most other developing countries benefit from the Generalised System of Preferences (GSP). Special agreements with individual countries (like Brazil) or groups of countries (like ASEAN) are of limited significance in the field of trade. Note that preferences are particularly generous when the EEC has a relatively strong competitive position.

This overall presentation of EEC foreign trade relations does not intend to suggest that its differentiated trade regime significantly distorts the directions of exchanges (trade diversion). To the extent that the margins of preferences granted to beneficiary countries are small in relation to competitiveness differentials, only minor distortions may occur (see below). This presentation does, however, give an indication of EEC political priorities.

Main trends

Over the past 20 years, EEC exports to and imports from Brazil have followed divergent trends (Table 4.1). Imports have tended to increase, from 1.5 per cent of total EEC imports in 1965 to 2.4 per cent in 1985, attaining the level of $7 billion. The dynamism of EEC imports from Brazil is particularly remarkable when compared with those from Latin America as a whole. While those from Brazil increased, imports from Latin America declined[2] from almost 9 per cent of EEC imports in 1965 to only 1985.

To some extent, this trend is also observed for total imports from LDCs, which fell from 40 per cent in 1963 to 35 per cent in 1985. Brazil now represents Latin America's biggest supplier to the EEC accounting for 37 per cent of the region's exports to the Community in 1985 (compared with only 18 per cent in 1965).

The picture is very different for EEC exports. Brazil's share of these increased from about 0.7 per cent in 1965 to 2.3 per cent in 1974, from where it declined by 1985 to the levels of 20 years earlier. This fall is essentially explained by the import-restriction policies adopted by Brazil as a result of her debt crisis. Similar trends are also observed for EEC exports to Latin America as a whole—these fell by 40 per cent in value between 1980 and 1985—but the shifting importance of Brazil as an export market

Table 4.1 EC trade with Brazil

	Exports to Brazil			Imports from Brazil		
	US$ billion	% of total exports	% of exports to Latin America	US$ billion	% of total imports	% of imports from Latin America
1965	215	0.6	10.0	616	1.5	17.5
1970	723	1.3	20.3	1085	1.8	24.2
1971	1016	1.6	24.9	1128	1.7	25.8
1972	1352	1.8	28.6	1513	2.0	31.1
1973	1770	1.8	31.4	2463	2.3	35.3
1974	3119	2.3	35.3	2685	1.7	31.8
1975	2868	1.9	29.9	2738	1.8	33.7
1976	2469	1.6	28.5	3017	1.7	32.7
1977	2465	1.3	24.4	4004	2.0	35.0
1978	2688	1.2	23.2	3952	1.7	32.1
1979	3260	1.2	22.7	5084	1.7	31.4
1980	3523	1.1	20.9	5888	1.6	30.5
1981	2817	0.9	16.9	5863	1.8	31.6
1982	2470	0.9	19.1	5998	1.9	33.5
1983	2575	1.0	25.4	6033	2.1	33.0
1984	2004	0.7	18.9	6855	2.3	36.1
1985	1937	0.7	18.6	7269	2.4	36.9

Source: Eurostat

in a Latin American context in recent years has been spectacular: her share of EEC exports to Latin America increased from 10 per cent in 1965 to over one-third in 1974, subsequently falling by 1985 to less than one-fifth.

Looking at individual Community member states, the importance of West Germany in EEC trade with Brazil is striking (Table 4.2), especially as an exporter. In 1985, West Germany accounted for 43 per cent of EEC exports to Brazil, a figure which is much higher than that of West Germany's share of total EEC exports (32 per cent). Note that in terms of imports, West Germany does not particularly specialise in trading with Brazil. The strong export position of West Germany is linked to the fact that she is the second most important investor in Brazil (with 15 per cent of total foreign direct investment). In 1984, five West German firms (Bayer, BASF, Hoechst, Volkswagen and Mercedes-Benz) located in Brazil were responsible for more than 17 per cent of total Brazilian imports from West Germany. Among the main changes that occurred in recent years, one can also single out the rising importance of France as an exporter to Brazil.

Table 4.2   Relative importance of individual EEC countries in trade with Brazil (per cent of total)

	D	F	I	UK	NI	B	DK	IRL	GR
					1965				
Imports	33.3	13.3	14.4	12.7	9.6	7.5	7.3	0.5	1.3
Exports	41.2	13.9	10.7	13.4	7.9	8.3	4.6	0.0	0.0
					1975				
Imports	32.8	12.1	16.3	14.2	13.2	5.9	4.5	0.4	0.7
Exports	42.0	12.5	16.8	12.4	6.3	6.7	1.2	0.1	0.0
					1985				
Imports	27.3	14.6	19.3	12.1	14.6	7.8	3.0	0.3	1.0
Exports	42.5	20.6	11.2	14.1	6.6	3.5	1.0	0.5	0.0

Source: Eurostat

Table 4.3   Degree of openness and importance of Brazil in international trade (per cent)

	Exports/GDP	Exports/World exports*
1950	9.2	1.9
1955	7.0	1.8
1960	5.43	1.1
1965	6.0	1.0
1970	6.2	1.0
1975	7.2	1.1
1980	10.0	1.0
1981	8.0	1.3
1982	7.2	1.2
1983	10.5	1.3
1984	12.9	1.5

*   Excluding Comecon countries.
Sources: Brasseul (1982); and Banco do Brasil

The EEC in Brazil's foreign trade

In spite of a rapid development of its exports during the last decade, the degree of openness of Brazil to international trade remains limited (Table 4.3). The export to GDP ratio tended to follow a declining trend in the 1950s and in the first half of the 1960s. It is only since the 1980s that a degree of export openness similar to that observed in the early 1950s was attained (10 per cent of GDP). With 1.5 per cent of world exports, the importance of Brazil in international trade is smaller than that of countries like Belgium (2.9 per cent) or the Netherlands (3.7 per cent), two countries with one-tenth of the population of Brazil. The relative weight of Brazil in world exports is also smaller than it was in the early 1950s. This makes Brazil essentially a price-taker in the world economy, except in the case of a few primary commodities such as coffee.

Area distribution of Brazilian trade

The geographical structure of Brazilian imports has changed dramatically over the past 15 years. Between 1970 and 1984, the share of developed countries in total imports fell by half, to 40 per cent of the total. This was not only the result of the oil shocks (which increased the OPEC share from 6 per cent in 1970 to 37 per cent in 1984), but also of growing South–South trade. Presently, about 20 per cent of Brazilian imports come from non-oil LDCs, compared with 13 per cent in 1970. Imports from the EEC (12.6 per cent of the total) are now less than from the Latin America Free Trade Association (ALADI) (15 per cent). Although the United States and Japan have also lost importance among Brazil's foreign suppliers, the United States remains the major source of imports, with 16.1 per cent of the total in 1984 (see Figure 4.2 and Table 4.4).

Brazilian exports are still more directed towards the developed world, which absorbed 63.6 per cent of the total in 1983, compared with 76.2 per cent in 1969–73. The most interesting change has been with the relative decline in importance of the EEC in Brazil's exports, from 35.3 per cent in 1970 to 23.0 per cent in 1984. The US market has overtaken the EEC as Brazil's now largest export market, with 28.5 per cent its total exports (24.7 per cent in 1970). Note that while there has been a continuous erosion of the EEC's relative position, exports to the United States have expanded considerably since the early 1980s. It is not clear if these divergent trends can only be explained by the recent growth differentials between the US and the EEC markets and by exchange-rate misalignments or whether more fundamental factors, come into play.

Composition of trade by product categories

The composition of Brazilian exports and imports by broad product categories is reported in Table 4.5. Important differences between the EEC, the United States and Japan appear both on the export and on the import side.

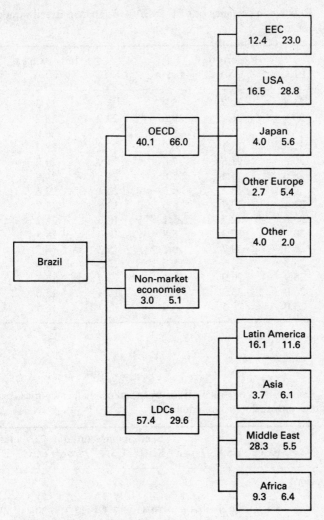

* Figures on the left (right) refer to imports (exports)

Basic products still represent a major share of Brazil's exports to the EEC, about one-half of the total, compared to less than 20 per cent for exports to the United States. On the other hand, almost 100 per cent of Brazils imports from the EEC consist of manufactured products, against only two-thirds of imports from the United States. The rapid growth in the role of the United States as a supplier of basic materials (essentially wheat) to Brazil is striking. Brazil also imports from the United States tungsten ore for transformation in Brazil.

Table 4.4 Relative importance of EEC, USA and Japan in Brazil's trade (percentage of total)

		Exports to			Imports from	
	EEC	USA	Japan	EEC	USA	Japan
1970	35.3	24.7	5.3	28.6	32.3	6.3
1971	33.4	26.2	5.5	29.9	28.8	7.0
1972	34.5	23.3	4.5	30.9	28.0	7.7
1973	37.3	18.1	6.9	27.7	28.7	7.9
1974	30.8	21.8	7.0	24.9	24.2	8.8
1975	28.0	15.4	7.8	24.6	24.9	9.3
1976	30.7	18.2	6.3	20.1	22.6	7.1
1977	32.4	17.7	5.6	19.3	19.8	7.1
1978	30.0	22.7	5.1	18.6	21.2	8.9
1979	30.1	19.3	5.8	18.0	18.3	6.0
1980	26.3	19.7	6.1	15.2	18.7	4.3
1981	25.3	20.5	5.2	13.5	16.9	5.1
1982	26.9	20.0	6.4	12.6	14.7	4.5
1983	26.0	23.3	6.5	12.3	15.6	3.6
1984	23.0	28.5	5.6	12.4	16.5	4.0

Source: Eurostat

Table 4.5 Composition of Brazil's trade by broad product categories (percentage of total traded with each block or country)

		Basic			Semi-manufactured			Manufactured	
	EEC	USA	Japan	EEC	USA	Japan	EEC	USA	Japan
Brazilian exports									
1975	71.8	50.3	86.1	7.1	7.3	2.2	21.1	42.3	11.7
1980	59.2	40.0	65.6	10.4	12.3	12.3	30.4	47.7	22.1
1984	54.1	16.9	52.5	7.9	8.4	18.3	38.0	74.6	29.2
Brazilian imports									
1975	2.3	15.3	0.2	4.3	4.5	8.6	93.4	80.2	91.2
1980	2.1	21.2	2.7	1.7	4.8	0.3	96.2	74.0	97.0
1984	2.5	32.8	0.3	2.4	3.4	0.3	95.0	63.8	99.4

Source: Banco do Brasil

Table 4.6   Brazil's exports to the EEC in detail

	% of total	Cumulative total (%)
Animal feedstuffs	16.5	16.5
Coffee, tea	16.2	32.7
Metallic ores	11.9	44.6
Oil seed	7.3	51.9
Preparation of fruit	4.4	56.3
Boilers, machinery and mechanical appliances	3.9	60.2
Tobacco	3.4	63.6
Vehicles	3.2	66.8
Cotton	2.6	69.4
Iron and steel	2.6	72.0
Meat products	2.5	74.5
Organic chemicals	2.2	76.7
Meat	2.1	78.8
Wood	1.9	80.7
Paper-making material	1.6	82.3
Animal and vegetable fats and oils	1.5	83.8
Cocoa	1.5	85.3
Miscellaneous edible products	1.4	86.7
Footwear	1.0	87.7
Raw hides, skins and leather	0.9	88.6

Source: Eurostat

Although Brazil's exports are more diversified than those of the other Latin American countries, they are still highly concentrated in a few products. Four products (coffee, animal feed stuffs, iron ore, and orange juice) make up 55 per cent of Brazil's export to the EEC. (A detailed presentation of the composition of Brazil's exports to the EEC is given in Table 4.6.) Exports to Japan are even more concentrated, with iron ore and steel plate counting for almost 40 per cent of the total. Note also that Brazilian exports of orange juice and of leather shoes to the US market make up close to one-quarter of its total exports to that country.

THE ROLE OF TRADE POLICIES

The dynamics of trade commented on above reflect the influence of firms' strategies, government trade policies, as well as domestic and foreign macroeconomic developments. In this section we illustrate major trade issues concerning the EEC and Brazil. They are typical of relations between mature industrial countries and newly industrialised countries (NICS).

Looking at Brazil, the main question is the extent to which NICS still deserve special treatment under GATT. The pressure for *reciprocity* in trade concessions will undoubtly grow in the coming years.

Looking at the EEC, the major question is the extent to which mature industrial countries can postpone necessary adjustments in agriculture and sunset industries by means of trade policies. Claims for better market access for LDCs will mirror the claims for reciprocity on behalf of the most competitive LDCs.

Brazil's trade policy

A comprehensive evaluation of Brazil's trade policies is difficult because one has to weigh the effects of a *changing* system of export incentives with those of important restrictions, which act as incentives for firms established in Brazil to sell on the Brazilian market. A permanent characteristic of Brazil's trade policies is that, in spite of a vast system of export incentives, an anti-export bias is usually found, due to the domestic price effects of import restrictions. In other words, nominal rates of protection tend to exceed export subsidies, biasing resource allocation towards the domestic market.

Shifts in Brazil's trade policies can be summarised in three main phases. In the post-war period successive reinforcements of trade barriers were intended to attract important foreign direct investment in manufacturing industries and especially in capital-goods production. Unlike in other LDCs (such as South Korea and India), foreign direct investment was welcomed as the main channel of transfer of technology. The main problem was that in a large captive market such as Brazil multinational enterprises often adopted technologies which do not correspond to the host country's factor endowment. Inefficiences in production processes resulted. A consequence of the policy was that exports tended to stagnate, the degree of openness of the economy to international trade declined. By the early 1960s, when the potential for additional import-substitution became limited, trade policy was redirected towards export promotion. A striking feature of the measures implemented was their selective orientation, the objective being the diversification of exports away from traditional products (primary commodities and semi-processed goods). The measures included a reduction of corporate income taxation by the share of exports in total sales, a drawback system to waive import duties, a lifting of non-tariff-barriers conditional upon export performance criteria, export-tax credit, exemptions from indirect taxes, and concessional credit for exporting companies. These measures were supported by an exchange-rate policy which, from 1968, consisted in preserving price competitiveness through frequent devaluations in line with domestic inflation. Processed agricultural exports such as soybeans and cocoa products, yarn and cloth were also favoured. Although the incentive system for import-substitutions was kept in place, the policy was successful in diversifying exports, since for selected products the anti-export bias was considerably reduced. The share of manufacturing exports increased substantially from 7 per cent of total exports in 1967 to 18 per cent in 1973.

The experiment with export-orientated policies came to an end with the first oil shock in 1974. The high dependency of Brazil on imported oil and economic recession in its main export markets produced a sharp deterioration in Brazil's trade balance. Given the abrupt character of the imbalances, import restrictions were difficult to avoid. They had, however, the undesirable effect of making export activity less attractive for domestic producers. For example Tyler (1983) finds an anti-export bias for Brazil averaging 43 per cent for the manufacturing sector, resulting from a nominal average protection of 68 per cent and an average export subsidies of 25 per cent. Foreign banks' loans permitted some smoothening of balance-of-payments adjustment over time, until the second oil shock, together with the interest-rate shock (induced by a sudden shift in US monetary policy) hit the Brazilian economy both on the merchandise side and on the services side of the balance of payments. Drastic cuts in imports have since intervened to the extent that the value of Brazilian imports in 1984 was not higher than in 1978. Trade and payments restrictions included taxes on purchases of foreign exchange (1980), strict ceilings on public sector imports (1980), an import licensing system (1981) and a comprehensive foreign exchange budgeting system (1983). Here it should be noted that, unlike in other Latin American countries, prolonged overvaluation of the currency did not occur in Brazil. A major devaluation was decided in 1983. During these difficult years, exports continued to diversify, manufacturing attaining in 1983–4 one-third of total exports, the highest in Latin America. Estimates of effective rates of protection by industrial sectors (Table 4.7) show, however, that the protection of manufacturing activity in Brazil remains very high, even if it has been declining since the late 1960s. The anti-export bias also implies that foreign direct investments did not create strong export links with home countries. The structure of Brazil's foreign trade with the EEC by categories of firm is reported in Table 4.8. It appears that multinationals are particularly active in Brazilian imports.

A list of the 25 most important firms involved in trading with the EEC is given in Table 4.9. One sees (except for Fiat) that the role of European multinationals as exporters to the EEC is rather limited. This tends to confirm that EEC direct investments in Brazil have been made above all to exploit a large captive market or (to a lesser extent) as a base for re-exporting to third countries, but certainly not for re-exporting to the Community.

Table 4.7   Effective rates of protection in Brazilian industry (per cent)*

	1967	1980
Food products	40	26
Beverages	173	1
Tobacco	124	6
Textiles	162	37
Clothing	142	47
Leather and products	85	14
Footwear		60
Wood products	25	18
Furniture and fixtures	124	53
Paper and products	59	−19
Printing and publishing	67	32
Industrial chemicals	42	86
Other chemicals	35	104
Petroleum refineries		64
Petroleum and coal products		−43
Rubber products	116	−21
Plastic products	58	28
Pottery, china, etc.	39	
Glass products	39	27
Non-metal products	39	
Iron and steel		
Non-ferrous metals		
Metal products	36	44
Machinery	32	93
Electrical machinery*	97	129
Transport equipment	75	−7
Professional goods		
Other industries	72	172
Manufacturing average	66	46

* Effective rates of protection refer to duties on value added, thus on the transformation activity.
† Not elsewhere classified.
Source: Havrylyshyn and Alikhani (1982)

Article 18 of the GATT is the legal basis for LDCs' import-substitution policies, which involve quantitive restrictions and licensing schemes. So far, safeguard actions taken for *development* purposes have been considered in a very flexible way by the developed countries. For example, economies undergoing a process of industrialisation to correct an excessive dependence on primary production would be allowed to take such measures. Part 4 of the GATT, which was added in 1985, also provides for developed countries not to expect reciprocity for commitments made by

Table 4.8   The structure of Brazil's trade with the EEC by types of firm, 1984 (per cent of total)

	Imports*	Exports[†]
Brazilian state enterprises	23.8	13.6
Private firms	31.8	57.5
Multinationals	44.4	28.9
(of which EC multinationals	(34.6)	(17.5)

* Based on a sample of 75 firms representing 60% of total imports from the EEC.
† Based on a sample of 75 firms representing 54% of total exports to the EEC.
Source: Raw data from Banco do Brasil.

Table 4.9   The EEC's 25 most important trading partners, 1984 (per cent of total trade)

Exporting firms		Importing firms	
Fiat (I)	5.02 (M)	Fiat (I)	5.76 (M)
CVRD	3.63 (S)	PETROBRAS	3.99 (S)
Ferteco Min.	2.27 (M)	Ford (USA)	3.66 (M)
Tristao	2.24 (P)	Emp. de Nav. Mercantil.	3.56 (P)
Citrosuco	2.09 (P)	Engesa Engenheiros Esp.	2.13 (P)
INTERBRAS	1.87 (S)	Cia Hidro do Sao francisco	2.06 (S)
Samarco Min.	1.65 (P)	Emp. de Nav. Aliança	1.87 (P)
Sucocitro	1.55 (P)	Bayer (D)	1.84 (M)
Ceval	1.49 (P)	Kammar	1.57 (P)
Cargill Citrus (USA)	1.33 (M)	BASF (D)	1.48 (M)
Inter Continental	1.30 (P)	Valesul	1.45 (S)
Anderson Clayton (USA)	1.29 (M)	Hoechst (D)	1.39 (M)
Aracruz Celulose	1.19 (P)	Fluvac	1.33 (P)
Souza Cruz (UK)	1.17 (M)	Verolme (NL)	1.24 (M)
Unicafé	1.09 (P)	Philips (NL)	1.21 (M)
Braswey	1.08 (P)	NUCLEBRAS	1.18 (S)
Bozzo Brasil	1.01 (P)	Equip. Villares	1.03 (P)
Sanbra (ARG)	0.96 (M)	Centrais Electr. do Sul	1.01 (S)
Esteve Irmaos	0.95 (P)	ICI Brasil (UK)	1.00 (M)
PETROBRAS	0.95 (S)	Pirelli (I)	0.95 (M)
Coop. Triticola Ser.	0.93 (P)	Cia Indus. St. Matilde	0.91 (P)
Itabrasco	0.90 (P)	Volkswagen (D)	0.87
Comind	0.87 (P)	Itaipu Binacional	0.81 (S)
Swift Armour	0.81 (P)	Centrais Eletr. do Norte	0.79 (S)
Resgue	0.80 (P)	Mercedes-Benz (D)	0.78 (M)
Total	38.45	Total	43.87

(M) = Multinational firm; (S) = State firm; (P) = Private Brazilian firm.
Source: Banco do Brasil

them in trade negotiations to reduce or remove tariffs or other barriers to trade with LDCs (article 36). During the Tokyo Round the EEC adopted a more favourable attitude to LDCs than the United States by not insisting on developing countries making reciprocal concessions. In the present multilateral trade negotiations, however, this benevolent attitude may change. The principle of *graduation*, whereby trade preferences are being reduced as an LDC advances, has applied since 1981 (see below).

EEC trade policy

Traditionally, the EEC has been very open to international trade, with the exception of a few products which are, however, of great importance to countries such as Brazil. There are five major sources of policy-induced distortion which potentially or effectively affect Brazil's trade with the EC: the Common Agricultural Policy (CAP); the special preferences granted to the ACP and the Mediterranean countries, which may divert some trade from non-ACP LDCs; the EEC steel policy; the Multi Fibre Agreement (MFA); and the Generalised System of Preferences (GSP). Additional effects resulting from the accession of Spain and Portugal will only be felt progressively, given that the transition to their full membership has yet to run its full course. These issues illustrate the difficulties of adjustment of mature industrial countries in the face of rather small shifts (macro-economically) in comparative advantages, and the gap between declarations of goodwill and trade realities. In the framework of the GATT, a major issue in the present multilateral trade negotiations will be the EEC's demand for more selectivity in the implementation of trade-restricting measures. In particular, the EEC may ask for a revision of article 19 which presently imposes the non-discriminatory application of safeguards. Brazil has, on the other hand pushed for a limitation of safeguards, notably in cases where stabilisation programmes (for balance-of-payments reasons) are in effect.

The impact of the CAP

While from the beginning the CAP has been very protectionist for most non-tropical products, its effects on Brazil have not been constant. Over time, large productivity gains induced by a generous system of Community price-support have led progressively to generalised self-sufficiency in agriculture and, for a growing number of products, to structural excess supply. At the same time, third countries have been squeezed out of the EEC market or even world markets, to the extent that EEC agricultural surpluses are exported. Below, we examine a few agricultural products which are significant in the trade distortions induced by the CAP.

Table 4.10   EEC imports of cereal substitutes (million tonnes)

	1974	1978	1982	1983	1984	1985
Soya*		14.5	18.5	18.3	16.4	18.6
Total cereal substitutes	4.6	11.9	16.2	14.1	13.6	14.7
Manioc†	2.1	6.0	8.1	4.5	5.3	6.3
Maize-gluten feed	0.7	1.7	2.8	3.6	3.7	3.5
Citrus pellets	0.3	1.0	1.3	1.4	1.3	1.5

*   Soya cake equivalent of soya in the form of grain and cake.
†   Cassava or tapioca.
Source: EEC Commission (1987).

Animal feed.   Paradoxically, Brazil's main export to the EEC is an agricultural product used in animal feed. Under the CAP, animal feed substitutes or complements are subject to limited (or no) protection, which cereals (coarse grains and feed wheat) are not. High EEC cereal support prices, together with a policy encouraging intensive forms of beef production, have rapidly increased farmers' demand for cheap substitutes (mainly tapioca and maize-gluten feed) and of protein-rich products (soya cake, rape, field beans, peas, lupins, and so on). In the end, the Commission has found itself being obliged to purchase at the guaranteed prices (which are set well above world prices) the excess supplies of cereals produced in the Community. By the end of 1986 EEC stocks of cereals attained 37 million tonnes. Imports of animal feed represent today about 20 per cent of total consumption. The main beneficiaries of this loophole in the CAP have been the United States (which is the major supplier of soya and maize-gluten feed), Brazil (with about one-third of total EEC imports of soya), and Thailand (for tapioca). EEC imports of cereals substitutes and complements are reported in Table 4.10.

Brazil is thus highly vulnerable to a change in the CAP, but so far it has benefited from the fact that the United States is also a major exporter of soya to the Community. It is indeed difficult for the EEC to restrict imports of soya for fear of US retaliation. In the meantime, Europeans have been accusing Brazil of dumping soya cakes. Thailand, which exports a substitute for maize-gluten feed (a major US export), to the Community has not been so lucky. Since September 1982 her exports have been restricted by a quota (although financial compensation was provided). The EEC–Thailand agreement stipulated that the EEC would ensure that Thailand's position as an exporter would not be significantly undermined by a substantial increase in imports of tapioca from other countries. As a result, other suppliers saw a potential market become restricted. Brazil's quota of tapioca is 145,000 tonnes, compared to Thailand's 5.25 million, although the Brazilian share in world production of tapioca is 17 per cent compared with Thailand's 15 per cent.

Beef.   Another example of the distortions which are induced by the CAP concerns international trade in beef. Traditionally, the EEC has been a net importer of beef. In particular, Brazil's exports to the EEC used to be highly specialized in beef, which represented 6.1 per cent of its exports to the Community in 1969–73, compared with 3.5 per cent of its exports to the world. As for EEC production, the high price guaranteed to Community beef producers, combined with the possibility of importing cheap inputs (see above), produce a situation of growing self-sufficiency and finally of excess supply. Excess supply was partly absorbed by stocks (700,000 tonnes by the end of 1985) and by exports, thanks to export subsidies (the so-called 'refunds'). While remaining an important beef importer (an average of 431,000 tonnes per year in 1980–85) the EC has also become a major exporter (with an average of 668,000 tonnes). This has the effect of depressing world market prices, by an estimated 17 per cent in 1984 (see Bureau of Agricultural Economics 1985). It should be noted that in 1986 the EEC *exported* a total of 200,000 tonnes of beef to Brazil at prices well below those of the most competitive producers—Brazil itself, Argentina and Uruguay. The price averaged 43 ECUs per 100 kg compared with the EC support price of 350 ECUs per 100 kg. Clearly, this produced tensions with Latin America and in Brazil itself. In view of the interest of the Community in maintaining harmonious commercial relations with the third country concerned, that is Brazil (EEC Commission 1986a), the Commission proposed to open for 1986 a special quota of 8,000 tonnes of high-quality beef. The opinion of the Committee on Agriculture of the European Parliament (European Parliament 1986a) was favourable—contrary to a similar measure decided in favour of Argentina—but claimed that further information should be supplied by the Commision on rumours which suggested that a large proportion of the beef exported to Brazil might be reimported into the Community as processed meat (corned beef) (EP 1986a, p. 9).

Sugar.   The EEC has never been a traditional market for Brazil's sugar exports, even when a net importer of sugar, because of the preferential access allowed to its members' colonies or former colonies. Special preferences granted to the ACP countries under the sugar protocol (concluded in 1974) of the Lomé Convention permit the beneficiary countries to export 1.3 million tonnes at the Community-guaranteed price which in 1985 was five times the world price. Most of Brazil's exports of sugar to the developed countries are directed to North America, but the market shrank when the United Stated allowed the high-fructose corn syrup industry to expand behind an import quota for sugar (Table 4.11).

In contrast with the US, it is on third markets that the EEC's sugar

Table 4.11   Structure of Brazil's sugar exports by destination (per cent of total)

	OECD	EEC	USA	Japan
1969–73	64.4	4.9	51.0	5.7
1974–78	47.8	12.6	19.2	6.3
1979–83	34.1	4.4	27.1	0.2

Source: International Sugar Organisation

policy had the most damaging effects on countries such as Brazil. Due to its system of price incentives, the EEC progressively became a net exporter of sugar from 1977 onwards, capturing 7.3 per cent of world net exports in 1977–9, and 13.9 per cent in 1980–4. In 1984–5, the EEC exported 4 million tonnes of sugar, compared to Brazil's 3.6 million tonnes. While Brazil has not seen its relative position as a major exporter threatened by the EEC, the Community has contributed to the destabilisation of world sugar prices by exporting as much as 30–50 per cent of its production in recent years. Brazil's share in world sugar exports increased from 4.5 per cent in 1960–9 to 9.5 per cent in 1970–9, and to 11.3 per cent in 1980–84. in value terms. However, results have been much weaker because of unfavourable price developments. The share of sugar in total Brazilian exports has been falling from 7.1 per cent in 1969–73 and 8.3 per cent in 1974–8 to only 3.9 per cent in 1979–83. US and EEC agricultural policies have both implied growing economic costs to non-ACP developing countries. A study by Zietz *et al.* (1984) estimates that industrial countries' sugar policies cost Latin America about $3.4 billion in lost export revenue in 1983 and increased price instability by about 25 per cent. EEC export subsidies on sugar have been the subject of attack by Brazil, in terms of Article 16 of the GATT, claiming that the EEC scheme had enabled it to obtain more than an equitable share of world trade in sugar. Although the GATT panel was not able to reach a definite conclusion on this it recognised the destabilising effects of EEC policies (1981). The panel also concluded that the EEC had failed to comply with its obligations by not collaborating with Brazil to further the principles set out in favour of LDCs (Part 4 of the GATT).

2. Iron ore and steel products

The EEC and Japan are Brazil's main customers for iron ore, purchasing respectively 37 and 34 per cent of its exports. In recent years, steel products tended to catch up with iron-ore exports in total Brazilian trade: almost absent in the 1970s, steel exports increased to 33 per cent of Brazil's exports in 1983, compared with 6.9 per cent for iron ore. However, this diversification of exports from basic commodities was not favoured by the

Table 4.12   Brazil's exports of iron ore and steel plate (as a percentage of exports to selected countries or groups of countries)

	Iron ore				Steel plate			
	World	EEC	USA	Japan	World	EEC	USA	Japan
1979	8.4	10.9	2.6	46.5	0.9	0.3	2.0	0.7
1980	7.8	10.7	1.7	44.3	1.2	0.5	3.4	0.1
1981	7.5	11.9	1.3	46.7	1.0	0.6	2.3	0.3
1982	8.8	12.3	0.6	49.5	1.8	1.3	1.9	2.3
1983	6.9	9.8	0.7	35.6	3.3	0.3	4.9	5.8

Source: COMTRADE databank, Geneva.

EEC, which restricts imports of steel. In 1983, steel plate represented 0.3 per cent of Brazilian exports to the EEC compared with 4.9 per cent of exports to the United States and 5.8 per cent of exports to Japan (Table 4.12).

The steel policy followed in the Community after the first oil shock has implied a high level of government intervention. Between 1974 and 1977, EEC steel production fell by about 20 per cent while third countries increased their market shares in the Community from 5 per cent to 10 per cent. From 1977 onwards, EEC steel policy combined adjustment subsidies (33 billion ECUs between 1980 and 1985) with unilateral and contractual measures to limit imports. The unilateral measures concerned surveillance of imports and the introduction of anti-dumping and countervailing duties. The contractual arrangements conducted with the main suppliers induced them to respect the minimum price levels guaranteed to the Community steel-makers (steel product prices are set 10–50 per cent above the world prices). In return, the Community guaranteed traditional export levels to foreign suppliers. Such an arrangement was also concluded with Brazil and subsequently renewed. The result of this policy was a 27 per cent fall in imports originating from countries with an arrangement with the Community between 1977 and 1983–5, essentially as a consequence of the pricing arrangement. The share of steel imports in total consumption fell from 11 per cent in 1977 to 9 per cent in 1981–5. This is low compared with other industries in Europe or with US imports of steel (which represent 22 per cent of its consumption).

In spite of drastic cuts in production capacities in the Community (17 per cent between 1980 and 1985) prospects are still not encouraging, so that it is likely that steel imports will continue to be monitored. In a recent report the European Commission (1986, p. 26) considered that the bilateral arrangements represent the best means of avoiding distortions of competition and maintaining traditional trade flows. Such a view, which singles out traditional exchanges, is particularly unfavourable to the most dynamic

Table 4.13   World steel exports (per cent of total)

	1985	2000
EEC	37.4	28.3
Brazil	4.6	6.7
Japan	19.4	14.0
South Korea	3.7	8.2
USA	0.4	0.3
Rest of world	34.5	42.5

Source: European Commission (1986, p. 25)

newly industrialised countries, which start from a low trade position but with great expansionary potential.

Two specific factors will act in favour of the persistence of steel protection in the EEC. First, the EEC will continue to see its market share in world steel exports decline in the next 10–15 years (Table 4.13). Given the importance of steel exports for Community producers, the pressure will persist to compensate declines on third markets with a preservation of domestic shares.

A second reason may be related to the EEC's involvement in the development of iron-ore mining in Brazil. In July 1982, the Commission agreed to make a loan of $600 million to the Brazilian company responsible for the development of the Carajás Project to get access to top-grade iron ore (see Coffey 1985). Although this was a new initiative favourable to non-ACP LDCs (traditionally the Commission limited its lending activities to ACP or Associated countries) the long-term delivery of basic materials to the Community steel industries tends to justify their own subsistence.

Textiles and clothing

The case of textiles and clothing is interesting because it concerns one of the few manufacturing industries in which LDCs in general have gained strong export positions and also because it led to the introduction of the concept of 'market disruption' into the GATT in 1959–60. Under GATT's safeguard clause sectoral restrictions may be authorised if 'any product is being imported . . . in such increased quantities and under such conditions as to cause or threaten serious injury to domestic producers'. The country invoking article 19 has the choice of imposing quantitative restrictions or higher tariffs. The concept of market disruption broadened the application of article 19 as *potential* increases of imports would now be sufficient. Also the origin of imports could be singled out as the main cause of sectoral problems. Under the GATT, trade restrictions in textiles first took the form of a Short-Term Arrangement Regarding Trade in Textiles (1961–2), then of a Long-Term Arrangement Regarding International Trade in

Textiles until 1973. Pressure to bring into the GATT restrictions on non-cotton textiles and clothing led to the first Multi-Fibre Agreement (MFA I, 1974–7) which was rather liberal. MFA II (1978–81) and MFA III (1982–6) resulted in a significant tightening of imports from LDCs. In spite of developed countries' assertions that restrictions would be temporary, a fourth MFA has been concluded. In the meantime, policies followed in European countries have increasingly encouraged modernization of plants, and R & D funds have been redirected with the intention of regaining lost comparative advantages (in this respect, see the Community BRITE programme).

Like most developing countries, Brazil has been part of the successive MFAs. Unlike other Latin American countries (such as Peru) or to South-East Asian countries, the share of textiles and clothing in Brazil's total GDP is relatively small (2–3 per cent). In terms of exports to the EEC, textiles and clothing represent about 3 per cent of the total, a figure which has been rather stable.

The Generalised System of Preferences

The principle of generalised tariff preferences was formally accepted at UNCTAD II in 1968 with the objective of increasing LDCs' export earnings, promoting industrialisation and accelerating economic growth by means of non-reciprocal, non-discriminatory tariff concessions. The EEC, which already granted preferences to its members' former colonies, introduced the GSP on 1 July 1971 (a few years before the United States) for an initial period of ten years. In 1981 an extension of the system for a new ten-year period was effected. A major change was thereby introduced, namely the principle of *graduation* of preferences which aims to preserve preferential access to the least competitive LDCs, and thus implies limitations *vis-à-vis* the more competitive LDCs.

The Community offer of preferential access covers almost all manu-factures and semi-manufactures, as well as a number of processed agri-cultural products. It is rather liberal in terms of product coverage and in terms of tariff exemptions for industrial products. For example, the EEC GSP includes textiles and clothing, shoes and leather products, which are not under the US offer. For agricultural products the EEC GSP tends to be less favourable than the US scheme, but the situation is improving. In 1972, agricultural products accounted for only 4 per cent of the Community offer; in recent years they have averaged about one-fourth.

The tariff concessions are, however, limited by quotas or ceilings. Initially, Community tariff quotas or tariff ceilings fixed quantitative limits (generally in ECUs) to preferential imports. Under the tariff ceilings individual EEC countries may demand a reintroduction of tariff when the ceilings are reached, while under the tariff quotas tariffs are automatically reintroduced once the quotas have been reached. In 1981, the *global* Community quotas were replaced by *country-specific* limitations of preferential imports. The reason was to avoid the most competative LDCs' capturing all the benefits of the preferences. Indeed, in 1973 the ten most important suppliers accounted for 87 per cent of total GSP trade. This figure currently runs at about two-thirds. Brazil is often singled out as the leading beneficiary of the Community GSP, with a share of 10 per cent of total GSP trade. But it is also true that if one considers total *dutiable non-GSP* imports of the EEC, as much as one-fourth originates in Brazil. This is due to the fact that important Brazilian exports are not under GSP: fats and oils, orange juice and base metals. In spite of the GSP, 52.2 per cent of Brazilian manufactured exports to the EEC are still affected by trade measures in 1983, against 37.3 per cent for exports to the United States (Anjaria *et al.* 1985). A significant example concerns orange juice, on which the EEC introduced in November 1986 specific surveillance measure (European Commission 1986d). In view of the 'serious disturbances' resulting from the competition from third countries, 'all release for free circulation in the Community of orange juice . . . shall be subject to the presentation of an import licence' (p. 14). Articles 2 and 3 of the Commission regulation are worth quoting. Article 2-1 says:

Import licences shall be issued subject to the provision of a security of 2 ECUs per 100 kg net. Article 3 says that:

Application for import licences must be accompanied by particulars as follows:
(i)   the concentration of the product . . . ;
(ii)   the price of the product as stipulated in the contract;
(iii)   the method of preservation;
(iv)   the form of packaging.
Those particulars must be notified by means of a document in duplicate in accordance with the model in the Appex. . . .
The competent authorities shall indicate on the contracts the quantities in respect of which import licences are issued. The quantities indicated shall be endorssed by the competent authority's stamp.

In assessing the impact of the GSP on its objectives, one has to take into account the following two aspects. First, preferences may produce trade creation effects via growing imports from LDCs and trade diversion effects via a shift in the sources of developed countries imports, in favour of LDCs. These effects may also occur *among* LDCs since preferences are now granted on a country-product-specific basis. Above all, the impact of preferences depends on the extent to which they succeed in reducing competitiveness gaps between developed countries and LDCs. For example, in 1982 the margin of preference—the difference between the MFN tariff and the GSP tariff concession (which is zero for most manufactured products)—was, on average, 7 per cent. Obviously, this may not be sufficient to turn a number of LDCs into competitive suppliers. Moreover, the administrative barriers implied by the preferential regime (rules of origin, and so on) also reduce the scope of the scheme. A striking feature of the GSP has been the relatively low utilisation rates by beneficiary countries. As a proportion of total EEC imports, GSP trade remains small: 30 per cent of total EC imports originate from the GSP countries, 6.7 per cent are eligible for tariff concessions, and only 2.8 per cent have effectively benefited from the preferences. It is significant that major Brazilian exports to the EEC or to the United States are not under the GSP. For example, exports of leather shoes are essentially to the US market which does not provide preferential access, which the EEC does (albeit limited by a quota). On the other hand, Brazil's exports of orange juice to the EEC have rapidly increased to about 4 per cent of its total exports to the Community, although the product is not under GSP.

Secondly, the margins of preferences have to be considered in a dynamic perspective. On one hand, reductions in the MFN tariffs under the GATT rounds as well as the development of non-tariff barriers in developed countries (not considered under the GSP) have tended to reduce the relative value of the preferences. For example, the preference margin fell from an average 10 per cent in 1973 to 7 per cent in 1982. This erosion of preferences was the result of the tariff cuts agreed during the Tokyo Round. On the other hand, the more competitive LDCs have seen their relative position *vis-à-vis* the lesser competitive LDCs eroded by specific limitations.

In spite of an extensive use of the GSP scheme by Brazil in comparison with other LDCs, Brazil's preferential exports to the EEC represented only 14.4 per cent of her total exports to the region in 1984, while the percentage share of the products *covered* under the GSP was 30.5. Since 1979 there has been no significant change in the relative importance of Brazilian exports benefiting from tariff concessions.

In its mid-term review of the GSP the European Commission (1986b, p. 1) called on the Council of Ministers

to respond to the emerging challenge of suppliers . . . which . . . must be considered to have become fully competitive with the EC's own industries and no longer therefore to need the GSP advantage. In such situations, the logical conclusion to the EC's present policy of differenciation in the allocation of the benefits in sensitive industrial products is *exclusion* . . . on the basis of criteria which have been carefully drawn up to be objective, coherent and fair.

A concrete step was taken in 1986 with a 50 per cent reduction in the 1985 value of product or country quotas. The criteria used to base selective productive country exclusions were that the supplying country was responsible for at least 20 per cent of the EC total imports of that product; and that its total exports into the EEC reached at least ten times the value of the quota.

The four countries concerned were Brazil, Hong Kong, Singapore and South Korea. Two major products for Brazil were affected by this new rule: leather and leather shoes. For leather the quota was 4 million ECUs and actual exports to the Community 57.5 million ECUs in 1985; for leather shoes the quota was 2.5 million ECUs and actual exports 66.6

million ECUs. Both quotas were reduced by half. Note that the tariff is 7 per cent for leather and 8 per cent for shoes.

In its opinion on the GSP scheme for 1987, the Committee on Economic and Monetary Affairs and Industrial Policy of the European Parliament suggested that 'reciprocity, (greater access to Community goods to the beneficiary's markets) might be a possible alternative to exclusion of a country's products from the application of the Community GSP'. (European Parliament 1986, p. 14). Similar views have been expressed in the United States. The GSP may thus become a means used by industrial countries to obtain a substantial liberalisation of trade in the more advanced developing countries.

The trade agreements signed between the EEC and Brazil are of little practical significance. A first agreement concluded in 1973 after the enlargement of the Community to include the UK, Ireland and Denmark gave Brazil the benefit of MFN status and preferential access (limited by safeguards) for beef, coffee and cocoa butter. This tended to compensate Brazil from the negative effects of the adoption by the UK in particular of the common external tariff. Lengthy discussions were held on the status of Brazil as an LDC during the renewal of the agreement, which entered into force on 1 October 1982. In the preamble of the agreement it is mentioned that Brazil is a member of the 'Group of 77'. The agreement is similar to the one signed between the EEC and Mexico in 1975. It reaffirms the MFN status and provides for preferences for cocoa and soluble coffee. The objective of the agreement was to develop and diversify trade and to reduce non-tariff barriers. Measures include trade promotion, economic co-operation through joint ventures, the creation of favourable conditions for investment activities, and collaboration with investors in third countries. The Trade and co-operation agreement is much less favourable than the agreements concluded with the ACP or the Mediterranean countries. The trade promotion measures include financial support for trade fairs, study tours, training and advisory services in matters relating to customs procedures, and training of commercial attachés. Aid is, however, very limited. It was concentrated on the promotion of contracts to purchasers, information on market outlets, and training. In 1985 Brazil got 625,000 ECUs in trade-promotion aid.

The effects of enlargement

The gradual abolition of customs duties and non-tariff barriers between the EEC's 1985 members and Spain and Portugal will shift the position of the new members in the hierarchy of preferences to the most favourable status. Studies on the *direct* effects of the enlargement conclude generally that the net effect on Latin America will be negative, despite a few positive aspects. Favourable effects should result from the adoption by Spain and Portugal of the Common External Tariff, which is on average lower for industrial products. The Community GSP scheme will also have to be adopted by the new members. In a few sectors, but particularly important for Latin American countries, the enlargement will imply an *increase* in the level of protection. This concerns products such as tobacco, beef and veal, sugar, cereals and cotton. The preferential access of Spain on the Community market will also imply negative effects on Brazil's exports of transformed agricultural products. The adoption by Spain and Portugal of the EEC special preferences in favour of the ACP countries may further divert some trade from countries such as Brazil.

The long term *indirect* effects of the enlargement are very uncertain, although they may be far-reaching on LDCs and in particular on the NICs.

CONCLUDING REMARKS

EEC–Brazil trade relations are a typical example of the difficulties of adjustment encountered by two economies which are subject to rapid shifts in comparative advantages. While this chapter does not cover all aspects of EEC–Brazil trade relations (for example, services are not considered) the issues it examines illustrate the importance of trade and industry policies on exchanges. In particular we have stressed: problems of access to the EEC market (for steel, textiles and clothing, beef and sugar); problems of competition on third markets (sugar); problems of trade-creating distortions (animal feed); problems of product vulnerability (commodities and transformed agricultural products); problems of trade-policy-induced price destabilisation (sugar, beef); problems of preferential access (GSP *versus* MFN, ACP and Mediterranean countries, enlargement); problems of foreign direct investment in large captive markets; and problems of rules of conduct in international trade (classification of countries, reciprocity, and selectivity in the application of safeguards).

NOTES

1 Throughout the paper, intra-EC trade is not considered in trade statistics. All figures refer to the EEC minus Spain and Portugal.
2 Figures for Latin America refer to the following 20 countries: Mexico, Guatemala, Honduras, El Salvador, Nicaragua, Costa Rica, Panama, Cuba, Haiti, Dominican Republic, Columbia, Venezuela, Equador, Peru, Brazil, Chile, Bolivia, Paraguay, Uruguay, Argentina.
3 Effective rates of protection refer to duties on value added.

BIBLIOGRAPHY

Arakalian, F. (1985). 'Commerce et Coopération entre le Brézil et la CEE', *Problémes d'Amérique Latine*, no. 75, Paris.
Anjaria, S., Kiriman, N., and Petersen, A. (1985), 'Trade Policy Issues and Developments', IMF Occasional Paper, no. 38, July.
Banco do Brasil, (1985). *Brasil 1984 Commercio exterior*, Serie Estatisticas.
Bekerman M., (1986) 'La Promocion de Exportaciones en Brasil', *Comercio Exterior*, vol. 36, no. 5, Mexico.
Borrmann, A., Borrmann, C., Langer, C. and Menck, K.-W., (1985). *The Significance of the EEC's Generalised System of Preferences*. Institut Für Wirtchaftsforschung, Hamburg.
Brasseul J., (1982). 'L'Internationalisation de l'industrie Brésilienne depuis 1964', *Problèmes d'Amérique Latine*, no. 65, Paris.
Brodin, J., Crétien, Y., Molinier, G., Pirtone A. (1986). L'Aide au développement' in *Le Droit de la Communauté Economique Européene*, J. Megret, M. Waelbroeck, D. Vignes and J.-L. Dewost (eds), Editions de l'Université de Bruxelles, Brussels.
Bureau of Agricultural Economics (1985). *Agricultural Policies in the European Community*, Canberra.
Carvalho, J. (1986–7). 'Liberación de las Restricciones Comerciales en Brasil', *Comercio Exterior*, vol. 35, no. 12, and vol. 36, no .1.
Coffey P., (1985). 'A Case Study—The Carajás Project', Europa Instituut, University of Amsterdam, 12–13 December, (miméo).
EEC Commission, (1986a). *Bulletin of the European Communites*, vol. 19, no .5.
EEC Commission (1986b), *Proposals for Council Regulations Applying Generalized Tariff Preferences for 1987*. Documents COM(86)437 final, 16 September.
EEC Commission, (1986c). *Report from the Commission to the Council on the General Objectives. Steel 1990*. Documents COM(86)515 final, 7 October.
EEC Commission (1986d). 'Commission Regulation no. 3518/86 of September 1986 on specific measures applicable to imports of orange juice', *Official Journal of the European Communities* no. 1 325/14, 20 November.
EEC Commission, (1986e). *The European Community and Latin America*. Documents, COM(86) 720 final, 2 December.
EEC Commission (1987). *The Agricultural Situation in the Community 1986 Report*, Brussels.
European Parliament, 1986a Report Drawn up on Behalf of the Committee on External Economic Relations on the Proposal from the Commission of the European Communites to the Council for a Regulation Opening for 1986 a Special Import Quota for High Quality, Fresh, Chilled or Frozen Beef Rappporteur: S Roberts; PE DOC A 2-118/86, October 8.
European Parliament, 1986b. Report Drawn up on Behalf of the Committee on Development and Cooperation on the Proposal from the Commission Fixing the Community's Generalized Tariff Preferences Scheme for 1987. Rapporteur: M. Lehdeux. PE DOC A2-151/86, November 12.
European Parliament 1986c. Report Drawn up on Behalf of the Committee on External Economic Relations on Economic Relations Between the European Community and Latin America. Rapporteur: J. van Aerssen PE DOC A2-194/86/B, December 18.
GATT, 1984. Textiles and Clothing in the Western Economies Geneva, July.
Eurostat, (1981). *Analysis of Trade between the EC and the Latin American Countries, 1965-1980*. Luxembourg.
Eurostat, (1984). *Analysis of Trade between the EC and the Latin American Countries*. Luxembourg

Eurostat, *External Trade*, Series 6, Brussels.

Havrylyshyn O., and Alikhani I. (1982). 'Protection Levels and Policies in Developing and Industrial Countries', World Bank, Washington, mimeo.

Horta, M.H., (1985). *Sources of Brazilian Export Growth in the 70s*. Brazilian Economic Studies, IPEA, Rio de Janeiro.

IMF *International Financial Statistics*, Washington DC.

International Sugar Organization. *Annual Report*, various issues.

McGovern E., (1982). *International Trade Regulation*, Exeter, Globefield Press.

Morgan Guarantee Trust Company of New York, (1985). 'Latin America's Trade Policies', *World Financial Markets*, May, pp. 1–11.

Stevens, C. (1982). *EEC and the Third World: A Survey*, Hodder & Stoughton, London.

Tyler, W. (1983). 'The Anti-Export Bias in Commercial Policies and Export Performance: Some Evidence from the Recent Brazilian Experience', *Weltwirtschaftliches Archiv. Review of World Economics*, vol. 119, no. 1, pp. 97–108.

von Gleich, A., Ehrke, M. Petersen, H.J. and Hrubesch, P. (1983). 'The Political and Economic Relations between Europe and Latin America in view of the Southern Enlargement of the European Community due to the Entry of Spain and Portugal' *Arbeitsunterlagen und Diskussionsbeitrage*, no. 20, Institut für Iberoamerika-Kunde, Hamburg, June.

Zietz, J. and Valdés, A. (1986) 'The Potential Benefits to LDCs of Trade Liberalization in Beef and Sugar by Industrialized Countries' *Weltwirtschaftliches Archiv. Review of World Economics*, vol. 122, no. 1, pp. 93–112.

PART 3: CAPITAL INVESTMENT FLOWS

5

Direct Investment in Brazil: its role in adjustment and emerging issues

Gustavo H.B. Franco[1]

There has been a growing interest in the subject of foreign direct investment in Brazil in recent years. This might be due in part to the possible contribution it might offer to the country's balance-of-payments difficulties. It is well known, however, that this contribution, although significant, can hardly be considered decisive. The interest in direct investment has been revived to a great extent in view of its *real* dimension, namely its effects on the Brazilian industrial structure and technological base. This chapter addresses these two dimensions of foreign direct investment in Brazil, and seeks to identify emerging issues in both fields.

The chapter's first task is to provide indications on the role played by direct investment in Brazil in recent years. In this connection we examine the nature of the policies of adjustment adopted by the Brazilian government after the 1974 oil shock. Evidence is provided of the success of several sectoral import-substitution programmes, and of the very positive export performance achieved in these same sectors; it is then suggested that foreign involvement in the process was crucial for the development of competitiveness in a very short period of time. We then shift our focus to the recent discussions on industrial policy and the authorities' perceptions on recent trends in industrial restructuring for the 1990s. The existence of priority sectors, which are identified as high-technology industries, and modernisation and updating of existing plants are the key aspects of industrial policies to be pursued. The role of foreign capital is likely to be important in this framework, and the tendency is to the extension of the successful joint-venture experience to the new priority sectors. The much debated exception is the computer industry, in which specific policies were adopted; the outcome of this experiment may disturb the apparent consensus on the 'triple alliance', or between the articulation of domestic, foreign and state capital into joint ventures.

We then consider the financial aspects of direct investment, and its relations with the debt issue. Indications are provided of the magnitude of the contribution of direct investment flows to the balance of payments. We comment briefly on the recent trends in debt negotiations, and suggest that the successive frustrations collected along the 'muddling-through' process have contributed to a deterioration in 'investment climate', and thus to the depression of foreign direct investment. We consider the prospect of an enhanced opportunity for debt–equity swaps as crucial for the determination of inflows of direct investment in the years to come. The chapter ends with a summary of the main conclusions.

MNEs AND STRUCTURAL ADJUSTMENT

Most early perceptions of the Brazilian adjustment strategy towards the first oil shock characterised it as 'postponing' adjustment through debt, or simply evading the issue.[2] Indeed, Brazil did not choose the conventional reduced absorption cum real devaluation mix; Brazil's response to the new conditions was the launching of an extraordinarily ambitious multi-year investment programme explicitly designed to adjust the economic structure to the situation of oil scarcity, and to a new stage of industrial evolution.[3] The core of the programme was in fact a 'new round of import-substitution' —with special emphasis on energy, basic inputs, capital goods, and transportation—designed to 'correct imbalances in the industrial structure and to save hard currency.[4] One can hardly take this option to mean 'non-adjustment', for what ultimately redresses the transformation frontier is investment.[5] It has been lately recognised that 'sustained "adjustment" to the new strained external circumstances requires longer-term restructuring of *production* towards exports and import substitutes rather than continued repression of income and *demand*. And this restructuring requires more, not less, investment.'[6]

The motivation behind the initiative hardly reveals a sophisticated understanding of the nature of the process of structural adjustment. The wording of the plan easily supports interpretations taking it as an expression of an outdated 'nation-power project', soon to become a 'dead letter'.[7] Yet planners at that time, at least *ex post*, seemed to display more common sense than assumed by these interpretations.[8]

The role assigned to foreign capital by the programme was very substantial; it was mentioned that the new strategy was likely 'to consolidate a Brazilian model of industrial capitalism', in which Brazil would sustain a 'mature, pragmatic and realistic' position as regards Multinational enterprises (MNEs), from which there would follow an 'equilibrium' between state, private sector and foreign interest. Some of the priority sectors—energy, transport and communications—were mostly controlled by state enterprises, and were deemed to remain so. But in other sectors, the state would stimulate the formation of joint ventures to undertake the new projects. This mode of organisation would have many advantages: it prevents full foreign control, it increases opportunities to enter international markets and it accelerates the transfer of technology.[9] The forms of state participation varied, though the overall policy was to restrain control by foreign partners and to strengthen the position of local capital. Much has actually been written on this 'alliance' of interest; joint ventures in Brazil are actually older than the recent enthusiasm for 'new forms' of foreign direct investment.[10] Their diffusion would only accelerate, however, by the late 1970s and early 1980s; a recent study has related over 1,500 joint ventures in operation in the Brazilian economy in 1984.[11]

The results of the Brazilian adjustment plan were quite impressive by all standards. As regards infrastructure, or the sectors under state control, the more publicised outcome of the plan was Petrobrás' oil and gas exploration efforts: domestic oil production rose 54 per cent, and production of natural gas 156 per cent in 1973–82 (reserves grew 124 per cent and 180 per cent respectively in the same period).[12] As regards electricity, on the other hand, it is significant that the share of hydroelectricity in the total consumption of primary energy rose from 19 per cent in 1973 to 29 per cent in 1983. The share of electricity in the total industrial consumption of energy rose from 31.8 to 45.8 per cent in the same period.[13]

Performance as regards net export and import coefficients in some leading industrial sectors is summarised in Table 5.1.

The overall picture here is that of an uncommon combination of a further deepening of the much maligned import-substitution, but accompanied this time by a very sound export performance—exports are generated in the same sectors in which import-substitution is taking place. The evolution of the trade accounts is very much consistent with these trends. At constant prices, Brazilian exports rose by an average annual rate of 8.6 per cent in 1975–80,[14] while imports at constant prices fell 18.2 per cent during 1974–82.[15] Exports of manufactures (at constant prices) grew at an average annual rate of 16.6 per cent in 1975–80; the share of Brazilian exports of manufactures over total exports of manufactures of developing countries rose from 1.86 per cent in 1973 to 4.28 per cent in 1981.[16] It can readily be hypothesised that costly incentives and 'bad planning' (as regards domestic market expansion) could generate such performance.[17] But a detailed examination of this performance has concluded otherwise: 'the new exports of manufactures in the 1970s were not, in fact, an exclusive consequence of incentives to exports, but the 'natural' consequence of the maturing of the process of industrial growth'.[18] It follows that, to a significant extent, a 'mature' industry is thus displacing competitors at home and abroad; after all the shift of resources towards tradeables (and this is what adjustment should ultimately be) might go either way (import substitutes or exports) or even both ways.

The process of adjustment shown in Table 5.1 reveals a pattern of

Table 5.1 Import and export coefficients, selected industries, 1974-83

	Import coefficients				Export coefficients			
	1974	1978	1981	1983	1974	1978	1981	1983
Steel	39.1	5.7	6.0	1.0	2.2	5.4	13.9	37.8
Ferro-alloys	7.5	1.2	2.0	0.2	20.1	36.5	45.6	60.4
Refractories	25.3	4.8	14.9	5.1	8.4	10.1	17.6	17.1
Aluminium	50.4	26.3	12.0	2.3	1.6	2.0	8.2	40.0
Copper	72.2	80.0	79.2	40.4	2.5	11.8	27.2	15.9
Zinc	64.2	49.7	21.7	3.3	0.0	0.1	10.6	1.9
Silicon	94.2	0.5	0.0	0.0	46.1	31.9	71.2	70.4
Caustic soda	53.1	6.5	1.8	n.a.	n.a.	n.a.	n.a.	n.a.
Fertilizers[a]	60.4	44.1	30.3	n.a.	n.a.	n.a.	n.a.	n.a.
Petrochemicals[b]	41.0	22.0	6.0	2.0	1.9	4.9	14.6	12.2
Petrochemicals[c]	14.0	11.0	0.4	0.6	0.0	0.0	8.3	12.3
Thermoplastic resins	35.2	22.0	2.0	1.0	2.0	2.0	17.0	30.0
Synthetic fibres	21.6	10.2	5.0	1.1	1.3	2.2	12.3	9.6
Paper	20.4	9.8	7.8	n.a.	1.7	4.0	10.6	n.a.
Cellulose	16.6	4.4	1.0	n.a.	11.8	14.8	31.1	n.a.
Capital goods[d]	39.8	37.9	37.1[e]	n.a.	3.0	8.9	15.9	n.a.
Capital goods[f]	27.0	20.5	24.9[e]	n.a.	7.0	14.3	23.1	n.a.

a. Average for nitrogen and phosphate based.
b. Intermediate products.
c. Basic products.
d. 'On order'.
e. 1980.
f. 'In series'.

Source: Jorge C. Batista, 'A Estratégia de Adjustamento Externo do Segundo Plano Nacional de Desenvolvimento', Revista de Economia Política, vol. 7, no. 2 April–June 1987, pp. 73-5.

'learned' comparative advantage which is not commonly found; very little evidence has actually been gathered on the maturation of infant industries. According to a survey of micro-studies of infant industries' experiences,' the evidence shows that maturation is not automatic or instant: reaching and maintaining international competitiveness is not simply a matter of developing the right industry . . . It takes more than effortless learning-by-doing and requires the capability to manage continuous technological change'.[19] Along similar lines, cross-country comparisons of the process of acquiring indigenous technological capabilities reveal a mixed picture. Few are the generalisations, and three Brazilian success stories (Usiminas, Romi and Metal Leve[20]) provide some:

when the size of the domestic market led over time to the installation of large plants . . ., and when the global technological frontier has remained stable for some time, protection policies systematically maintained for at least two decades seem to have induced the development of competitive enterprises in LDCs based on sound indigenous technological capabilities.[21]

Since technological change is the crux of the matter it is important to observe that local subsidiaries of MNEs enjoy a number of advantages with respect to domestic firms as regards the development of technological capabilities,[22] and the same goes for firms with minority foreign participation. As argued above, the joint-venture mode of enterprise is explicitly designed, among other things, to facilitate the transfer of technology; very often in Brazil this was the only foreign contribution to the partnership. A significant example is the Usiminas steel plant, which stands as the most notable success story in the survey of infant industries mentioned above; Usiminas is a joint-venture of the Brazilian government and a group of Japanese investors that was very active in providing technical assistance in the project.[23] One is therefore led to conjecture whether the learning phenomenon of Table 5.1 was not independent of the structure of ownership of these projects.

The period covered by the table indeed witnessed a very important advance in the process of internationalisation of Brazilian industry. From 1973 to 1985 the book value of foreign direct investment in Brazil (at constant prices) grew at an average annual rate of nearly 12.6 per cent, the ratio between the stock of foreign direct investment and GDP nearly doubled, rising from 5.9 to 11.6 per cent.[24] The growth of net direct investment flows to non-oil developing countries in this period was only 3 per cent (in real terms)[25]; during 1975-9 Brazil received 7.1 per cent of world direct investment flows, a major increase with respect to 1970-4 (4.0 per cent) and 1965-9 (2.6 per cent).[26] In some cases the increased foreign participation in industry can be traced directly to the sectors listed in Table 5.1, as, for example, in petrochemicals, aluminum, paper and cellulose;[27] a full investigation, however, has yet to be conducted.

To summarise, Brazilian adjustment comprised a major effort of import-substitution for intermediary inputs and capital goods, along with heavy investments in changing the country's energy matrix. It is very significant that import-substitution was conducted without the anti-export bias it exhibited in the past; the export performance of these new industries was very impressive, suggesting that competitiveness was present from the start.[28] This sort of achievement is not to be found in the documented cases of successful infant industries; reaching competitiveness involves managing technological change, and such capabilities take time to develop. It is very likely, though, that foreign participation, under joint-ventures or 'traditional forms' of foreign investment, was a crucial factor in this export performance. This might be the case of intermediary inputs,[29] but probably less so as far as the capital-goods industry is concerned. 'Learning' is likely to proceeed along more evolutionary lines in this case; the coexistence of domestic firms and MNEs creates a pattern of oligopolistic competition favourable to innovation and efficiency. In these conditions competitiveness is likely to develop over time, given the size and growth of the Brazilian market and the potential for economies of scale. Export activity can be a natural development in such conditions, as recently suggested,[30] if, however, triggered by the proper price stimuli.

INDUSTRIAL RESTRUCTURING AND POLICY

The completion of the projects under the 1974 adjustment programme has led many observers to conclude that Brazilian industry 'has literally overcome its structural defficiences', or that 'it no longer fits the definition of underdevelopment'.[31] This notion appears very explicitly in the recent discussions on industrial policy within official circles. According to the *Grupo Interministerial*[32] appointed in the beginning of 1986 to produce an industrial policy proposal, 'the definition of an industrial policy for Brazil has to consider that the current industrial structure is practically *complete* relatively modern in technological terms and has several segments with strong penetration in international markets'.[31] A more recent entry in the debate would qualify this notion in an important way: 'the country's industrial structure has already reached a high degree of *maturity*. Thus, it is no longer possible to count on opportunities of investment for import-substitution in a sufficient magnitude to work to induce economic expansion'.[34] This could be interpreted as meaning that expansion is no longer constrained by bottlenecks, which boils down to saying that imports are now lower for a given activity level. In no sense is the foreign exchange 'gap' closed, as the experience of 1986 would plainly demonstrate. 'Maturity' should, therefore, mean a more 'balanced' structure, without any major sectoral defficiency, and consequently without an import-substitution agenda. This surely shifts the priorities of industrial policy away from establishing industries or sectors of strategic interest; the documents assign top priority to modernization and technological updating of established industries: 'permanent technological updating, especially through technologies generated domestically, appears as the main characteristic of the new pattern of industrialisation'.[35] The existence of a 'technological heterogeneity' is recognised, especially between export-orientated sectors and those directed to the domestic market.[36] Investment should therefore be directed to 'intensive incorporation of technical progress to industrial activity so as to assure efficiency and competitiveness' and 'to develop domestic technological capabilities'.[37]

Priority sectors are identified from two sorts of considerations: on the one hand, there is an attempt to replicate world trends in industry, from which top priority is assigned to high-technology industries—informatics, microelectronics, fine chemicals, new materials, biotechnology, and so on. On the other hand, there are concerns as to sectors approaching full capacity (paper, cellulose, fertilisers) and others requiring major rebuilding and updating (steel, segments of capital goods). Emphasis should be given to exporting industries, to the continuation of investments in energy (oil, gas and coal) and to some extent to wage-goods, especially textiles and footware.[38]

The role assigned to foreign capital in this framework has been evolving very significantly. Some early attempts by the National Industrial Confederation to establish guidelines for an industrial policy suggested a 'more transparent definition of the role to be played by foreign capital'.[39] The *Grupo Interministerial* was explicit as regards existing sectors, suggesting basically the continuation of the status quo. In terms of guidelines for the new sectors, it was argued that the contribution of MNEs 'should be predominantly directed to the generation of hard currency'; the formation of joint ventures would be supported provided control is maintained by nationals.[40] Shortly afterwards, the document produced by the Industry and Commerce Ministry would proclaim that 'the institutional framework in which the proposed policies will be executed is one of a market economy based on free enterprise . . . the role of industrial policy is to complement the market.'[41] The document proceeds to suggest that 'the private sector has effective and potential conditions . . . to lead the new round of industrialisation', and that the aim of industrial policy should be to 'increase significantly' the role of domestic enterprises. Yet the crucial point was to reaffirm the support to joint ventures with the majority of voting capital owned by domestic residents, but to establish that they 'must be considered as domestic enterprises by all means'.[42]

The very latest entry into this debate was a short piece authored by president José Sarney's influential son-in-law and personal secretary. The document identifies foreign willingness to participate in investments in the high-technology sectors, and suggests that this could be an asset in the debt negotiations. It then proposes to implement 'freedom of installation for all sorts of enterprise in the country', 'freedom for technology negotiations, associations and purchase', and 'release of [non-transferred] external debt [deposits] for conversion into equity, stimulating investment in priority sectors'.[43] Quite significantly, the President himself, on a couple of occasions, has mentioned the internationalisation of the economy as desirable, and also the possibility of establishing 'Export Processing Zones' in Brazil's North-Eastern region.

Internationalisation has been gathering strength also in sectors associated with industry; after all it can be taken as a *sine qua non* for modernization and continuous technological updating. Brazilian industry is surely already very 'international' as far as ownership is concerned, but it has had little exposure to world markets. Exporting experience is recent, and exports still represent no more than 12 per cent of GDP. There is a clear perception that tariff protection has become an anachronism, not only for the ridiculous situation of having local consumers subsidising 'learning' from infants bearing names such as General Motors and Toyota,[44] but also from the fact that there are infants that did fail to mature after three decades of full protection. The *Grupo Interministerial*, for example, has proposed a full revision of Brazilian tariffs in order 'to adjust the tariff structure to the profile of the existing industrial structure, introducing degrees of protection compatible with the levels of competitiveness reached in each sector.'[45] There should be no doubt, however, that import restrictions will be maintained mostly in view of the needs of the balance of payments. If any slack develops in the latter, that would surely help the cause of industrial modernisation, though this is hardly foreseeable.

The apparent consensus on the participation of foreign capital in the new priority sectors through the joint-venture mode might be disturbed by the experience of the computer industry, in which specific policies were followed. The so-called 'market reserve' consisted in closing the lower end of the sector (microcomputers) even to joint ventures; this generated an extraordinary mushrooming of domestic manufacturing firms, first of eight-bit machines and then of IBM PC clones. Only 18 micros were sold in 1979, but in 1983 this number reached 55,783; the fact that 'a fundamental technological breakthrough (the microprocessor) became available on the open market, [or that] it was controlled by firms with no proprietary interest on final demand sales'[46] was crucial for this success. In the minicomputer segment, however, where technology had to be obtained through licensing, this was definitely not the case; the number of units sold in 1983 was nearly 15 per cent less than in 1979.[47] As regards competitiveness, the microcomputer's success is a mixed one: domestically manufactured microcomputers, printers, disk drives and periphercals are priced between two and four times higher than the US equivalent (when still manufactured), and the downward trend of this ratio is slight at best.[48] Even so, the phenomenal sales success has generated much lobbying for extending the 'market reserve', which was initially conceived to be

Table 5.2 Direct investment, reinvestments and dividends in Brazil, 1978–86 (US$ millions)

	1978–82	1983–86	1986
A. Net inflows	1682	990	639
(% of exports%	9.5	4.1	2.9
of which:			
conversions	110	496	206
(% of net inflows)	6.8	50.1	32.2
repatriation	176	292	636
(% of total stock)	1.0	1.2	2.4
B. Dividends	492	928	1100
(% of total stock)	2.9	3.8	4.1
C = A − B	1190	62	−461
(% of exports)	6.6	0.2	−2.1
D. Reinvestments	881	570	449
(% of total stock)	5.0	1.8	1.7

Sources: Adapted from L.A. Corrêa do Lago, 'Investimentos Diretos no Brasil e a Conversão de Empréstimos em Capital de Risco', Departamento de Economia, Pontifícia Universidade Católica, Rio de Janeiro, 1987. Original figures from Banco Central do Brasil, *Boletim*, and *Brasil–Programa Econômio*, vol. 15, June 1987.

temporary, and also for adopting the model in other sectors. Yet the high tide of the market reserve appears to be passing; its association with former members of the National Information Service (the chief agency organising the military government's repressive policies) has made further concessions to the sector politically very costly. In sum, it is not likely that the computer model will reach other sectors, except in the event of a major political turnaround, to the left or right; interestingly enough both extremes of the political spectrum are sympathetic to the 'market reserve'.[47]

FOREIGN DIRECT INVESTMENT AND THE DEBT ISSUE

Direct investment has played a secondary role *vis-à-vis* bank lending in the Brazilian balance of payments in recent years; its contribution, however, is by no means unimportant. As shown in Table 5.2, the net inflows of direct investment reached an average of 8.8 per cent of exports in 1978–1982; the net foreign exchange result of all direct-investment-related transactions reached $1 billion, or nearly 6 per cent of exports, during this period. The dramatic reversal of this picture observed after 1982, which is clearly observed in the table, was in itself a significant part of the explanation of the recent Brazilian payments difficulties. It can be observed that net inflows in 1983–6 have been reduced to a third of their 1978–82 average, and nearly half of these entered through debt–equity swaps ('conversions'). Rates of repatriation and profit remittances have increased significantly, especially in 1986, relative to the earlier period; this is consistent with the observed reduction in the reinvestment rates. The net result of these influences was, therefore, that a positive inflow of around $1.5 billion has turned into an outflow of nearly $500 million.

Most observers of the debt problem have argued that it is very unlikely that direct investment flows could substitute bank lending as a mechanism to finance current account deficits in debtor countries;[50] so that one should not expect from direct investment but a minor contribution to resolve payments imbalances. In Brazil inflows of long-term loans during 1978–82 averaged $12.7 billion, an entirely different order of magnitude from those of inflows reported in Table 5.2. Yet foreign direct investment can surely help; gains, however small, in this area can improve the trade-offs involved in producing trade surpluses.

The deterioration shown in Table 5.2 has to do with a combination of domestic policies and developments on the debt front. On account of the former, the chaotic nature of macropolicies followed is very evident: violent shifts in policy have taken place since the inception of the 'New Republic' (the civilian government).[51] To the extent that overall macroeconomic policies affect direct investment flows, instability and the uncertainties generated by the workings of the Constitutional Assembly elected in November 1986 will probably divert investment away from Brazil in favour of other locations, at least temporarily.[52]

On the debt front, what is important to observe is that the tone of the negotiations has much to do with the 'investment climate' that supposedly governs foreign direct investment. In this respect, growing frustrations as regards the so-called 'muddling-through' strategy are producing a more confrontational stance from both sides.[53] The Brazilian moratorium on private banks' debts reflects these global tendencies, and has surely had a devastating effect on the 'investment climate'. There are definite signs of reversal on the part of the Brazilian government, but future developments are very difficult to predict; given the political uncertainties mentioned above there is no indication on who, and under what caveats, will be in charge of debt negotiations on a medium-term perspective.

In any event, there are three sorts of mechanism involved in the next few years' rescheduling exercises: (a) conventional 'muddling-through' re-scheduling, with its usual consequences—'frayed nerves, much bad feeling, pointless extra transactions costs, and increased uncertainty';[54] (b) 'securitisation', namely the exchange of old debt for long-term negotiable bonds at a discount, which turns out to be rescheduling cum write-offs; and (c) debt–equity swaps, again at a discount. Swaps are of interest here since direct investment is directly involved. Table 5.2 shows that most direct investment since 1982 has been entering the country through swaps; it follows that regulations regarding these operations can be of crucial importance for future inflows.

Debt–equity swaps can in principle reach a volume that is equal to the total net inflows of foreign direct investment; this could mean conversions after 1987 a little higher than the value of total inflows for 1978–82. It could be more, as a matter of fact, if dividends remitted are used to buy debt at a discount and re-enter the country through a conversion into equity. Gains in these operations can be substantial. By the same token, a significant volume of swaps can be made if the government allows the reinternalisation, again through debt purchase and conversion into equity, of past capital flights, estimated to reach some $9.0 billion.[55] Creditor banks themselves could, if regulations thus allowed,[56] be interested in turning substantial portions of their protfolios into equity; it is impossible to assess this willingness a priori, yet their interest on the issue hints that it could be large.

Swaps totalling around $2–3 billion yearly would mean annual reductions of around 2–3 per cent in the stock of debt;[57] it could surely make a difference over the years, especially if we note that the terms of the 'servicing' of the stock of direct investment are much better than those of loans. In 1986, for example, repatriations plus dividends represented a record high 5.9 per cent of total stock; in the same year the stock of debt was of $110.2 billion, amortisations came to $10.1 billion and interest payments $9.6 billion, together representing 17.9 per cent of total debt.[58]

Another beneficial aspect of a more extensive use of swaps is that it can offer a contribution to domestic capital formation; the benefits are those of ordinary foreign direct investment, namely, transfer of technology, access to foreign markets, and so on. These are likely to be especially relevant if swaps are governed by the priorities of industrial restructuring and policy discussed in the last section.

Objections to a larger-scale use of swaps come from concerns about the denationalisation of the economy. Yet the enforcement of the joint-venture mode, along with investors' increased willingness to engage in 'new forms' of international investment[59] should result in forms of involvement of foreign capital in domestic enterprises not especially vulnerable to nationalist concerns. The truly decisive objections to debt–equity conversions have been from the Central Bank, which is mostly concerned with monetary control. Three billion dollars in conversions, for instance, would imply an increase of around 50 per cent in high-powered money. This would not be a problem if inflation has this same magnitude, and under reasonably orderly public finances. But under a public deficit of about 8 per cent of GDP, there is little room for further pressures over domestic public debt. The problem is, therefore, not the unfeasibility of a large-scale debt–equity conversion programme in itself, but the fact that the huge budget deficit precludes this and other projects of the nation's interest.[60]

In sum, domestic policies and developments on the debt front tend to contribute negatively to the 'investment climate' and depress direct investment even further. A more extensive use of debt–equity swaps, which could, in principle, revive foreign direct investment, is blocked by domestic financial constraints imposed by an uncontrolled budget deficit. One cannot fail to be impressed by the amount of negative influences on direct investment generated domestically.

SUMMARY

This chapter has discussed real and financial dimensions of foreign direct investment in Brazil, considering briefly the experience of adjustment after the oil shocks and prospects for the future. A survey was made of Brazilian adjustment strategy after 1974, and on the basis of this evidence ways were suggested through which foreign involvement might have been important to the success of such policies. Next, the authorities' views on industrial policies and their perceptions as to the ways Brazilian industrialization is likely to proceed were discussed. Special attention was devoted to the issue of the role of foreign investors in this process, and the alternatives open to policy- makers. Lastly, the financial aspects of direct investment and its connections with the debt problem were examined. It was argued that the potential contribution of direct investment to a solution to the debt issue might be very significant, especially if the government chooses to make a more liberal use of debt–equity swaps.

NOTES

1. With the usual caveats, I would like to thank Luiz A. Corrêa do Lago and Winston Fritsch for comments and suggestions.
2. See, for example, C.G. Langoni, *A Crise do Desenvolvimento: uma estratégia para o futuro*, Apec, Rio de Janeiro, 1985.
3. *II PND: Plano Nacional de Desenvolvimento*, Brasilia, 1975, p. 12.
4. Ibid., p. 28.
5. The option certainly imples current account deficits for some time; yet it is perfectly 'sound' so long as investment is building capacity in the 'right' sectors, and its counterpart is a (discounted) flow of production of tradable goods. The fact that the Brazilian debt appeared 'sound' (at least in 1974–81) since it corresponded to an overly high investment activity was argued, for example, by J.D. Sachs, 'The Current Account and Macroeconomic Adjustment in the 1970s', *Brookings Papers in Economic Activity*, 1, 1981, p. 39.
6. G.K. Helleiner, 'Foreign Direct Investment and Balance of Payments Adjustment in Latin America', mimeo, 1987, p. 1 (emphasis in original).
7. C. Lessa, *A Estratégia de Desenvolvimento 1974–1976: sonho e fracasso*, UFRJ, Rio de Janeiro, 1978.

8. J.P. Reis Veloso, *O Ultimo Trem para Paris*, Rio de Janeiro, 1987. For a discussion of the rationality of the plan, see A.B. Castro and F.E. Pires de Souza, *A Economia Brasileira em Marcha Forçada*, Paz e Terra, Rio de Janeiro, 1985, pp. 30–47.
9. For foreigners the advantages would include overcoming lack of familiarity with local conditions, access to subsidies, etc. For a discussion see G.K. Helleiner, 'Transnational Corporations, Direct Foreign Investment, and Economic Development' in H. Chenery and T.N. Srinivasan (eds), *Handbook of Development Economics*, North Holland, Amsterdam, p. 40.
10. One interesting example is the Usiminas steel plant, a joint venture with Japanese associated founded in 1957. A more substantial experiment was undertaken in the petrochemical industry in the early 1970s; see J.T. Araujo Jr. and V.M. Dick, 'Governo, Empresas Multinacionais e Empresas Nacionais: o caso da industria petroquímica', *Pesquisa e Planejamento Econômico*, vol. 4, no. 3, December 1974; and E.A. Guimarães *et al.* 'Changing International Investment Strategies: the 'new forms' of foreign investment in Brazil', IPEA/INPES Internal Discussion Paper no. 45, January 1982. For a general view of the above-mentioned 'alliance', see Peter Evans, *Dependent Development: the alliance of multinational, state and local capial in Brazil*, Princeton University Press, Princeton, NJ, 1979.
11. J. Zoninsein, Política Industrial, Joint Ventures e Exportações, p. 17.
12. J.C. Batista 'Brazil's Second National Development Plan and its Growth cum Debt Strategy', Instituto de Economia Industrial, Federal University of Rio de Janeiro, 1986, p. 26a.
13. The share of oil was reduced from 30.2% to 14.4%. See ibid., p. 76.
14. M. Peñalver *et al*, *Política Industrial e Exportação de Manufacturados*, FGV, Rio de Janeiro, 1983, p. 17.
15. Batista, 'Brazil's Second National Development Plan', p. 44a.
16. And as a share of total world exports of manufactured goods, Brazilian exports passed from 0.22% in 1965 to 0.64% in 1980: see Peñalver *et al.*, *Política Industrial*, pp. 17, 28. See also Batista, 'Brazil's Second National Development Plan', p. 44a.
17. As proposed, in general terms, by Helleiner as regards the 'conversion' of import-substituting industries to exporting: see G.K. Helleiner, 'Manufactured Exports from Less-Developed Countries from Multinational Firms', *Economic Journal*, 83, March 1973, pp. 25–26.
18. S. Teitel and F.E. Thoumi, 'Da Substituição às Exportações: as experiências argentina e brasileira no campo das exportações de manufaturados', *Pesquisa e Planejamento Econômico*, vol. 16, no. 1, April 1986, p. 163.
19. M. Bell *et al.*, 'Assessing the Performance of Infant Industries', *Journal of Development Economics*, vol. 16, 1984, pp. 123–4.
20. They produce steel, conventional lathes and pistons, respectively.
21. Jorge M. Katz, 'Domestic Technological Innovations and Dynamic Comparative Advantage: further reflections on a comparative case study program', *Journal of Development Economics*, vol. 16, 1984, p. 32.
22. Katz, 'Domestic Technological Innovations', p. 23.
23. H. Nogueira da Cruz, 'Observações sobre a Mudança Tecnológica de Produto e de Processo na Setor Metal-Mecânico no Brasil' in *Anais do XII° Encontro Nacional de Economia*, São Paulo, 1984.
24. International Monetary Fund, 'Foreign Private Investment in Developing Countries', Occasional Paper no. 33, January 1985, p. 42.
25. Ibid., p. 3.
26. In 1980–1 this share was reduced to 4.7 per cent: see US Department of Commerce, *International Direct Investment, Global Trends and the U.S. Role*,

146   Gustavo H.B. Franco

August 1984, p. 47.

27. Zoninsein, Política Industrial, Joint Ventures e Exportações; Guimarã *et al.* 'Changing International Investment Strategies'; M.A. Suarez, 'A Evolućčo da Indústria Petroguímica Brasileira e o Modelo Tripartite de Empresa', *Revista de Economia Política*, vol. 3, July 1983; J. Zoninsein and A. Teixeira, 'Joint Ventures en la Industrialización Brasileña notas para el estudio de las formas de capital', *Economía de América Latina*, vol. 2, 1984.

28. The role of incentives and exchange rate policy for these results is much debated. See, for example, Teitel and Thoumi, 'Da Substituićão de Importaçóes às Exportações'.

29. A significant example is given by the cellulose industry. Brazil turned into an exporter with the establishment of a number of joint ventures in the 1970s; two of which, Cenibra and Aracruz (starting operations in 1976 and 1978 respectively) were alone responsible for 70 per cent of Brazilian exports of cellulose in 1982. Zoninsein, Política Industrial, Joint Ventures e Exportações, pp. 54–5.

30. There has been a tendency in the recent work in trade theory to obtain unorthodox results from dropping hypotheses of perfect competition and constant returns to scale. On this specific issue see Paul Krugman, 'Import Protection as Export Promotion: international competition in the presence of oligopoly and economies of scale' in H. Kierzkonski (ed.), *Monopolistic Competition and International Trade*, Clarendon, Oxford, 1984.

31. Castro and Pires de Souza, *A Economia Brasileira*, pp. 81–2.

32. Representatives from the Ministries of Planning, Industry and Commerce, Finance, Science and Technology.

33. *Política Industrial, Relatório do Grupo Interministerial de Política Industrial*, Brasilia, July 1986, p. 1 (emphasis added).

34. Ministério de Indústria e Comércio, *Política Industrial e Diretrizes Setoriais*, Brasilia, 1987, p. 7 (emphasis added).

35. Ibid., p. 8.

36. *Política Industrial, Relatório do Grupo Interministerial*, p. 1.

37. Ministério da Indústria e Comércio, *Política Industrial e Diretrizes Setoriais*, p. 6.

38. Ibid., p. 10.

39. Confederação Nacional da Indústria, Departmamento Econômico, *Política Industrial*, ENIND, September 1984, p. 34.

40. *Política Industrial, Relatório do Grupo Interministerial*, p. 42.

41. It is perhaps difficult for those not used to the tone of Brazilian official documents to evaluate the extent to which this liberal discourse represents dissent from the past: see Ministério da Indústria e Comércio, *Política Industrial e Diretrizes Setoriais*, p. 11.

42. Ibid.

43. J. Murad and M. Ethel, 'Estratégia para o Desenvolvimento', reproduced in *Jornal do Brasil*, 7 September 1987, p. 17.

44. An acute observation of C. Diaz-Alejandro, 'The Less Developed Countries and Transnational Enterprises, Economic Growth Center, Yale University, p. 21.

45. *Política Industrial, Relatório do Grupo Interministerial*, p. 24.

46. Peter Evans, 'State, Capital, and the Transformation of Dependence: the Brazilian computer case', *World Development*, vol. 14, no. 7, 1986, pp. 799, 803.

47. Ibid., p. 799.

48. L. Perine, 'Competitividade dos Periféricos Nacionais: unidades de disco (drive)', Instituto de Economia Industrial, UFRJ, May 1985; C. Piragibe,

'Competitividade dos Equipamentos Periféricos Fabricados no Brasil' Instituto de Economia Industrial, UFRJ, March 1985; and P. Tigre and L. Perine, 'Competitividade dos Microcomputadores Nacionais', Instituto de Economia Industrial, UFRJ, March 1985. Competivieness was apparently achieved in manufacturing some older microcomputer models such as Apple II, TRS-80, HP 85-A and HP 85-B, the latter two manufactured by the local subsidiary of Texas Instruments. Yet, this is only true for CPUs; configurations including CPU, monitors and drives were priced in May 1984 some 20–50 per cent higher than the US equivalent.

49.   This 'alliance' has produced much irony along with the debate.

50   For example D. Goldsborough, 'Investment Trends and Prospects: the link with bank lending' in T. Morand (ed.), *Investing in Development: new roles for private capital?*, Overseas Development Council, 1986; and Helleiner, 'Foreign Direct Investment', p. 8.

51.   President Sarney's government started with a monetarist economic team, then it sponsored a major 'heterodox' stabilisation experiment, which gradually took a populist orientation, and then switched to a more pragmatic, yet half-hearted, version of the 'heterodox shock', and the latest development in this area is the President's promise to double real wages by the end of his term.

52.   Goldsborough, 'Investment Trends and Prospects', p. 185.

53.   Edmar L. Bacha, 'Escaping Confrontation: Latin America's debt crisis in the late eighties', Departamento de Econômia, PUC-RJ, September 1987.

54.   Helleiner, 'Foreign Direct Investment'.

55.   Estimates of capital flights in Brazil are highly sensitive to the period chosen. Taking the cumulative sum of 'errors and omissions' for 1974–82 one gets insignificant values: see J. T. Cuddington, 'Capital Flight: estimates, issues and explanations', *Princeton Studies in International Finance*, 58, December 1986 Table 1. Taking 1978–82, R. Dornbush gets $1.9 billion, but adjusting his estimate for the change in international reserves observed in this period, one gets nearly $9.0 billion: see R. Dornbush, 'External Debt, Budget Deficits, and Disequilibrium Exchange Rates' in G.W. Smith and J.T. Cuddington (eds), *International Debt and the Developing Countries*, The World Bank, Washington DC, 1985, Table 8–3. This high value appears consistent with the observed magnitudes transacted in Brazil, in markets such as the 'black' market for dollars, gold markets, and recently created trust funds for 'cold' monet'. The recent performance of these funds has been very impressive: since their creation in 1986 their assets have reached nearly $2 billion, according to *Gazeta Mercantil*, 10 December 1987.

56.   Current provisions only permit the conversion of inter-company loans. See Corrêa do Lago, 'Investimentos Diretos no Brasil'.

57.   Recall that total debt is somewhat higher than $100 billion, running at actually $110.2 billion at the end of 1986. Yet conversions are made at a discount. A 10% discount, for instance, would mean that for each dollar converted debt would be reduced by $1.10; in this case $2 billion in swaps would mean an exact 2 per cent reduction in debt.

58.   These are contractual values only. The amounts actually transfered are much smaller.

59.   See Charles Oman, *New Forms of International Investment in Developing Countries*, OECD, Paris, 1985; and Guimarães et al., *Changing Investment Strategies*.

60.   For an illuminating discussion, see Bacha, 'Escaping Confrontation', esp. pp. 8–9.

6

Debt–equity swaps, foreign direct investment, and the Brazilian debt crisis

Heinz Gert Preusse and Rolf Schinke

Debt–equity swaps (DES) have attracted considerable attention in recent years. Proponents of debt swaps usually argue that debtor countries will reap appreciable benefits when foreign debts are swapped into equity capital. They maintain that the capital stock will be increased and the foreign exchange constraint relaxed. In this chapter the rationale for these hopes will be discussed, taking Brazil as a case study. First, some important aspects of the Brazilian debt situation are presented. Recent trends in the country's foreign direct investment (FDI) are then examined which point to the existence of a FDI gap. Based on this finding the potential contribution of debt–equity swaps as one of the possible ways of closing this gap is then analysed. It will be argued that a new and consistent strategy for economic growth and adjustment, rather than the application of financial tools, is the appropriate answer to the present crisis. Some features of such a strategy for growth and change are stylised in the concluding section.

THE DEBT SITUATION AND RECENT MACROECONOMIC PERFORMANCE

In 1985 Brazil's total external debt amounted to $106.7 billion, thereby accounting for more than one-tenth of the total indebtedness of all developing countries.[1] From 1970 to 1985 its foreign public debt grew on the average by more than 20 per cent per year. While the highest growth rates were in the 1970s, Brazil experienced the highest increases in absolute terms from 1980 to 1985 (see Table 6.1 and Figure 6.1). During this latter period its debt obligations rose substantially *vis-àvis* financial market institutions, most of it being involuntary lending, however.

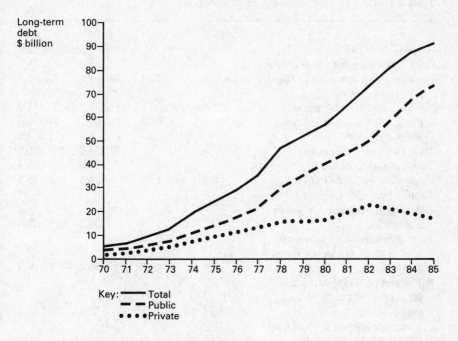

Long-term debt $ billion

Figure 6.1   Brazil's long-term debt, 1970–85

Sources: World Bank, *World Debt Tables*; IFS.

The increase in overall indebtedness was accompanied by a marked change in its structure. The share of variable-rate loans in total lending increased from 11.7 per cent in 1970 to 71.5 per cent in 1985. Concessional lending decreased from 47 per cent (1970) to an insignificant 2 per cent (1985). In the same period the share of commercial lending in public debts nearly doubled. A trend towards public guarantees is also discernible from Table 6.1

Such a high indebtedness implies a heavy burden on society. In 1985 Brazil's total debt accounted for more than half of GNP, public debt alone for more than a third. Servicing of the latter absorbed more than a quarter of the country's exports of goods and services, that of total long-term debts more than a third. As a result, factor incomes paid to foreigners accounted for more than 5 per cent of GDP.

From 1971 to 1980 debt accumulation was accompanied by extraordinarily high rates of growth of real GDP.[2] They were at the two-digit level before the first oil-price shock and declined somewhat afterwards. From 1981 to 1984, however, growth rates were close to zero or negative most of the time, leading to a serious decline in per-capita income. In 1985 and

Table 6.1   Debt ($ million) and debt indicators

	1970	1975	1980	1985
Debt outstanding and disbursed				
Public and publicly guaranteed long-term debt	3,431.9	14,132.3	40,105.4	73,893.6
vis-à-vis financial markets	972.6	8,988.1	31,227.0	57,451.3
Private non-guaranteed debt	1,706.3	9,592.9	16,605.3	17,200.0
Short-term debt	—	—	13,526.0	11,017.0
Total (without IMF credit)	—	—	70,236.7	102,110.6
Total debt as % of GNP	—	—	29.0	51.3
Public debt as % of GNP	8.2	11.6	16.6	35.5
Total debt service on public debt as % of exports of goods and services	12.5	17.9	34.5	26.6
Total debt service on long-term debt as % of exports of goods and services	21.8	43.2	56.4	34.9
Public and publicly guaranteed long-term debt as % of total long-term debt	66.8	59.6	70.7	81.1
Commercial lending as % of long-term public and publicly guaranteed debt (DOD)	45.0	71.2	82.9	81.0
Concessional lending as % of DOD	47.0	14.2	4.4	2.0
Lending at variable rates as % of DOD	11.7	52.0	61.0	71.5

Source: World Bank, *World Debt Tables 1986–87*, pp. 286.

1986 Brazil again achieved growth rates of more than 8 per cent of GDP which proved to be insufficient, however, to restore per-capita income to the pre-crisis level.

Development of real GDP is in part mirrored by that of the average propensity to invest. While investment (as a percentage of GDP) increased from 21.1 (1961–70) to 28.1 during the 1970s, it fell back to nearly its previous level in the period between 1981 and 1985.[3] With still high absolute increases in foreign indebtedness this is a rather clear indication that Brazil tried to smooth the decline in real consumption by financing deficits instead of adjusting further to the changed world-wide economic environment.

Besides the decline of the investment–GDP–ratio there is still another explanation for the decrease of the growth rate. As can be inferred from the rise in the incremental capital output ratio from 4 between 1974 and 1978 to more than 11 from 1979 to 1983 (see Table 6.2) investment

Table 6.2 Investment, savings, growth, and incremental capital output ratio

	1970–73	1974–78	1979–83
A. Investment*	0.26	0.28	0.21
B. Savings*			
Domestic	0.25	0.25	0.20
Foreign	0.01	0.03	0.01
C. Growth rate (%)	9.80	7.10	1.90
D. Incremental capital			
output ratio[†]	2.70	3.90	11.1

* Relative to GDP.
† (A/C)·100

Source: Own calculations. Data are taken from IMF, *International Financial Statistics*, various issues.

productivity has been insufficient since the second oil-price increase. One can conclude, therefore, that along with the quantity of investment there was also a marked decline in quality.

The rate of inflation grew from year to year; from 98 per cent in 1982 it reached 227 per cent in 1985.[4] In February 1986, when the annual inflation rate grew to 400 per cent, a stabilisation programme with a price and wage freeze brought it down to 60 per cent in the same year and raised production by about 8 per cent. Since the beginning of 1987, however, inflation rates have been rising again. Highly fluctuating rates of inflation provided strong incentives for capital flight. Transfers of this kind of capital were especially high and were estimated to be $7.9 billion from 1983 to 1986.[5] This identifies Brazil as being the second largest 'capital exporter' on this account in Latin America.

FINANCIAL CONSTRAINTS

It is tempting to relate this mixed performance to the debt difficulties and to the lack of external finance. In explaining the increase of Brazil's gross external debt from 1978 to 1982 Dornbusch[6] pointed out that more than 80 per cent of the accumulated current account deficit, which amounted to $58.4 billion, was matched by new loans. Of this only $4.7 billion was attributable to trade deficits. Most of this deficit originated from interest payments ($33.7 billion), a result of the accumulated indebtedness of the country in international capital markets and the rise in nominal interest rates since 1979. Nearly the same result is obtained by Bacha.[7] According to his analysis external shocks had been the single most important source of the deficits. Increases in interest rates form part of these shocks. When taken together with the effects resulting from the growth of indebtedness interest payments accounted for a growing part of the deficit, explaining 42 per cent of the deterioration of the current account–GDP–ratio in the period from 1978 to 1982.

Increasing indebtedness hardly provides any difficulties as long as exports grow at a rate higher than the interest rate.[8] Brazil's export growth, however, had been severely constrained by the retardation of world trade. As Bacha[9] has shown, this had increased the ratio of current account to potential GDP by approximately one-fifth in 1982. If in such a situation real interest rates increased a debtor country may quickly be regarded as insolvent[10] by the creditor banks who will then refuse to roll over loans.

If foreign capital is unavailable, private investment must equal the difference between private savings and the budget deficit. In times of increasing government deficits (as have occured in Brazil since 1984[11]) and without additional private savings, investment must decrease. In fact, in Brazil decreasing real interest rates and expectations of exchange-rate devaluations even provided incentives to lower private savings, when the country most urgently needed more of them.

The impact of these processes on savings and investments is revealed in Table 6.3. The decline in gross capital formation since 1975–7 by almost ten percentage points is mainly reflected in the decrease of gross national savings, whereas external savings are more or less constant. This decrease is only partly due to declining gross domestic savings. Further, it reveals the strong influence of net factor incomes paid abroad, thus showing a direct impact of indebtedness on capital formation in Brazil.

Furthermore, in a general credit squeeze serious efforts are necessary to bring the need for foreign exchange into line with availability. Most often the quickest way is a cut in imports either by depressing demand or by raising import restrictions. Countries with already low levels of imports relative to GDP face the problem that further import reductions will inevitably lead to difficulties in production and/or investment. In fact, Brazil experienced a decline in imports from an already low level in absolute as well as in relative terms. The share of imports of goods and non-factor services in GDP decreased from 9.4 per cent in 1981 to 7.9 per cent in 1984.[12] The geographical distribution of this decrease was relatively uneven. Whereas imports from industrial countries declined by 40 per cent, those from LDCs experienced a decrease of 36 per cent.[13] The higher decrease of imports from DCs is revealed in the change of the composition of imports. Whereas fuels increased by 2.3 percentage points, imports of machinery declined by 4.1 percentage points.[14] In these years of debt crisis Brazil tried to maintain production at the previous level, while adjustment via investment was postponed. Only since 1984 have there been indicators for a change in strategy. While imports from LDCs halved in the longer run (1981–6), purchases from DCs were at approximately the same level in 1986 as they had been in 1981. But even if this is interpreted as a sign of

Table 6.3 Savings and gross capital formation, 1975–77 and 1982–84
(percentages, based on values at current prices)

	Gross domestic savings	Net factor income	Ratio to GDP of Gross national savings	External savings*	Gross capital formation
1975–77	25.7	−1.9	23.8	3.7	27.6
1982–84	20.2	−5.5	14.7	2.6	17.3

*   Defined as net imports of goods and non-factor services less net factor income.
Source: UNCTAD, *Trade and Development Report*, 1986, p. 127.

rising investment (data are not available so far), it may still take quite a long time for growth rates to stabilise at 1970 levels.

The reason for this can be clearly seen in the results of Bacha's analysis mentioned above.[15] In an economy in which foreign exchange is constrained, like the Brazilian, the net worth of a dollar earned in foreign exchange is much higher than a dollar in domestic savings. Capacity underutilisation may result if additional savings cannot be transformed into higher foreign exchange. If this situation holds all measures that try to diminish current consumption are of less importance than those that increase foreign exchange.

Evidently inherent in this situation is a dilemma when an export promotion policy is implemented. Although in the short run higher exports may lead to more foreign exchange than would be available otherwise, thus raising capacity utilisation, they can imply at the same time, *ceteris paribus*, less foreign savings if the resulting increase in imports is sufficiently low to decrease the current account deficit. Foreign savings, however, may be necessary for expanding the production frontier in the long run if internal savings are low.

This conflict can only be avoided if foreign capital is available. However, as recent years have witnessed, it seems to be quite impossible to raise additional capital in the international capital markets unless creditworthiness has been restored. With long-term lending at concessional terms hardly available, Brazil is left with the necessity of raising foreign non-debt capital. The question to be discussed in the next section, therefore, concerns the possible role foreign direct investments can assume in an attempt to solve Brazil's current debt problems.

In this section we are going to make use of the following sources. First, data from the IMF, the European Community (EEC) and from Brazil will be used, along with data from the OECD and the UN Centre of Transnational Cooperation (UNCTC) to present a general picture of the development of Brazil's FDI position world-wide and with the EEC member states. Second, these data will be supplemented by an analysis of the more detailed statistics on FDI stocks which has recently been published by the Deutsche Bundesbank.

Recent trends in foreign direct investment with special reference to the European Community

From Table 6.4 it can be seen that FDI flows to LDCs grew steadily from 1970 to 1981 and the same is true for those to the Latin American countries and Brazil. In 1981 this trend broke down. Total FDI to LDCs dropped from $14.298 billion in 1981 to $11.318 billion in 1984. During this period FDI to Latin American decreased even further both in absolute and in relative terms. Thus, while LDCs suffered from a loss of $2.980 billion, or 21 per cent between 1981 and 1984, the Latin American countries registered a decline of $4.336 billion, or 57 per cent. Brazil followed with a time-lag of one year and then also was hit heavily. FDI dropped by 54 per cent from $2.922 billion in 1982 to $1.346 billion in 1985. This development is also reflected in the relative positions of Latin America and Brazil within the LDCs. While Latin American attracted about 50 per cent of all FDI in the 70s, it only received 29 per cent in 1984. Within the group of Latin American countries the decline of the Brazilian share to well below 50 per cent in the 1980s confirms the especially severe decline of its relative share *vis-àvis* all LDCs.

Drawing on preliminary OECD data for 1985 and 1986 indicates that another disastrous breakdown of FDI flows to LDCs took place in 1985. Again, these recent developments coincide for Latin America and the group of all LDCs. In both groups of countries, FDI dropped by more than one-third, while Brazil followed with another one-year time-lag. In 1986, FDI in Brazil was estimated to amount to $655 billion.[16] In this year a partial recovery can already be observed for the other LDCs.[17] It is especially worth noting that the $1.449 billion decline of FDI flows to Brazil between 1982 and 1985 is about half of the total loss which all LDCs together had to bear between 1981 and 1984. This still holds for 1986.

Thus, taking into consideration that Latin America alone accounted for a decline of $4.336 billion until 1984 and another $1 billion between 1984 and 1985 (which adds up to a 70 per cent decline since 1981), it becomes

Table 6.4 Foreign direct investment flows to less-developed countries,* 1970–85 (US$ million)

	Annual average 1970–4	1975–9	1980	1981	1982	1983	1984	1985	1986
LDCs	2,900.5	6,984.1	10,472	14,298	13,745	10,876	11,318	(7,481)†	(10,831)†
Latin America (LA)	1,467.8	3,447.2	6,116	7,618	6,471	3,781	3,282	(2,281)†	(2,826)†
Brazil (BR)	796.6	1,820.4	1,913	2,526	2,922	1,557	1,598		
						1,556	1,596	1,346	655‡
LA/LDCs (%)	50.6	49.4	58.4	53.3	47.1	34.8	29.0	30.5	26.1
BR/LDCs (%)	27.5	26.1	18.3	17.7	21.3	14.3	14.1	18.0	6.0
BR/LA (%)	54.3	52.8	31.3	33.1	45.2	41.2	48.7	59.0	23.2
(LA − BR)/LDC (%)	23.1	23.3	40.1	35.6	25.8	20.4	14.9		

*   Gross inflows plus reinvestments
†   Calculated on the basis of OECD data
‡   Calculated from Banco Central do Brasil estimates

Sources: Banco Central do Brasil, *Boletím Mensal*, vol. 22, no. 12, December 1986; IMF, *Balance of Payments Statistics Yearbook, 1986*, vol. 37, Part 1; D. Rosario, and S. Rivas, *Seleccón de Estadísticas Básicas sobre Concentración Global y Transnacionalisación*, CET/IPAL, Buenos Aires, 1985, Table II, p. 39; M.R. Agosin and V.B. Ribero, 'Inversiones Extranjeras Directas en América Latina: tendencias recientes y perspectivas', *Integración Latinoamericana*, vol. 12, no. 124, June 1987, Tables 1 and 2; OECD, *International Investmentand Multinational Enterprises*, Paris, 1987, Table III, p. 10.

clear that the crisis of FDI flows to LDCs in the early 1980s is, by and large, a Latin American crisis with Brazil as the most prominent contributor.

From all FDI flows, which were going to Brazil in 1984, more than one-third originated in the United States, about one-quarter in the EEC and 9 per cent in Japan.[18] In the following some details of the EEC FDI flows will be analysed.

Total EEC[19] net FDI flows to Latin America (Table 6.5) rose from $289.51 million in 1975 to $619.04 million in 1985. As with its world-wide performance, Brazilian FDI could not keep pace with this development. FDI rose slowly from $211.91 million in 1975 to a 1983 peak of $401.44 million and then dropped to $220.59 million in 1985. Consequently, the Brazilian share in total EEC flows to Latin America dropped from about 75 per cent before 1978 to an average 35 per cent thereafter.

The decreasing importance of Brazil within Latin America can basically be explained by the increasingly cautious investments of West German enterprises since the mid-1970s. France and the UK only started to rein in their engagements in Brazil in 1981 and 1983, respectively. The latter year can also be indentified as the one in which the general decline of FDI to Brazil started. A reversal of the flows can be observed for Belgium/Luxembourg (1984 and 1985) and West Germany (1986).

Table 6.5 Net foreign direct investment flows between the European Community and Latin America, 1976–85 ($ million, current)

	European Community* to:			West Germany to:			France to:			United Kingdom to:		
	Latin America (LA)	Brazil (BR)	BR/LA (%)	Latin America (LA)	Brazil (BR)	BR/LA (%)	Latin America (LA)	Brazil (BR)	BR/LA (%)	Latin America (LA)	Brazil (BR)	BR/LA (%)
1971				56.8	35.4	62.3	31.7	4.7	14.8			
1972				54.9	45.6	83.0	57.3	15.1	26.4			
1973				104.2	60.6	58.2	96.9	26.5	27.3			
1974				130.1	112.8	86.7						
1975	289.51	211.91	73.1	153.0	128.2	83.8	69.0	44.6	64.6			
1976	524.38	344.54	65.8	266.9	231.5	86.7	106.7	55.6	52.1	58.5	33.1	56.6
1977	437.34	331.15	75.7	302.5	208.8	69.0	95.7	47.4	49.5	116.6	42.9	36.8
1978	1,887.37	582.86	30.9	336.0	241.0	71.7	192.7	42.1	21.8	−32.2	68.4	—
1979	768.37	256.04	33.3	315.4	144.8	45.9	238.0	60.0	25.2	1,355.5	294.2	21.7
1980	725.65	177.85	24.5	204.2	74.0	36.3	354.9	82.7	23.3	181.6	22.3	12.4
1981	801.30	359.90	44.9	158.4	211.3	—	450.2	81.8	18.2	164.1	24.5	14.9
1982	776.79	315.35	40.6	265.8	153.8	57.9	278.8	78.6	28.2	175.5	56.2	32.0
1983	967.20	401.44	41.5	383.6	297.1	77.5	200.9	41.8	20.8	214.4	78.8	36.8
1984	826.69	287.14	34.7	341.1	222.5	65.2	110.3	13.2	12.0	337.1	53.9	16.0
1985	619.04	220.59	35.6	174.0	168.6	96.9	221.6	19.6	8.8	(1,126.5)	(192.1)	(17.0)
1986				−61.3	−11.5	(18.7)						

* West Germany, France, United Kingdom, Belgium/Luxembourg and Denmark

In order to gain some more insight into the evolving structure of European FDI to LDCs and to Brazil in particular, more detailed regional statistics and sectoral breakdowns are needed. These are, at present, not available for most of the EEC member states. Fortunately, however, comprehensive new statistics on FDI stocks[20] for West Germany exist which now extend from 1976 to 1985.[21] We will draw on these data which are based on yearly reports of German enterprises to the Deutsche Bundesbank.[22] Some reservations have to be made concerning the use of these data, because they cannot be used as a perfect mirror of total FDI of EEC in LDCs and Brazil. Nevertheless, their use can be justified by the quantitative importance of West German FDI in Brazil relative to the other EEC countries.[23]

The major findings are presented in Tables 6.6 and 6.7. West Germany tripled its FDI stocks between 1976 and 1985 from $16.883 billion to $49.444 billion. A major and increasing part of these investments was located in industrialised countries, so that from 1976 to 1985 the share of LDCs and that of Brazil, in particular, declined from 16.5 to 12.8 per cent and from 9.4 to 5.5 per cent, respectively. Looking at LDCs, excluding Brazil, reveals that their share of West Germany's total stocks did not decline. In fact, leaving aside the especially bad performance of 1985, this share increased slightly from 7.1 per cent in 1976 to 8.3 per cent in 1984. It is still more surprising that this trend also holds for the other Latin American countries which did suffer a serious decline in FDI world-wide. This means that the relative decline of West German capital stocks in LDCs can, by and large, be explained by the diminishing activites in Brazil. Nevertheless, Brazil was and, despite the relatively slow growth of FDI stocks since 1976 (remember that net inflows have stagnated since 1975–6), still is the single most important recipient of West Germany's FDI in LDCs which, in turn, are highly concentrated in Latin America.

Table 6.8 presents some structural characteristics of West German FDI in Brazil. First of all, the overwhelming majority of these investments were undertaken in the manufacturing sector. On average, this sector received 93 per cent of total West German FDI as compared to 75 per cent from private investors world-wide.[24] West German investors are not very heavily engaged in mining and agriculture, the traditionally important sectors for FDI of the industrialised countries. Neither did they use the rising growth potential of the emerging new service industries which accounted for 19 per cent of total FDI in Brazil in 1984 but only for 3.4 per cent of West Germany's activities. West German FDI, instead, is concentrated in a number of industrial manufacturing sectors which also form the country's major export industries. In 1981, 81 per cent of total manufacturing FDI was undertaken in machinery, motor cars, electrotechnical and chemical industries. Only two of these, however, the chemical and the electrotechnical industries, continued to grow during the first half of the 1980s. The machinery and automotive industries still had lower FDI stocks

Table 6.6 Regional distribution* of West Germany's foreign direct investment, 1976–85 (stocks in $ million, current[†])

	World	Industrialised countries	Less-developed countries (excl. OPEC)	Latin America (incl. OPEC)	Brazil	Less-developed countries (excl. Brazil)	Latin America (excl. Brazil)
1976	16,883	12,484	2,792	2,328	1,581	1,211	747
1977	21,309	14,674	3,063	2,551	1,758	1,301	793
1978	24,164	18,032	3,760	3,072	2,182	1,578	890
1979	29,699	23,194	4,183	3,415	2,100	2,083	1,315
1980	35,712	27,553	5,406	4,398	2,379	3,027	2,019
1981	38,245	29,228	5,823	4,686	2,600	3,223	2,085
1982	40,774	30,889	6,099	4,806	2,983	3,116	1,823
1983	45,247	34,878	6,270	4,807	2,684	3,586	2,122
1984	49,914	39,237	7,149	5,641	2,978	4,171	2,663
1985	49,444	39,818	6,351	4,932	2,737	3,614	2,192

* According to Deutsche Bundesbank classification
† At IMF average yearly rates

Table 6.7 Regional distribution of West Germany's foreign direct investment, 1976–85 (percentage shares of stocks)

	% of world total							% of LDC total (excl. OPEC)					
	ICs	LDCs (excl. OPEC)	Latin America (incl. OPEC)	Brazil (BR)	LDCs (excl. OPEC and BR)	LA–BR	SEA-NICs + India	LA	BR	LA–BR	SEA-NICs + India	LA–BR / LDC–BR	BR/LA
1976	73.9	16.5	13.8	9.4	7.1	4.4	1.3	83.4	56.6	26.8	7.6	61.7	67.9
1977	68.9	14.4	12.0	8.2	6.2	3.7	1.2	85.2	57.4	25.9	8.2	60.1	68.9
1978	74.6	15.6	12.7	9.0	6.6	3.7	1.4	81.7	58.0	23.7	9.0	56.4	71.0
1979	78.1	14.1	11.5	7.1	7.0	4.4	1.4	81.6	50.2	31.4	9.7	63.1	61.5
1980	77.2	15.1	12.3	6.7	8.4	5.7	1.6	81.4	44.0	37.6	10.7	66.2	54.1
1981	76.4	15.2	11.9	6.8	8.4	5.5	1.7	80.5	44.7	35.8	11.3	65.0	55.5
1982	75.8	15.0	11.8	7.3	7.7	4.8	1.6	78.8	48.9	29.9	10.7	58.5	62.1
1983	77.1	13.9	10.6	5.9	8.0	4.7	1.6	76.7	42.8	33.8	11.8	59.2	55.8
1984	78.6	14.3	11.3	6.0	8.3	5.3	1.7	78.9	41.7	37.2	11.7	63.8	52.8
1985	80.1	12.8	10.0	5.5	7.3	4.4	1.6	77.7	43.1	34.5	12.2	60.7	55.5

NICs = Newly industrialising countries
ICs   = Industrialised countries
SEA = South-East Asia

Table 6.8 Distribution of West Germany's foreign direct investment in Brazil*, by sector, 1981–85 (stocks in $ million, current)

	1981	1982	1983	1984	1985
Total	2,600	2,983	2,699	2,978	2,736
Mining	—	6	21	6	40
Manufacturing					
industries	2,509	2,842	2,466	2,757	2,500
Chemical industries	491	589	592	622	562
Iron and steel	278	305	223	231	209
Machinery	365	438	329	365	320
Motor vehicles	817	850	752	878	709
Electro-technical					
industries	356	427	373	390	399
Service industries	50	61	97	100	98

* Classified according to sectors of operation in Brazil

in 1985 than in 1981, dropping from 47.1 to 41.2 per cent. Altogether, FDI stocks in the manufacturing sector were lower in 1985 than in 1982.

Is there a foreign direct investment gap in Brazil?

FDI flows to Brazil, along with those to most other LDCs, slowed down during the world-wide recession of the early 1980s. However, the former were already growing at a slower rate than the latter throughout the 1970s. After 1976, this relatively weak performance put Brazil behind the rest of Latin America. Did these differing rate-of-growth trends lead to a FDI gap in Brazil? In order to answer this question it must be considered that many LDCs have had rather ambiguous views on foreign venture capital in the past, for economic as well as political reasons,[25] and have discriminated in various ways against the multinationals. The growth rate of FDI that prevailed throughout the 1970s should therefore be considered as a minimum figure. This is underlined by the fact that during this period the internationalisation of the world economy has also led to a most rapid increase in capital flows between the advanced industrialised nations. Provided that world economic growth recovers to a rate similar to that of the 1970s, FDI flows to LDCs as a whole should, therefore, be expected to increase (at least) in line with the trend rate that was established during the 1970–82 period.[26]

However, Latin America, and Brazil in particular, are said already to have relatively high levels of foreign economic penetration and might, therefore, face a ceiling on further expansion. What can be seen as a reasonable trend for all LDCs might, from this point of view, be over-ambitious for Latin America, and especially for Brazil.

Looking at some overall indicators of foreign economic involvement in Brazil does not appear to support this contention. Thus, in 1977, FDI accounted for only 2.1 per cent of total investment in Brazil. Despite the fact that this figure placed Brazil well above the LDC average of less than 1 per cent, such diverse countries as Singapore (10.1 per cent), Zaire (9.3 per cent), Peru (7.4 per cent) and Mexico (3.3 per cent) were still further ahead.[27] But the concentration of FDI in Brazil in the industrial manu-facturing sector (world 75 per cent, West Germany, 95 per cent) suggests that, within this sector the foreign impact is far more pronounced. In fact, in 1977, multinational companies provided 32 per cent of the industrial manufacturing production[28] and 23 per cent of employment.[29] Moreover, they are among the largest companies and they are concentrated in only a few sectors.[30] This heavy concentration of FDI in some manufacturing sectors does not only reflect the fact that entrepreneurs from industrialised countries tend to invest in those industries where they can expect to have a comparative advantage and dispose of exclusive product, production and management know-how. Besides these preferences, it also has to be recognised that many potentially important industries in Brazil are nation-alised or prohibited from being run by foreigners. Thus, computer hard-ware and software industries, telecommunications and other modern high-technology industries have recently been heavily protected and the share of state-owned firms has grown considerably. Despite the fact that in Brazil state-owned enterprises are, to some extent, allowed to form joint ventures with foreign firms, discrimination against foreign capital in some of the most important industrial sectors remains and hinders the inflows of FDI and know-how. Furthermore, it forces existing companies to stick to their original industry so that their investments are limited to the performance of their specific markets. Both developments are a hindrance to growth and will negatively affect FDI and technology transfer in the future.

From these considerations one can conclude that FDI in Brazil will not become a dynamic force as long as sectoral limitations and other forms of discrimination remain as restrictive as they are at present.[31] There is no saturation with foreign capital to be expected in the near future, however, when multinationals are allowed to spread their activities more evenly among all industrial sectors. This is especially so when they are allowed to penetrate into the new growth industries, where foreign know-how is most urgently needed. Under the condition that Brazilian economic policy will open up towards the world market again and will follow the general LDC trend towards a more liberal treatment of foreign venture capital, we can calculate the potential FDI gap by comparing the actual performance of Brazil with trend figures for all LDCs from the 1970s.

Drawing on OECD figures[32] the trend rate of growth of FDI to all LDCs in 1970–82 was 10.4 per cent per annum. This means that Brazilian FDI would have grown to $4.325 billion in 1986 if the pre-world-recession trend had prevailed—with Brazil participating proportionately. Actually, these flows amounted to only $655 million so that the potential yearly FDI gap is $3.670 billion. According to real term data from the World Bank[33] net direct investment to LDCs grew at an annual rate of 5.8 per cent in 1970–80. Using this yardstick, the FDI gap still amounts to $3 billion, and even using the World Bank's pessimistic scenario of 2.6 per cent[34] for the 1985–95 period, a gap of $2.5 billion would have accumulated during the early 1980s. In the light of these data, and taking into consideration that the 1986 low value of FDI to Brazil is still biased upward because of the dollar depreciation, an FDI gap of well above $3 billion at current prices can be seen as a conservative estimate.

CAN DEBT–EQUITY SWAPS CLOSE THE GAP?

From this analysis it seems straightforward to look for additional channels to attract FDI. One such possibility seems to be embodied in debt–equity swaps. Proponents of DES usually maintain that they will increase foreign investment.[35] They base their argument on the high returns which are obtained when the proceeds of the swaps are invested in high-priority projects. Thus for instance, the Chilean 'Chapter 19' DES yields are about 26 per cent.[36] In the Mexican programme net returns may be even higher (up to 30 per cent).[37]

Additional profits of this size may constitute an incentive to invest in those countries which are heavily engaged in DES. The profitability of these transactions is based on the fact that developing-country debts are traded in the secondary loan market at high discounts. An investor who needs the currency of a debtor country may buy this country's debts on the secondary market and present them to the respective authorities of the debtor country for redemption in local currency. Net gains from this transaction depend on the difference between the prices he paid for the loan and the prices he gets from the local authorities. Normally they will not pay him the face value of the loan but substract a discount. But as the price of the loan on the secondary market is usually much lower than the price he receives, a substantial profit margin per unit of loan remains for the investor. Assuming that capital markets are efficient this profit is paid by the debtor country.[38] The investor will look at it as a subsidy for his investment. This subsidy may compensate for the disadvantages and risks associated with investments in the debtor country.

On this account Brazil may have several disadvantages. While in 1976–83 direct returns from investments yielded 6.6 per cent, those obtained in Chile and Argentina were considerably higher (27.7 and 18.7 per cent, respectively).[39] Further, additional risks may be expected if one recognises the increasing dislike of FDI among the Brazilian public. This may lead to decreasing legal protection of foreign property. Considering recent economic policy in Brazil may also raise questions as to its credibility, consistency and continuity in the future. Furthermore, the recent decline of the price of Brazilian debt instruments by 30 percentage points in the secondary loan market[40] indicates a serious loss of Brazil's creditworthiness. This implies that creditors expect to receive significantly less in debt service payments from Brazil. As restrictions on debt service are usually accompanied by those on capital flows in general, investors may associate a price decrease of Brazilian debts on the secondary loan market with increased risk of investment in Brazil. All this demonstrates that possible losses on behalf of these effects are to be expected.

At present there is no formal DES programme in Brazil. Debt swaps, as executed since November 1984, mainly concern swaps of inter-company loans into equity. Rarely can bank loans be used for this purpose. At present, the amounts swapped are rather low, amounting to $20 million a month; in 1986 it is contended, $600 million were converted.[41] Brazil's reluctance to execute DES is at least partly explained by the Central Bank's conviction that foreign investments would have come in anyway.[42] In view of the weak performance of new capital inflows in recent years this argument appears to be rather weak, however (see above). Another reason for opposing DES is that, as stock prices are rather low, banks may be able to substitute bad loans for highly profitable equity.[43] Although management of the current DES system is rather restrictive, it might assume larger volumes if some of the main obstacles are abolished. Proposals for a new system are under review.[44] Thus, a more general discussion of the advantages of DES in attracting FDI is called for.

In order to do this, it must be emphasised that the alternative to DES is a conventionally financed FDI,[45] where the funds are converted at the official exchange rate and the investor gets a subsidy equivalent to that implied by DES.

Starting from the assumption that higher returns are necessary to attract additional foreign investment, the improvement in profitability can be traced back to gains in direct or indirect returns. The latter may be split into higher subsidies and reductions in risk which may stem from increased legal protection of property, better use of macroeconomic policy especially in the field of foreign exchange and external debt, and so on. Generally DES affect returns via the same channels as conventional methods of financing do. Taking conventional methods of financing foreign investments as a point of reference, it is difficult to see where additional direct returns should come from. There is no direct additional advantage for the investor using DES because it is assumed that the funds are allocated to the same use irrespective of how the investment is financed. Hence, additional returns could only be explained by the non-equivalence of the subsidies or by a different impact of DES on risk reduction. Thus it may be possible that the investor reaps additional returns from DES if one or several of the following conditions hold.

First, it may happen that there is political opposition in the debtor country to overt as opposed to more covert DES subvention. In this case higher subsidies may result from DES schemes. (Note, however, that increasing hidden subsidies may itself be counter-productive—just as the whole subsidy may be.[46])

Second, the assumption of equal transaction costs may be violated. This may imply a higher subsidy net of transaction costs in the DES case.

Third, there may be an improvement in creditworthiness if financing by DES affected it more positively than conventional methods of investment finance did. Then, investors might feel that the risk of future exchange restrictions is diminished.[47]

Summarising the discussion so far leads to the conclusion that lower transaction costs or reduced resistance to disguised forms of subsidy paid to foreigners may lead to an increase in returns and, therefore, to more foreign investments than otherwise could be realised, if they are financed by DES. The empirical relevance and the logical consistency of these arguments for DES seem to be small. First, it seems unlikely that transaction costs will be lower when investments are financed by DES, compared with those financed conventionally. Although spreads and commissions for DES transactions have been lowered substantially[48] they are still considerably higher than in normal foreign exchange transactions. Further, the second argument rests on the assumption that individuals have illusions about the true nature of DES and therefore react irrationally. Besides the fact that perceived irrationality points to errors in model-building, whether or not individuals have illusions and, if so, how long they will persist, is an empirical question.

However, if DES lead to higher FDI, one may ask whether they are a reasonable policy tool for this objective. At least in some cases DES can imply rather high opportunity costs, for example, when the foreign investment would have come in anyway at some point in the near future. This would imply a waste of government resources. It may happen, however, that the DES-financed investment is diverted from another country.[49] The country that loses foreign investments may itself introduce countervailing subsidies. Thus, a competition for FDI by increasing subsidies may be introduced, leading to a waste of resources.[50]

Another argument also has to be considered. It was argued earlier that in Brazil a dollar earned in foreign exchange has a higher value than a dollar's worth of additional savings. In this respect DES clearly possess a disadvantage when they are compared with a conventionally financed FDI:[51] While the latter may lead to additional foreign exchange, DES do not. Further, it is questionable whether a country using DES will gain from not paying debt service. Usually the transfer of dividends and that of the principal is restricted for some years only and these restrictions may be circumvented by over- and underinvoicing. Further, dividends may be higher than interest payments.

Thus, one is finally left with the result that DES will most probably not lead to higher investments. However, if they do. this could only be at the expense of the debtor country. Further, the opportunity costs may be too high and result in a negative net present value. There may be, however, one exception. DES may increase the creditworthiness of the debtor country more than a conventinally financed investment. This result can be obtained when both means of financing foreign investments affect the determinants of creditworthiness in a different way. In an empirical analysis of the Chilean swap system it has been demonstrated that creditworthiness would be enhanced far more if, instead of DES conventional methods of financing foreign investments were used.[52]

FOREIGN DIRECT INVESTMENT AND THE CHANGING CONDITIONS FOR ECONOMIC GROWTH

From the above analysis the conclusion can be drawn that swapping foreign debt into equity will not contribute significantly to the solution of the debt problem. Rather than subsidising FDI via complicated debt–equity schemes and similar financial arrangements (see, for example, the 'Uriquidi Plan' for Mexico[53]) with no or negligible impact on the real 'sphere', a comprehensive new economic programme is called for which is aimed at the reintroduction of adequate macroeconomic conditions and a sound long-term strategy. Although it is beyond the scope of this chapter to.outline such a strategy in detail, some final comments on a few of the major areas of concern may be appropriate.

First of all, the disastrous outcome of the 1986 'Cruzado Plan' does not lend support to those who believed that a 'heterodox shock',[54] which predominantly operates by means of a wage and price freeze, will be sufficient to restore macroeconomic stability in a country like Brazil.[55] Rather, with 'formal' and 'informal indexation' around for many years,[56] there is no way out of inflation without adjustment of the major deformations of the system of relative prices and the public sector disequilibrium. This implies that at least some of the groups of economic agents will have to cut back their real claims on total product during the adjustment process. For purely quantitative reasons (not to mention profound theoretical arguments) it appears to be an illusion that this can be done by squeezing rent capital alone.[57]

Second, economies which are facing severe structural rigidities tend to be manageable more easily when growth is under way and as long as economic agents are orientated to nominal claims.[58] While the latter condition is likely to be disrupted with rising rates of inflation and adapting expectations, the former will be weakened if the international environment deteriorates or if a national growth strategy is misguided. Thus, as long as the international environment is conducive to growth a failure of national economic policy may only have a limited impact on the economy's total performance. But it will become a major point of concern when external shocks arise.

As far as Brazil's national growth policy is concerned, there are three major areas which should be considered as prime candidates in a reformulation of the present strategy. Two of these areas—the industrial manufacturing sector and the trade regime—can be identified right away from recent experience with development strategies in an increasingly interdependent world economy,[59] and they are closely related to each other. Modern development theory suggests that the only successful way for an average newly industrialising country to keep up further with the economically advanced nations is to develop its industrial manufacturing and technological know-how and to exploit its comparative advantages in the international market.[60]

Following this concept would mean for Brazil, first, absorbing modern technology intensively from abroad by trade, FDI and the various new arrangements in venture capital and know-how transfer; second, diversifying and upgrading its productive capacity along the dynamic scale of comparative advantages and expanding and enriching its exports of manufacturing products. Mining and agriculture, though generally of importance for a resource-rich country like Brazil and of specific interest, in the case of agriculture, because of its occupational and migrational effects, does not find a strategic position within this framework. These long-term considerations get even stronger support when they are complemented by an analysis of the weak prospects of commodity markets in the near future.[61]

There is no unanimous opinion as to exactly which strategy has been followed by Brazil in recent years. While Fendt and Salazar-Carillo[62] claim that since 1981 a restructuring has taken place away from energy and import-intensive products towards mining—for the Grande Carajá Programme along an investment of $62 billion has been scheduled[63]—and agro-industries (the latter being closely linked to the highly subsidised alcohol programme), Fishlow does not interpret these events as a shift of emphasis but as one towards a 'no-strategy': 'The government attempted not merely to satisfy new priorities in agriculture, but to satisfy all priorities simultaneously. The list . . . included virtually every other claim that was seen as politically valid. . . . It was an abortive effort to produce another miracle.'[64] No matter which of these interpretations comes closer to reality, there is no doubt that the Brazilian development strategy in the 1980s, rather than opening up further to the world market and supporting (or, at least, not discriminating against) future growth industries, tends to overemphasise the primary commodity sector, to fall back into protectionist sentiments and to misspecify its industrial incentive system.[65]

In addition to these problems the enormous increase of the share of state-owned enterprises in total economic activity has been emphasised as another obstacle to growth for a number of reasons.[66] Even if state participation is considered inevitably from a political point of view, these enterprises will have to be organised and controlled independently and they must be allowed to charge market clearing prices in order to diminish one of the major sources of the Brazilian public sector deficit.

A development policy which is designed along these principles would, most certainly, contribute to a rise of FDI and its implicit know-how transfer without relying on costly subvention schemes with uncertain outcome. It would also help to reactivate complementary capital inflows from official and private sources and improve the availability of external finance on a broad front. The foreign debt of $107 billion in 1985, which constitutes so serious a problem in the present situation, would, in fact, soon become economically immaterial, if such a new environment of growth and development could be established.

Needless to say that the success of any such switch in economic policy will basically depend on the maintanance of free world markets and that it will be much easier to implement if it is accompanied by international financial support.

NOTES

1. World Bank, *World Debt Tables 1986–87*, Washington DC, 1987, pp. viii, 286.
2. IMF, *International Financial Statistics*, Supplement on Economic Indicators, 1985, p. 16.
3. Inter-American Development Bank, *Economic and Social Progress in Latin America. 1986 Report*, Washington DC, 1986, p. 24.
4. Data are from the Central Bank of Brazil, cited in E.A. Cardoso and R. Dornbusch, 'El Plan Tropical del Brasil', *El Trimestre Económico*, vol. 54, 1987, p. 662.
5. *The Economist*, 8–14 August 1987, p. 71.
6. R. Dornbusch, 'External Debt, Budget Deificits, and Disequilibrium Exchange Rates' in G.W. Smith and J.T. Cuddington (eds), *International Debt and the Developing Countries*, World Bank, Washington DC, 1985, p. 216.
7. E.L. Bacha, 'External Shocks and Growth Prospects: The Case of Brazil, 1973–89', *World Development*, vol. 14, no. 8, 1987, p. 923.
8. M. H. Simonsen, 'Developing Country Debt Problem', in Smith and Cuddington, *International Debt*, p. 105.
9. Bacha, 'External Shocks', p. 923.
10. R.N. Cooper and J.D. Sachs, 'Borrowing Abroad: The Debtor's Perspective', in Smith and Cuddington, *International Debt*, p. 22.
11. Cardoso and Dornbusch, 'El Plan Tropical', p. 662.
12. IMF, *International Financial Statistics*, July 1987.
13. IMF, *Direction of Trade Statistics, Yearbook 1987*, p. 111.
14. United Nations, *International Trade Statistics, Yearbook 1985*, vol. 1, p. 190.

15. Bacha, 'External shocks', pp. 925.
16. According to the Banco do Brazil, FDI were $327.7 million for the first half of 1986. See Banco Central do Brazil, *Boletím Mensal*, vol. 22, no. 12, December 1986, p. 28.
17. The recovery in 1986 which, in nominal terms, appears to be nearly compensating for the 1985 loss, is far less impressive when the recent US-dollar depreciation is taken into account.
18. UN/CEPAL, *Banco de Datos sobre Inversión Extranjera Directa en América Latina y el Caribe*, vol. 2, LC/L. 386/Add.1, 25 March 1987, p. 21.
19. The data do not cover all EEC member states. However, from the most important venture capital exporters, only Italy (which has about the same share as France) is missing. Spain is another prominent investor in Latin America, but due to its historical background, does not have important links with Brazil. Thus, by and large, the countries used in this analysis account for about 80–85 per cent of European FDI to Latin America and Brazil, respectively.
20. By FDI stocks are meant foreign-owned capital stocks.
21. Deutsche Bundesbank, 'Die Kapitalverflechtung der Unternehmen mit dem Ausland nach Ländern and Wirtschaftszweigen', supplement to *Statistische Beihefte zu den Monatsberichten der Deutschen Bundesbank*, third series, Zahlungsbilanzstatistik, no. 3, March, various years (1980–7).
22. For a detailed description of the accounting procedures and definitions, see 'Stand der Direktinvestitionen Ende 1976, *Monatsberichte der Deutschen Bundesbank*, vol. 31, no. 4, April 1979, pp. 26–40.
23. In 1984, West Germany contributed nearly 50 per cent to the total FDI stock of EEC member states in Brazil, followed by the United Kingdom, Italy and France, which altogether accounted for about the same share. World-wide, West Germany, accounting for 12.2 per cent in 1984, is second only to the USA, which holds about one-third of all foreign-owned stocks in Brazil. See Banco Central do Brasil, *Boletím Mensal*, November 1985.
24. UN/CEPAL, *Banco de Datos*, p.20.
25. W. Bear, 'Foreign Investments in Brazil: Their Benefits and Costs' in R. Fendt Jr. and J. Salazar-Carillo (eds), *The Brazilian Economy in the Eighties*, Pergamon Press, New York, 1985, pp. 127–137.
26. In fact, the rise of global interdependencies in trade and capital flows during the last decade points to an even more pronounced increase.
27. UN, *Transnational Corporations in World Development, Third Survey*, New York, 1983, Annex Table II.14.
28. UN/CEPAL, *Banco de Datos*, p. 107.
29. Ibid., p. 109.
30. Baer, 'Foreign Investments', pp. 132–3.
31. For a more detailed analysis see D.V. Coes, 'Imperfect Capital Mobility, Exchange Risk and Brazilian Foreign Borrowing' in Salazar-Carillo and Fendt, *The Brazilian Economy*, pp. 12–24.
32. OECD, *International Investments and Multinational Enterprises, Recent Trends in International Direct Investment*, Paris, 1987, p. 186.
33. World Bank, *World Development Report 1986*, p. 56.
34. Ibid.
35. Morgan Guaranty Trust Company, 'Debt–equity Swaps', *World Financial Markets*, June–July 1987, p. 12.
36. F. Garces Garrido, 'Comentarios sobre Conversiones de Deuda Externa en Chile', *Banco Central de Chile, Boletín Mensual*, no. 710, April 1987, p. 867.
37. 'Profile of Debt–to–Equity Conversion Programs Worldwide', *Business Latin America*, 20 April 1987, p. 124.

38. For a fuller discussion see G. Franke, 'Economic Analysis of Debt–Equity Swaps', Paper presented at the New Institutional Arrangements for the World Economy symposium held in Konstanz, West Germany, 1–4 July 1987.
39. World Bank, *World Development Report 1985*, p. 135.
40. *The Economist*, 19 September 1987, p. 82.
41. R. Bruce, 'Who Are Debt/Equity Swappers?', *Euromoney*, May 1987, p. 117.
42. A. Marton, 'The Debate over Debt-for-Equity Swaps', *Institutional Investor*, February 1987, p. 117.
43. The Economist Intelligence Unit, *Country Report, Brazil*, no. 3, 1987, p. 17.
44. Ibid., p. 10.
45. This has been discussed at more length in Franke, 'Economic Analysis' p. 4; and R. Schinke, 'Debt Equity Swaps, Investment and Creditworthiness: The Chilean Example', Discussion Paper no. 43, Ibero-Amerika Institut für Wirtschaftsforschung, Göttingen, 1987, p. 2.
46. This argument is discussed at more length in Schinke, 'Debt Equity Swaps', p. 9.
47. A more complete discussion and empirical analysis is given in ibid., pp. 14ff.
48. M. French, 'Swapping Debt—Just Hot Air?', *Euromoney*, May 1987, p. 115.
49. Note that in this case a deviation from a world-wide optimal allocation of resources may result.
50. Note that a debtor country can raise the subsidy simply by implementing a bad debt policy. The latter will most likely lead to a lower price of the country's debts on the secondary market. These problems are dealt with at more length in Schinke, 'Debt–Equity Swaps', p. 11; and in R. Schinke 'Wirkungen von Debt Equity Swaps auf Wachstum und Kreditwürdigkeit', Arbeitsberichte des Ibero-Amerika Instituts für Wirtschaftsforschung no. 24, Göttingen, forthcoming.
51. Opponents of DES usually argue that debt swaps threaten monetary or financial stability because they involve either an increase in money supply or a rise in public indebtedness (if the increase in money supply is neutralised by selling government bonds). Thus it may happen that interest payments in domestic currency are higher than those on the original foreign currency denominated debt (see Morgan Guaranty Trust Company, 'Debt Equity Swaps', p. 12). Rising instability may cause a drain on the country's international reserves. Note, however, that the same arguments apply to conventional FDI. Therefore, based on the stability argument, DES have no advantage or disadvantage when compared with conventional FDI.
52. Schinke, 'Debt Equity Swaps', pp. 15.
53. V.L. Urquidi, 'Una Propuesta para Establecer un Sistema de Pago Parcial, en Mondeda Local, de los Intereses de la Deuda Externa,' *El Trimestre Económico*, vol. 53, no. 211, July-September 1986, pp. 627–30.
54. L. Bresser Pereira, 'Intertial Inflation and the Cruzado Plan', *World Development*, vol. 15, no. 8, 1987, pp. 1035–44.
55. P. Meller, 'Apreciaciones Globales y Específicas en Torno al Plan Cruzado', *Apuntes Cieplan*, vol. 62, March 1987, pp. 26–27.
56. W. Baer, 'The Resurgence of Inflation in Brazil, 1974–1986', *World Development*, vol. 15, no. 8, August 1987, p. 1009.
57. Evidence for US FDI in Latin America suggests that there has been a tremendous decline in profits in 1980–4 which even brought a net loss for some sectors; see M.R. Agosin and V.B. Ribero, 'Inversiones extranjeras directas en América Latina: tendencias recientes y perspectivas', *Intergración Latinoamericana*, vol. 12, no. 124, June 1987, pp. 21–37, Table 4.
58. Brazil, therefore, stepped into real trouble when previous levels of external finance were reduced in late 1982 and domestic contraction had to be enforced:

see Bacha, 'External Shocks'.
59. R. Agarwala, 'Price Distortions and Growth in Developing Countries', World Bank Staff Working Paper no. 575, Washington DC, July 1983. J. Riedel, 'Trade as an Engine of Growth in Developing Countries, Revisited', *Economic Journal*, vol. 94, March 1984, pp. 56–73.
60. For a more detailed presentation and interpretation of the 'continuum of dynamic comparative advantages', see M. Michaely, 'Income Levels and the Structure of Trade' in S. Grassmann and E. Lundberg (eds), *The World Economic Order: Past and Prospects*, London and Basingstoke, 1981, pp. 121–61; H. D. Tuong and A. Yeats, 'On the Relation between Income Levels, Industrialization and the Future Composition of Developing Country Exports', *Development and Change*, vol. 11, 1980, pp. 531–44; H. Hesse, H. Keppler, H.G. Preusse, 'Internationale Interdependenzen im Weltwirtschaftlichen Entwicklungsprozess,' no. 22, Ibero-Amerika Institut für Wirtschaftsforschung, Göttingen, 1985, pp. 74–9.
61. 'Revitalizing Development, Growth and International Trade, Assessment and Policy Options', Report to UNCTAD VII, New York 1987, Ch. 3.
62. F. Fendt Jr. and J. Salazar-Carillo, 'Brazil and the Future: Some Thoughts on the Eighties' in Salazar-Carillo and Fendt, *The Brazilian Economy*, p. 14.
63. A. Hall, 'Agrarian Crisis in Brazilian Amazonia: The Grande Carajás Programme', *Journal of Development Studies*, vol. 23, no. 4, July 1987, p. 533.
64. A. Fishlow, 'Comment on Fendt/Salazar-Carillo' in Salazar-Carillo and Fendt, *The Brazilian Economy*, p. 35.
65. W.G. Tyler, 'Effective Incentives for Domestic Market Sales and Exports: A View of Anti-Export Biases and Commercial Policy in Brazil, 1980–81, *Journal of Development Economics*, vol. 18, nos. 2–3, August 1985, pp. 219–42.
66. World Bank, *World Development Report, 1987*, p. 66.

PART 4: THE SECOND ENLARGEMENT OF THE EEC: POSSIBLE CONSEQUENCES FOR BRAZIL

7

The entry of Portugal and Spain into the EEC and Euro-Brazilian trade

Helson Braga and Gilda M.C. Santiago

In 1986 Portugal and Spain formally joined the European Economic Community (EEC), after a protracted period of preparation and negotiations. This meant that the EEC now represented a market of more than 320 million consumers with a high purchasing power and a per-capita income of over 8,000 ECUs.

The changes that are taking place in the largest market in the world would in themselves justify speculation as to their implications. Furthermore, to the extent that they involve countries, particularly Portugal, to which Brazil is closely linked by historical and cultural ties, an evaluation of the possible effects on the Brazilian economy of this latest addition to the EEC becomes even more necessary. That is the main objective of this chapter. The analysis focuses on two principal questions. The first is to examine the most likely impact on the flow of goods and capital between Brazil and the Iberian countries. The second is to assess to what extent it is valid to expect that Portugal and Spain can be utilised to facilitate access to the Community market.

For a good part of the analysis, the arguments are developed in a wider context, encompassing, on one side, the Latin American countries and, on the other, the whole EEC. This is not only because similar ties exist between Spain and the Spanish American countries, but also because of the fact that Brazil–EEC relations very often fit into the context of Latin America–EEC relations.

Before moving on to the actual analysis of the above mentioned implications, we provide a quantitative view of the economic relations between Brazil and Portugal and Spain, with the basic objective of establishing the magnitude of the questions involved. A final section summarises the main conclusions of the work.

FEATURES OF BRAZIL'S ECONOMIC RELATIONS WITH PORTUGAL AND SPAIN

Portugal and Spain do not figure among Brazil's major trading partners: in the 1982–4 period, they absorbed only 0.5 and 2.1 per cent, respectively, of Brazilian exports and supplied 0.1 and 0.4 per cent of its imports. From the perspective of the Iberian countries, trade with Brazil is also of little significance: in the same period, Brazilian exports to Portugal and Spain represented only 1.5 per cent of imports of the former and 1.7 per cent of the latter; while Brazil acquired only 0.8 per cent of South Portugal's and Spain's exports.

Brazil has traditionally enjoyed a surplus balance of trade with these two countries, as shown in Table 7.1 and 7.2: the average surplus for the 1983–5 period was $464.9 million with Spain and $122.8 million with Portugal. And, as can be seen from these tables, there has been a clear increasing tendency over the last ten years. As one would expect, this fact has already led to a growing pressure on the part of both countries, particularly Spain, for a greater equilibrium in the flows of trade.

Besides the limited volume, another important characteristic of Brazilian trade with the Iberian countries is the high concentration on a few products, particularly on the export side (see Tables 7.3–7.6). The figures for 1985 show that two products taken together—soybean seeds (29.3 per cent) and coffee beans (23 per cent)—accounted for more than half of Brazil's exports to Portugal; all the remaining products had shares below 5 per cent. These two products are also among the most significant items on the list of exports to Spain, coffee beans representing 19.4 per cent, and soybean seeds 17.8 per cent; other important items are soybean feed (18.4 per cent) and iron ore (10.4 per cent).

As regards imports, the traditionally most important items among those supplied by Portugal are olive oil, whose share was around 23 per cent in the three-year period 1983–5, and table wine and chestnuts, both with an average of 14 per cent in the same period.

Of the products most regularly imported from Spain, the most important are garlic (averaging 9 per cent in the period 1983–5), magnetic tape (8 per cent) and potassium chloride (5.5 per cent). Some items appear sporadically but account for a predominant proportion of these imports, such as soybean oil in 1985 (24.8 per cent), and ships in 1983 (40 per cent).

A third important characteristic of Brazilian trade with Portugal and Spain is the concentration on primary products (Brazilian exports) or on those with a low level of processing (imports). Besides coffee, soybeans and iron ore, Brazil exports demerara sugar, cotton thread, sisal, cowhides, and so on, to Portugal, and cocoa beans, beef and chicken, pig-iron, and so on, to Spain. This aspect is extremely important considering that (as will be seen below) the entry of these countries into the EEC will bring about a tendency to substitute Brazil with other countries which could

Table 7.1   Brazil's trade with Portugal, 1976–85

	Exports		Imports		Balance	
	US$ million (fob)	Increase (%)	US$ million (fob)	Increase (%)	US$ million (fob)	Increase (%)
1976	40.422	—	18.807	—	21.615	—
1977	121.955	201.7	21.965	16.8	99.990	362.6
1978	63.778	−47.7	26.459	20.5	37.319	−62.7
1979	71.508	12.1	37.865	43.1	33.643	−9.9
1980	153.856	115.2	37.855	−0.0	116.001	244.8
1981	103.637	−32.7	43.331	14.5	60.306	−58.0
1982	67.719	−34.7	20.494	−52.7	47.225	−21.7
1983	106.369	57.1	13.133	−35.9	93.236	97.4
1984	161.785	52.1	9.352	−27.4	152.253	63.3
1985	136.006	−15.9	13.144	37.9	122.862	19.3

Source: CACEX, Banco do Brasil.

Table 7.2   Brazil's trade with Spain, 1976–85

	Exports		Imports		Balance	
	US$ million (fob)	Increase (%)	US$ million (fob)	Increase (%)	US$ million (fob)	Increase (%)
1976	441.131	—	101.586	—	339.545	—
1977	485.501	10.1	107.140	5.5	378.361	11.4
1978	294.943	−39.2	92.052	−14.1	202.891	−46.4
1979	323.757	9.8	135.028	46.7	188.729	−7.0
1980	521.333	61.0	197.765	46.5	323.368	71.4
1981	372.428	28.6	93.505	−52.7	278.923	−13.8
1982	370.841	−0.4	88.429	−5.4	282.412	1.3
1983	526.573	42.0	69.842	−21.0	456.731	61.7
1984	495.427	−5.9	36.047	−48.4	459.380	0.6
1985	532.534	7.5	54.003	49.8	478.531	4.2

Source: CACEX, Banco do Brasil.

Table 7.3 Brazil's exports to Portugal, 1983–85

Product	1983 US$ million (fob)	Increase (%)	1984 US$ million (fob)	Increase (%)	1985 US$ million (fob)	Increase (%)
Soybean seeds	—	—	44.538	27.5	39.829	29.3
Unprocessed coffee beans	11.750	11.0	14.416	8.9	31.259	23.0
Unrefined demerara sugar	10.302	9.7	8.782	5.4	6.749	5.0
Raw cotton	10.414	9.8	8.638	5.3	9.597	7.1
Raw sisal	7.735	7.3	7.582	4.7	5.881	4.3
Cowhides	4.899	4.6	10.463	6.5	8.2916.1	
Internal combustion engines	—	—	3.405	2.1	3.210	2.4
Books and magazines	6.086	5.7	5.082	3.1	5.314	3.9
Automobiles with diesel engines	—	—	—	—	2.279	1.7
Parts for moulding machines	—	—	8.451	5.2	—	—
Casting machines	—	—	6.660	4.1	—	—
Refined sugar	—	—	5.312	3.3	—	—
Refined cocoa paste	4.452	4.2	3.182	2.0	1.970	1.4
Other	50.371	47.7	35.275	21.8	21.627	15.9
Total	106.369	100.0	161.785	100.0	136.006	100.0

Source: CACEX, Banco do Brasil.

Table 7.4 Brazil's imports from Portugal, 1983–85

Product	1983 US$ million (fob)	Increase (%)	1984 US$ million (fob)	Increase (%)	1985 US$ million (fob)	Increase (%)
Purified or refined olive oil	3.096	23.2	2.717	28.5	2.320	19.2
Chestnuts, with shells, fresh or dried	1.722	12.9	1.524	16.0	1.639	12.5
Aluminium cables	—	—	—	—	1.625	12.4
Table wines	1.339	10.0	532	5.6	2.030	15.4
Books and magazines	2.621	19.7	1.729	18.1	1.859	14.1
Olives in brine	492	3.7	254	2.7	648	4.9
Fresh pears	333	2.5	420	4.5	—	—
Natural untreated cork	261	2.0	244	2.6	221	1.7
Other	2.469	26.0	2.102	22.1	2.602	19.8
Total	13.333	100.0	9.532	100.0	13.144	100.0

Source: CACEX, Banco do Brasil.

Table 7.5 Brazil's exports to Spain, 1983–85

Product	1983 US$ million (fob)	1983 Increase (%)	1984 US$ million (fob)	1984 Increase (%)	1985 US$ million (fob)	1985 Increase (%)
Unprocessed coffee beans	111.779	21.3	92.759	18.7	103.392	19.4
Soybean feed	73.862	14.0	101.993	20.6	99.118	18.4
Soybean seeds	126.652	24.0	110.687	12.3	94.742	17.8
Agglomerate iron ores	39.314	7.5	98.298	9.8	55.453	10.4
Cocoa beans	30.493	5.8	26.442	5.3	35.979	6.8
Frozen poultry	6.667	1.3	9.268	1.9	11.680	2.2
Frozen beef	15.881	3.0	10.874	2.2	9.644	1.8
Hematite	6.835	1.2	7.400	1.5	7.608	1.4
Pig-iron	3.511	0.7	3.173	0.6	6.943	1.3
Sheet iron or steel	560	0.1	–	–	6.914	1.3
Peanut seeds with shells	–	–	–	–	5.993	1.1
Other	110.019	21.1	84.553	17.1	95.078	17.9
Total	526.573	100.0	495.427	100.0	532.534	100.0

Source: CACEX, Banco do Brasil.

Table 7.6 Brazil's imports from Spain, 1983–85

Product	1983 US$ million (fob)	1983 Increase (%)	1984 US$ million (fob)	1984 Increase (%)	1985 US$ million (fob)	1985 Increase (%)
Unrefined soybean oil	2.174	3.1	–	–	13.400	24.8
Fresh or refrigerated garlic	3.678	5.3	5.003	13.9	4.182	7.7
Potassium chloride	3.410	4.9	1.887	5.2	3.377	6.3
Other	60.580	86.7	29.157	80.9	33.044	61.2
Other	69.842	100.0	36.047	100.0	54.003	100.0

Source: CACEX, Banco do Brasil.

supply them and which would benefit from the preferential treatment granted by the Community.

As can be seen in Table 7.4, Brazil also imports basic products from Portugal, such as olives, pears and cork; magazines and books also make a significant contribution. The list of imports from Spain is, on the other hand, much more diversified. As shown in Table 7.6, in 1985 imports of organic chemical products represented 10.7 per cent of the total, and boilers, mechanical machines and appliances, 9 per cent; books, electrical machines and appliances, medicines, can also be mentioned. In that year, manufactured goods represented 47.7 per cent of Brazilian imports from Spain.

The low level of activity, in terms of trading relations, observed between Brazil and these two countries, is also a characteristic of the flow of capital between the two blocs. The stock of direct investments (including reinvestments)by Portugal and Spain registered in Brazil were, respectively, $55.2 million and $88.5 million at the end of 1985. This corresponded to about 0.2 and 0.3 per cent of the total foreign investments registered in the country at that time. For obvious reasons, the flow of capital in the opposite direction is practically non-existent.[1]

EXPANSION OF THE EEC: IMPLICATIONS FOR BRAZIL AND LATIN AMERICA

Implications for Latin America in general

Relations between Latin America and the EEC have never been particularly close, despite the apparent efforts of both sides to promote greater integration between the two regions, especially since the second half of the 1960s. At that time, Latin America, which until then had remained very much a zone of American influence, became deeply dissatisfied with the allegedly inadequate economic support provided by the United States to the countries of the region. This discontent culminated in the Declaration of Viña del Mar, in 1969, in which the Latin American countries proposed a change in the relationship with the United States and closer links with the EEC. To implement the latter decision the Latin American states set up a Joint Committee with the EEC, which did not, however, achieve the results expected (see Muñiz 1980).

Two lines of approach were adopted to promote greater integration between Latin America and the EEC: the first, through community association, that is to say, establishing a single form of treatment for the Latin bloc as a whole; and the second, adopting a more restricted view, through bilateral agreements, with one or more countries of the region.

To explain the failure of the first type of strategy, the two sides involved offer different reasons. From the Latin American viewpoint, such a failure to achieve the objectives proposed by the Joint Committee was due mainly to factors of institutional order and to lack of regular direct contact between the two sides. On the hand, the European group pointed to the lack of unity of the Latin countries as the main cause of the difficulty in formulating a global policy towards Latin America (Muñiz 1980, p. 58).

As to bilateral agreements, several were signed, such as that between Brazil and the EEC in 1973. Brazil, along with Argentina, also participated in an agreement on the use of atomic energy for peaceful ends. It is also a member of the group of countries which benefit from the Generalised System of Preferences (GSP), conceded by the Community. Compared with the other Latin American countries, Brazil occupies a prominent position in terms of trading relations with the EEC, as it offers a more attractive market and a more developed industrial base. Nevertheless, it is still far from enjoying a privileged position along the lines of the countries of the third Lomé Convention.

The entry of Portugal and Spain into the EEC in January 1986 brought new prospects for relations between the Community and Brazil. Generally speaking, there are optimistic expectations with respect to the development of such relations, made possible by the new paths opened up by the two Iberian countries.

However, the expectation of turning the Latin American countries into a new group along Lomé Convention lines, as a result of the historical roots which link this continent to Portugal and Spain, has no realistic basis, as simply being an ex-colony does not in itself justify privileged access to the EEC market. When the Treaty of Rome was signed in 1957, the founder members (France, West Germany, Italy, Holland, Belgium and Luxembourg) defined a special type of Community association with their former African territories which, during the negotiation stage, were undergoing a process of political independence. Community association was so tied to the concept of colony that, with the political rupture of the African countries, an official approach was made to these countries concerning their political interest in remaining in the association. The provisions laid down in the Treaty continued in force until 1963, when they were replaced by the Yaoundé Agreement, encompassing the 18 African states and Malgache Associations (EAMA) in a type of free-trade zone (Tamames 1986, p. 155). However, the economic disparity between the EEC and EAMA soon revealed the inadequacy of this associative model, which was restructured in 1974 on a more protectionist basis, in the context of a system of preferences to products coming from those countries.

The entry of the UK into the EEC in 1973 strengthened the group of beneficiaries with the inclusion of the Commonwealth countries. When the first Lomé Convention was signed in 1975, the group consisted of the old members of EAMA, the Commonwealth, and Tanzania, Kenya and Uganda, to form the Africa, Caribbean and Pacific (ACP) group.

With each agreement, new terms are negotiated, always taking into account the economic situation of these countries, which demands a greater participation by the European countries in their process of social and economic development. From being a simple free-trade zone the association has gradually turned into a strong commitment on the European side to the problems of the Third World countries of the ACP.

This is the fundamental difference in relation to Latin America. Some ACP regions are classified by the Europeans as areas of absolute poverty, requiring maximum help to overcome their difficulties, while Latin America is characterised as a less needy region.[2] Besides this, the African countries do not represent a danger to the commercial transactions of the EEC countries. Latin America can represent a strong competitor not only for the African countries, in the European market, but for the Community themselves. This is particularly true of Brazil and Argentina, which, in view of their more advanced state of development, are perfectly competitive in a wide range of industrial products. It should be mentioned that the former French colonies and the Commonwealth countries did not constitute, at the time of their association, an economic force capable of jeopardising the foreign trade of the EEC. Thus, France and the UK were easily able to curb the resistance of the other members, such as Italy, who were against this type of integration.

Another reason why one should not expect preferential treatment for Latin America, following Portugal and Spain's entry into the EEC, is based on a comparison with what happened to the UK's trading partners after it joined the Community. The UK's entry not only introduced the Commonwealth countries into the EEC orbit, but also changed the relations between the EEC and the European Free Trade Association (EFTA), of which the UK had been a member, together with Ireland and Denmark, which also joined the EEC. For EFTA, the withdrawal of these three countries, particularly the UK, seriously affected the trading relations of the other member countries—Portugal, Switzerland, Sweden, Finland, Norway and Austria—to such an extent that it became necessary to reach an agreement with the new EEC to get round possible problems arising from this change. A list was drawn up of products which would be subject to a gradual process of decreasing import duties, until these were completely eliminated. Portugal, because of its weaker economy, received different treatment, and concluded two agreements, one with the EEC and the other with the Coal and Steel Community (EEC Commission 1978).

A decline in the level of trade, arising from the loss of an important trading partner, is reason enough to begin talks with the EEC, but not sufficient to ensure a satisfactory solution a priori. In the case of EFTA, commercial transactions were guided by the same free-trade principle, the volume of business was considerable and both the remaining EFTA countries and the newly incorporated members of the EEC possessed considerable economic and political power to exert pressure on the six to accept their demands.

In the Latin American case, the impact of this new expansion of the

EEC has not been very considerable, according to various quantitative studies that have been carried out (see, for example, Granel 1981; Ashoff 1982; and Alonso and Donoso 1983). Added to this is the fact that the Latin Americans and the Iberians do not form a sufficiently strong group to face countries such as the UK, France and Italy. The great differences in UK–EFTA and Portugal-Spain–Latin America trading relations demonstrate how inappropriate it would be to use the EEC–EFTA agreement as a reference for the pattern of future links between the EEC and Latin America.

In sum, community association between the EEC and the countries of Latin America has little chance of coming to fruition as a result of the new structure of the EEC for four basic reasons: there are no strong ties of political and economic dependence with the new members of the Community; to European eyes, the economic situation of Latin America is not so pressing as that of the ACP countries; the effects arising from Portugal and Spain's entry on trade with Latin America will not be very substantial; and the political force of the new members cannot be compared to that of the others, making any form of pressure even more difficult.

Implications for Brazil in Particular

Optimistic forecasts concerning bilateral agreements between Brazil and EEC countries are based on similar arguments to the preceding: the close link that exists between Brazil and Portugal might favour integration in view of the entry of Mozambique and Angola into the group benefiting from the preferential regime of the third Lomé Convention;[3] and, if not under such favourable conditions, at least Portugal and Spain might act as intermediaries in specific questions.

In relation to the first arguement, the same considerations put forward for Latin America as a whole also apply to the case of Brazil (the lack of a dependent relationship, not being characterised as a needy country, its insignificant trading ties, as seen in the previous section, and its insufficient political power to impose conditions on EEC member countries). In addition, Brazil is the Latin American country that looks the most dangerous in terms of competitive potential, not only for the associaited African nations, but also for some EEC countries such as Italy, Greece and even Spain itself, on account of the degree of industrial development it has achieved.

Another question frequently mentioned in analysing these repercussions on the Latin American countries—and on Brazil in particular—is the possibility of the new members taking on the role of intermediaries in defending the interests of their ex-colonies during negotiations with the other EEC countries. Even if this should happen, it would still be necessary to assess the capacity of Portugal and Spain to come forward as representatives of Brazil in the EEC. According to Ashoff,[4] this capacity is severely limited by the fact that the two countries had to comply, at the time they joined the EEC, with the full range of Community commitments.[5] These obligations, of course, have transformed the external panorama of the Iberian countries which, since then, have started to take new variables into account in defining their external relations. Henceforth, these relations will be determined not only by the prospective advantages, but also by the limits imposed by the need to harmonize conflicting interests between traditional and recent trading partners.

Moreover, the political power of the parties involved has once more to be taken into consideration. Throughout the negotiations to join the Community, Spain was careful to obtain commitments from the EEC in connection with maintaining its preferential trading ties with Latin American countries, particularly with regard to financial co-operation and the inclusion of Ibero-American interests in future redefinitions of the GSP. Despite all the Spanish efforts, the only result was the inclusion of a common declaration of intentions regarding development and closer relations with Latin American countries, and agreement concerning the differential treatment, on a temporary basis, of imports of cocoa, coffee and tobacco from those countries.[6]

Spain remains determined to raise the question of these three products in future revisions of the GSP. However, despite such a determination, it is easy to foresee not only a weakening of its efforts due to a transformation in its external relations, but also a reduction in its influence, owing to the strength of the other members, who are opposed to the idea of granting benefits to Latin American countries without receiving a profitable return.

Access of Brazilian products to Portuguese and Spanish markets , and EEC markets in general, is likely to become more difficult as a result of the effects on their competitive position of the application of the Common External Tariff (CET), the imposition of non-tariff barriers, and possible increases in the list of 'sensitive products'. Brazilian products may lose their competitiveness in Portuguese and Spanish markets in two situations, which both result from the accession of the two countries to the EEC: in relation to the associated countries (ACP, the Mediterranean countries, EFTA, and so on), principally affecting farm products, and, in relation to the other EEC countries, who will have preferential access to those two markets. Furthermore, Brazilian exports to the Ten could be adversely affected in two situations: if they are displaced by Portuguese and Spanish products which will no longer be subject to CET and in the possible exclusion from the GSP of products considered sensitive by the new members. On the other hand, the adoption of the GSP by Portugal and Spain may increase the export of products which are included in this system. Irrespective of whether the final figure is positive or negative, the fact remains that, given the relative insignificance of trade between Brazil and Portugal and Spain, it can be concluded that the effects should be of rather minor importance.[7] Consequently, in the most likely event of negative effects outweighing positive ones, Brazilian external transactions would not be seriously threatened. Even so, if prejudicial effects are detected, Brazil could take advantage of the transition period given to Portugal and Spain to adjust to EEC norms[8] and to adopt measures to attenuate negative impacts.

Another aspect, in relation to which there might be changes, concerns the migratory currents between Brazil and Portugal, regulated at present by extremely simplified laws,[9] which, from the point of view of the other member countries, might represent a threat of invasion by workers from less-developed countries and an increase in unemployment levels. In recent years, the EEC countries, led by West Germany, have established stricter norms to stem the inflow of foreign labour, to which Portugal is now subject. The question carries some importance, in view of a growing migration trend of Brazilians to Portugal, at present stimulated by the unsettled economic situation of Brazil and by the mobility within Europe which Portugal's entry into the EEC has facilitated.

Finally, there is the question of the impact on direct investments, both Portuguese and Spanish, in Brazil, as well as Brazilian investment in Portugal and Spain. In the first case, there is the possibility of an increase of direct investments in Brazil as a result of the latest expansion of the EEC. Such reasoning is based on the supposition that Portuguese and Spanish companies will have a greater facility to penetrate the Brazilian market for cultural reasons and because of the language. This may lead to associations of European companies with Portuguese companies with this objective (see Morcillo and Rodrigues 1986). However, if one considers that the factors which attract foreign capital are various and also that Portugal and Spain's participation in Brazil is still very small, such associations would possibly not result in any significant growth in direct investment in Brazil. Direct investments in Portugal and Spain may represent the best way for Brazil to benefit from the new EEC. Spain, in the period since its entry into the EEC, has witnessed a considerable increase in direct foreign investment from many different parts of the world, motivated by grants, fiscal and customs advantages and an extremely liberal attitude in relation to foreign capital. Encouragement given to the setting up of joint ventures in these countries which are much closer from a cultural point of view, will certainly facilitate penetration in the EEC.

CONCLUDING REMARKS

In this chapter an evaluation of the impact on the Brazilian economy of the recent accession of Portugal and Spain to the EEC has been attempted.

The analysis has been essentially speculative in character, since the time which has elapsed is too short to permit a more definitive evaluation.

The study concentrated on examining the likely effects of the enlargements of the EEC on trade and investment between Brazil and Portugal and Spain, and whether it is realistic to suppose that Brazil can benefit from closer relations with these two countries to obtain easier access to the rich EEC market.

The first of these matters is partially addressed when one ascertains the small relative importance of trade and capital movements between Brazil and these two countries: for example, Portugal absorbed only 0.5 per cent of Brazilian exports in the 1982–4 period, and Spain not more than 2.1 per cent. In terms of foreign investments in Brazil, Portugal and Spain's shares are equally unimpressive: 0.2 and 0.3 per cent, respectively, of the foreign stock of capital registered in Brazil in 1985. Thus, even in the most likely hypothesis of a net negative effect on Brazilian exports—which might be displaced both in the markets of Portugal and Spain by products coming from other member and associate countries of the EEC, as well as in the EEC market itself, by competitive exports from Portugal and Spain—the loss would be of little significance. Besides this, there is no reason to expect any substantial alteration in the level of investments by the two countries in Brazil.

As to the second matter, an analysis of the previous attempt to establish a Latin America–EEC community association, as well as the experiences of associations already undertaken by the EEC with other group of countries (ACP, EFTA, and so on), show that it would be unrealistic not only to expect the concession of preferential treatment to Latin America, due to its ties with Portugal and Spain, but also to believe that these countries could be used as a doorway to the EEC market. The most promising alternative for extracting some benefit from Portugal and Spain's entry into the EEC seems to be the formation of joint ventures with companies in these two countries, to tap the European market—a possibility which undoubtedly will be facilitated by greater cultural affinities and by language.

NOTES

1. At the beginning of 1987, there were nine Brazilian companies operating in Portugal, in such fields as watch-making, civil construction, pencil manufacture and supermarkets (Simonetti 1987).
2. Muñiz (1980, p. 58) cites the comment made by Sir Roy Deuman, Director General of External Relations of the EEC, about Latin America in the 1970, defining it as 'the middle class of the world'.
3. The Portuguese ex-colonies of São Tomé and Principe, Guinea-Bissau and Cape Verde, have already joined the ACP group.

4. The author specifically deals with the case of Spain in relation to the Latin American countries. It is obvious that the same reasoning is also valid for the case of Portugal–Spain–Brazil.
5. This consists of the automatic acceptance of the obligations taken on in the context of Community association with the countries that signed the Lomé Convention, the Generalised System of Preferences, and agreements of various kinds.
6. For tobacco, progressive adjustment to the Community's rules was to be reached within seven years; for cocoa and coffee, adjustment was restricted to five years; in this case, however import quotas were fixed (Tamames 1986, p. 159).
7. This conclusion has been reached by many writers who have carried out quantatitive studies of Latin-American exports.
8. This period of transition has been fixed at between five and ten years, depending on the issue.
9. Nowadays, after five years' residence in Portugal, the Brazilian immigrant is entitled to citizenship.

REFERENCES

Alonso, José Antonio and Donoso, Vicente (1983). 'Efectos Comerciales de la Adhesión de España a la CEE sobre América Latina', *Pensamien to Ibero-americano*, no. 3, January–June.
Ashoff, Guido (1982). 'Konsequenzen der EG-Süderweiterung für die Beziehungen zwischen Lateinamerika und der EG, Vorläufige Fassung' (1982), quoted in Alonso and Donoso (1983).
EEC Commission (1978). *Report of the Comission to the Council concerned with Portugal's Request of Entry*, vol. 2, no. 2, May.
Granel, Francisco (1979). 'El Futuro del Comercio Hispano-Latinoamerica no ante el Ingresso de España a la CEE', *Comercio Exterior*, vol. 29, no. 1.
Morcillo, Patrício and Rodrigues, Jose.aa. M. (1986). 'La Integración en la Economía Mundial: El Caso Español', *Pensamiento Iberoamericano*, no. 10, July–December.
Muñiz, Blanca (1980). 'EEC–Latin America: A Relationship to be Defined', *Journal of Common Market Studies*, vol. 19, no. 1, September.
Simonetti, Conrado (1987). 'Portugal: Parceiro e Ponte para a CEE', *Indústria e Desenvolvimento*, April.
Tamames, Ramón (1986). *Guía del Mercado Común Europeo—España en la Europa de los Doce*, Madrid, Alianza Editorial.

Index

Supplementary Index of Tables

194 Supplementary Index of Tables